11.9̓

Roissy Express

V

Roissy Express

A Journey Through the Paris Suburbs

---◆---

FRANÇOIS MASPERO

Photographs by
ANAÏK FRANTZ

Translated by Paul Jones

VERSO

London · New York

This book has been published with the financial assistance of
the French Ministry of Culture.

First published as *Les passagers du Roissy-Express*
© Editions du Seuil 1990
Translation © Paul Jones 1994
This edition © Verso 1994
Postface © François Maspero 1994
All rights reserved

Verso
UK: 6 Meard Street, London W1V 3HR
USA: 29 West 35th Street, New York, NY 10001-2291

Verso is the imprint of New Left Books

ISBN 0-86091-698-7 (pbk)
ISBN 0-86091-373-2

British Library Cataloguing in Publication Data
A catalogue record for this book is available from the British Library

Library of Congress Cataloging-in-Publication Data
Maspero, François, 1932–
[Passagers du Roissy-Express. English]
Roissy Express : a journey through the Paris suburbs / François
Maspero ; photographs by Anaïk Frantz ; translated by Paul Jones.
p. cm.
ISBN 0-86091-698-7 (pbk)
ISBN 0–86091–373–2
1. Maspero, François, 1932–   –Journeys–France–Paris Region.
2. Paris Region (France)–Pictorial works.   3. Suburbs–France–
–Paris Region–Social conditions.   4. Railroad travel–France–
–Roissy-en-France Region.   I. Title.
DC707.M384413   1994
914.4'3604839–dc20

Typeset by Solidus (Bristol) Limited
Printed in Great Britain by Biddles Ltd

Contents

Contents

PART III   Hurepoix

PART I

Plaine de France

The train in question left the desert plateau once a year, on 20 February, and reached its destination, a small summer resort in the hot lands, between 8 and 12 November. The journey was 122 kilometres long, and consisted mostly of a descent between misty mountain slopes covered entirely in eucalyptus.

ALVARO MUTIS, *The Journey*

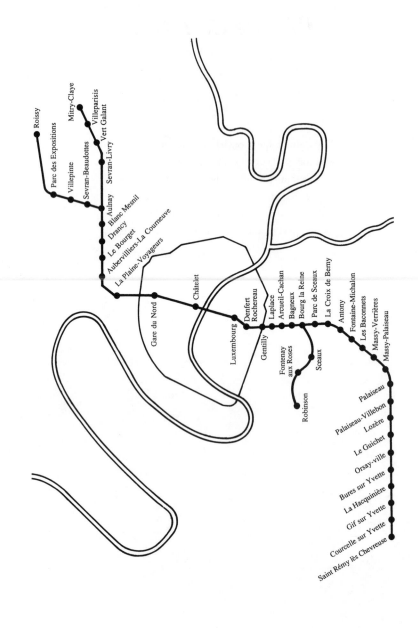

1

Châtelet station and the phantom of the Opera.
– Crossing a desert of several million people?
– Birth of a project. – Roissy-in-concrete
and Roissy-village.

TUESDAY 16 MAY 1989. They have arranged to meet at 9 a.m. on the northbound platform at Châtelet-Les Halles, deep underground. Their first stop will be Roissy-Charles de Gaulle international airport, their launch pad into the wide-open spaces of their great adventure. They will be away for a month. For a month, then, farewell Paris.

They have fastened their travel bags, taking care not to pack them too full; they must be easy to carry but must also have room for those extras that will be needed even more than necessities: spare clothes (who knows what the capricious spring climate has in store?), evening reading, maps and playing cards.

They come face to face at the end of the platform, trapped between two banks of television screens – one giving the driver an end-to-end view of the train, the other featuring people in improbable colours gesticulating to the sound of rhythmic gurgling noises for the passengers' entertainment or education – who knows? Pollution in its purest form.

Face to face, harbouring those secret little apprehensions that are present at the start of a long journey, vague anxieties they must not confess to each other, about everything and nothing. What have we forgotten? What sort of weather will we have, or not have? What kind of people will we meet, or not meet? Where will we sleep tonight? How am I going to put up with him, or her, for weeks on end? And won't this adventure, in practice, in stark reality, turn out to be absurd, insignificant, nonexistent? Who knows if, at the end of some endless day, we won't think: Let's go home, there's nothing to see? Maybe everyone will shout: Go home! There's nothing to see!

Will the journey stay on the rails?

*

François likes the moment in accounts of great ocean voyages when the author breathes for the first time the smell of unknown lands; as in a small blue book he has just read in which Jean-Louis Vaudoyer, heading for Havana on a handsome steamer sixty years ago, tells how 'once we crossed the Tropic of Cancer, the breath of the West Indies filled the air with an organic fragrance'. But you don't have to cross a Tropic to enjoy such a sensation: an organic aroma wafts permanently around Châtelet-Les Halles. François's friend Yves Lacoste, the great geographer, who knows his geostrategy and geopolitics inside out, told him: 'The RATP engineers are tearing their hair out but they can't find out where it comes from – they've tried everything, but they haven't got a *clue.*' Along with the millions of people who use the station, Anaïk is sure that it's the sewers. As one of the traveller's basic maxims is to beware of blindingly obvious explanations, François, who always looks for the cultural angle, suggests that it comes all the way down the tunnel from Auber metro station: the phantom of the Opera is the culprit, out rowing on the underground lake of the Grange Batelière, the boat barn, and stirring up the pestilential mud with his oars.

For the last ten years, the suburban express trains of the RER have had four-letter nicknames according to their destination. Those beginning A to J are all northbound; from K to Z, they head south. Or the other way round, I can never remember. Some are affectionate: LILY, EMMA, PAPY. Others, like KNUT, are plain fierce. There used to be a PONG, and then one fine day, who knows what got into the eggheads at the RATP (or the SNCF – don't forget that PONG was an *interconnexion*), one fine day, poof! PONG vanished into thin air. PONG, KNUT, PAPY, LILY. Each of these nicknames corresponds to a 'mission': between Gare du Nord and Aulnay-sous-Bois, for instance, GUSS doesn't stop at the stations where EPIS stops, except Le Bourget, and of course vice versa. Or the other way round, I'm not sure. These trains play at leapfrog. *Mission*: that's probably what modern vocabulary is. There's a Wells Fargo side to it as well; drivers need to feel a bit like Saint-Exupéry, flying the old airmail lines across the South Atlantic and the Andes, with not another soul in the world – the mail must get through. Or holy missions, the Marchand mission to Fachoda, mission lands, and martyred saints. Mission and missionary mean many things, including 'we're going where the savages are'.

The train pulls into the station: it's painted red, white and blue, as they all are – *vive la France*. They're in luck: it's EMIR, a through service which doesn't stop before Aulnay, and the carriage is nearly empty. At this time of day the great morning migration is almost over, and in any case, it flows in the other direction.

It's fine weather for a springtime journey: the cloudless sky is truly blue only at its zenith, then slowly turns mauve, mauve-grey, steel-grey, down to lead-grey on the horizon. It is not the cleanest of skies, especially when you look behind you, towards the back of Sacré-Cœur. But don't forget that the train windows are themselves tinted a greyish colour. There's no chance of sunburn on the RER – our bald engineers have thought of everything.

And where are the people? There is barely a human being to be seen. Plenty of cars, though: cars driving bumper-to-bumper along the motorway which crosses the Canal Saint-Denis; rows of cars in station parking lots, as far as the eye can see; new cars piled on goods trains, waiting down a siding. Is there a face anywhere? The windows of the big clusters of buildings are too far off to be made out. The streets closer by are deserted. A single human being? Further up the line towards Roissy, on green or bare expanses of land dotted with rectangular sheet metal and cement constructions, and scraggy trees, our travellers will soon spot a rabbit. And near Aubervilliers-La Courneuve they had passed big blue irises beside the tracks, and poppies in between.

In the old days, not so long ago, the railway landscape proclaimed social and political convictions. Near Blanc-Mesnil, an age-old inscription declares that together the workers won't let a factory die, though time has worn away its name. In the landscape today, only the ad-men's voices can be heard, mostly shouting a shade saucily about household appliances, property, electrical products. But in reply there are the tags. Or the graffiti, which sometimes knock you for six. They're everywhere – on walls, bridges, platform shelters. In the trains, even. Sometimes it's attractive, but a little too often it's sinister, belting you between the eyes, in the scorching sun through the lead-coloured windows. At Parc des Expositions station, the tags are already devouring the posters for the Trotskyist group *Lutte ouvrière* – at long last, a reference to politics and social affairs. The *Fête de la Lutte ouvrière* was held yesterday. Our travellers didn't go this year. 'Do you remember . . . the bright sunshine, a real party atmosphere, lying stretched out on the grass under the immense sky with clouds scudding by, the live duck raffle, the speech by Arlette Laguiller, the sack race, the debate on imperialism and the Third World, the delighted children, and adults, and this world of ours to be made, and remade, differently?' 'No,' says Anaïk, 'I don't remember. I've never been to the *Fête de la Lutte ouvrière*.'

At Roissy station, they take the coach shuttle to airport Terminal 1, the one shaped like a cheese in which you go round and round and round. At 10.30 they are in front of the big departure board. Anaïk chooses Brazzaville; François hesitates between Singapore and Cork. Anaïk complains how ugly the terminal is, and François complains about Anaïk's powers of complaint.

'You wear me out with your grouchiness. Don't start.'

'But *you* started. This *is* a good start.'

They discuss the idea of an attractive airport. Is there such a thing? asks one – or the other. François waxes lyrical about the time when, the time where: Orly in its first year – was it 1963? – with its gleaming high steel-blue outline, pure and clean, standing alone at the end of the motorway rushing towards it, into it, under it: he used to finish work at midnight and drive from the centre of Paris to Orly; the inside of the airport was huge and brilliantly lit, the echoes crystal-clear; as the last flights took off, there was time for one last cup of coffee, and there was a pair of Chinese ducks in the Japanese garden by the bend in the escalators, between the big departure lounge and the terraces. They would stand on the dark terraces, dreaming away, surrounded by the orange light from the big projectors, and they would feel a little bit happy. But where are the ducks of yesteryear? They've been eaten, of course, like the ducks of *Lutte ouvrière*. 'You wear me out with your memories,' says Anaïk. 'But what's the point in going on journeys,' says François, 'if they don't bring back memories?' 'An attractive airport,' Anaïk continues, 'might just be a hangar at the end of a runway: Ziguinchor, say, with the delighted children surrounding an old DC3 at the end of the tarmac?' 'Or Murmansk,' François goes on, 'a hut in the Far North in the midnight sun during that strange stopover I made on the winding road to Havana?' 'In any case,' says Anaïk, 'it *isn't* Roissy – here I feel like a mouse in a maze.' 'A rat, more like,' says François. 'And in a cheese, of course.' 'Don't rub it in,' says Anaïk.

On the morning after Whit Sunday there are no crowds; life is just ticking over. They make their last-minute purchases. At a bookshop they find the map they've been looking for all over Paris, the precious 1:15,000 Michelin map, the magical No. 19 which covers in fine detail virtually all of the first half of their itinerary – saved in the nick of time.

They sit down for a cup of watery coffee. Anaïk is unable to obtain a glass of water. Let's get this straight from the start: Anaïk never has coffee without *its own* glass of water. Indeed, it seems that the rules for drinking establishments in France are quite clear on the subject: every customer is *entitled* to a glass of *cold* water; this is free for the client, obligatory for the owner.

They write their last postcards before the real departure, feeling slightly emotional. Finally they have to go – it's boarding time. They make their way towards the stop for the shuttle that will take them back to the SNCF railway station. They want to get to Roissy-village. Have you ever been to Roissy-village?

*

This journey was his idea. Of course it had been lurking, hibernating inside him for a long time, years even. Maybe it had already occurred to him, three years ago for instance, in deepest China, when three of them had been dragging themselves about, together with a Nagra, microphones and tapes, dragging round an escort of guide-interpreter-cops (the Nagra is the world's most professional tape-recorder, the *nec plus ultra*, the tool favoured by Radio-France, whose speciality is sending you to the ends of the earth to do ultra-light reports with this ultra-heavy machine – the Chinese cops were there to keep an eye on the Chinese interpreters, who were there to translate for the Chinese guides, who were there to keep an eye on . . .); and he had said to himself: You poor fool, you want to tell other people about other people's worlds, but you can't even be bothered to tell yourself about your own world – you can always look competent and professional when announcing that people in Shanghai have two metres square living space each, but what do you know about the way people live half an hour from the towers of Notre-Dame? You make fun of all those people who race round China and bring back a book, but what could you bring back from La Courneuve or Bobigny-Pablo Picasso, termini on the metro lines you use every day in the country you live in? Being a good Frenchman, you talk so much about everything and nothing, but have you ever got off at Sevran-Beaudottes or Les Baconnets, stations you've been going through so often for so many years, just to have a look around . . .

But he knows when he got the clear idea for *this* journey. He can name the year, the day, the time and even the minute (he would need only to consult an old RER Line B winter timetable): it was a 2 January at 3.30 p.m., between Parc des Expositions and Villepinte.

That morning, he had got a call from Roissy: a friend was between flights. She had arrived from one continent and was leaving for another. He had gone to meet her for such a short time, in that space outside of real time and space. They hadn't seen each other for so long: as always, they had so many things to tell each other that they found nothing to say. And it would be so long before they saw each other again. They might never even see each other again. As with each time they met, they sat there wondering, though saying nothing, how it could be so, why oh why? They had once dreamed of living together and going on great journeys, for they complemented each other, each one knew how to see the world with the other's eyes, and to talk and listen as the other talked and listened. And they had each gone on living and travelling in different places, knowing that they would always miss each other's eyes and voice, simply miss each other, everywhere. They ate an absurd lunch in the ridiculous luxury of the airport restaurant, heavy with the emotion of words left unspoken, the look in their eyes, barely touching skin, soft lips, and already it was time to say farewell. Her flight was called, he had walked with her to the final control, then gone and taken the train back to Paris.

And it was on the return journey through grey rain, feeling abandoned in the empty off-peak carriage, that he had suddenly had the idea for this journey – it seemed so obvious – because he was looking through the RER window at the shapes of the suburbs, his eyes aching with loneliness, staring at the dead landscape of that winter's afternoon, because he was looking at it like an outside world he might have crossed in a diver's mask. That was that: he'd had enough of great intercontinental journeys; enough of clocking up the miles without seeing any more than you would through the misted-up windows of the Trans-Siberian Express; enough of droning through skies above the clouds and oceans. All the journeys have been done. They are within reach of anyone who can afford a charter ticket. All the accounts of journeys have been written, and Monsieur Fenouillard, Georges Colomb's globe-trotting diplomat, has long since summed up the entire philosophy of travel, from Paul Morand to *Si Yeou Ki* with a passing nod to Christopher Columbus. Secret places were there before his eyes, waiting to be discovered, unknown even to those who travelled through them daily and often to those who lived there; incomprehensible, disjointed spaces which used to be pieces of geography which we really must try and rewrite. They were secret and unknown, these lands, they really were. A far cry from the Lima–Titicaca–Machu Picchu package deal, or the Châteaux of the Loire.

And maybe too, as the train slowly filled with travellers of every colour, grey, white, brown, black, yellow and pink, maybe it was reading and pondering Maurice Nadeau's article in the last number of *La Quinzaine littéraire* about a 'studiedly nonchalant' book, 'the account of a both initiatory and sentimental journey, an enchanting discovery': *Danube* by Claudio Magris, from a publisher with such an attractive name – L'Arpenteur, the surveyor. This is what he had read between Aulnay-sous-Bois and La Plaine-Voyageurs:

> The project is something like the one we were given in geography class, in the last year at junior school: follow the course of the Rhine, or the Mississippi, or the Danube, and talk about what you find along the way. It was a most enjoyable task, but one which required much head-scratching, with our scant knowledge. Claudio Magris has been to see the lie of the land for himself. . . . And, in addition, the colour of the sky, the atmosphere of Vienna's Central Café, the width of the Danube at Budapest, a (car) ride into the Hungarian

pusztas or the thistles of the Baragan....

Take an atlas. Choose a country that the Danube runs through, or for which it acts as border: ...

When he got home, he had taken out an atlas, but, sure enough, couldn't find what he was after, so he had spread out the Michelin map 'The Outskirts of Paris' (the green one, 1:100,000, in truth far too small a scale), then traced in bright pink felt-tip the route of the RER B-line, the one which runs north–south through Paris – or, to be precise, north-east–south-west, from Roissy-Charles de Gaulle to Saint-Rémy-lès-Chevreuse, and looked at the places it passed through: the line set off from deep in the Plaine de France to arrive deep in Hurepoix: at least these lands, with their smell of the soil, are definitely ours. Right at the top were the Valois forests where Gérard de Nerval had sung, danced and kissed goodness knows whom (before going to hang himself not far from Châtelet-Les Halles station, in rue de la Vieille Lanterne, an extension, now gone, of rue de la Tuerie, which they demolished long ago, before hanging himself on a winter's night so much colder than this one: 'Don't wait for me this evening, the night will be black and white'), and right at the bottom were the meadows of Beauce where Péguy went walking, praying and Lord knows what else (before being killed by a bullet through the forehead on the banks of the River Ourcq, on the far side of the map, one sunny September day in 1914 – killed shouting: 'Shoot, in God's name shoot').

He had then consulted the plan of the metro express network and seen that the line numbered 38 stations, including those under Paris; was about 60 kilometres long; and that at the rate of a station a day, skipping those in Paris and missing out a few small ones, he would need close on a month to complete the journey. A month, he had decided, during which he would never return to Paris.

And at the end of this long journey he could visit the family home of his childhood, three kilometres from Saint-Rémy-lès-Chevreuse, at Milon-la-Chapelle, and at last live as happy as Ulysses – or even: 'Leben wie Gott in Frankreich'.

It would be a real journey: every evening a hotel would need to be found; or he could stay with friends. Come to think of it, did he have many friends round Massy-Palaiseau or Aubervilliers? He had also seen that he would be travelling through new housing estates and old suburbs, industrial areas and maybe others that were still agricultural, it wasn't too clear on the maps (on the one published by the Institut Géographique National and *Le Nouvel Observateur*, to the right of the Picardy-bound motorway near Roissy, 'Fields of Tulips' are marked; he would have to check up on that); and all over that area, staying quite close to the railway, lived a good two million people, not counting Paris, spread over five departments. Would it be possible to find under all that traces of the past, traces of the Plaine de France and Hurepoix? But which interested him more, the surface or what was underneath? The past or the present?

He then picked up the telephone, called Anaïk, and asked her what she thought of his idea – yes, he knew it was a bit strange, maybe a bit silly too. . . . 'I'm your man,' she said.

Yes, that's how the project took shape and they decided to make the journey together.

*

They have known each other for years. One day, in those far-off times when François made other people's books, he had seen Anaïk arrive with a big packet of photos taken in the Chemin des Alouettes shantytown at Carrières-sur-Seine, where she had lived for several months for reasons she didn't give; he didn't publish the photos – he never published photos, and was wrong not to. And maybe Anaïk's photos, some of the first she had taken, still had an incomplete feel to them, but he would have had no idea how to explain it, and she, at the time, no idea how to understand it.

Shortly afterwards, one day when he had gone to see his friend Georges Pinet, a lawyer in a collective – it was the time when lots of friends believed in collective work, when people believed in generosity, which means we're going back a long way – one day, then, when he had gone to see Georges Pinet in his molehill of left-wing lawyers in boulevard Ornano, while he was waiting his turn in the queue, the switchboard operator with the fascinating blue fingernails suddenly asked him: 'I'd like you to explain what you think of my photos.' His eyes had moved up from the blue nails to the blue eyes and discovered that the operator was actually the photographer called Anaïk; he explained to her that he couldn't explain to her why he couldn't explain, and his explanations were probably convincing, because from that moment on they didn't stop seeing each other and she didn't stop showing him her photos; and he always used to say that he loved them, but he couldn't say why or how, he just did, like a natural reaction and attraction, certain that when he looked at them something happened, that they went straight to his heart. Sometimes they didn't see each other for months. Years might go by when the only signs of life she gave were occasional sets of prints through the post: bargees run aground on the oxbow lake at Conflans, Annecy gypsies, the old grocerwoman in rue de l'Ouest; they were like pages of a family album, a way of passing on news. He knew that there would come a moment when she would show him the others. He used to wait for them, and it was always the same anxious and happy discovery.

Anaïk lived in impasse de l'Ouest, but she spent her life on frontiers. For that she might go to Africa, as she did one year, but might just as easily not leave the XIVth arrondissement in Paris. Where she lived was not the Montparnasse of the boulevard, the lights and the tower, but a far-flung neighbourhood of modest streets and modest people. When she was eighteen, this area became her first photographs and her only family. That old *quartier* is no longer there today. Anaïk followed its demolition, street by street, house by house, until it was the turn of hers to go. She saw the old people leave, exiled to suburbs they found frightening. She saw the arrival of the building-site labourers, Portuguese and North Africans. She saw passengers in transit settle in doomed accommodation: tenants in precarious circumstances, squatters, homeless families, African and Asian immigrants. Illegal immigrants and drug-pushers were always lurking around. When it was all finished, when other inhabitants, faceless ones this time, had taken possession of the brand-new tower blocks, sheltered behind electronic codes and intercoms, when she herself had managed to be rehoused in a 1920s council block in the *ceinture des Maréchaux*, a series of boulevards named after Marshals of the Empire, just inside the *périphérique*, on the very edge of her XIVth arrondissement, Anaïk's family had grown immeasurably: branches had sprouted in metro station passages, on the rusty rails of the *petite ceinture*, the inner railway loop round Paris, in dormitory towns, in small detached *pavillons*,[1] in the hospital-asylum-hospice-knacker's yards for old people at Kremlin-Bicêtre and Nanterre, at the homes of prostitutes from Pigalle and gypsies from Porte de Vanves – on all the paths which, in cities, apparently lead nowhere and which people in a hurry don't use or know.

Each of Anaïk's photos had a long story behind it. They never took people by surprise, were never muggings. Her pictures were not rush jobs or photographic rape. Nothing was for show either. The faces did not spring from nowhere only to melt back into anonymity: each one had a name, each one was linked to memories, confidences, meals, some shared human warmth or hours spent together. The stories they told were always *to be continued*. For these reasons, François used to say that they had something in common with Arab tales or an African palaver. They were photos that took their time.

Going for a walk in Paris with Anaïk always meant, sooner or later, being stopped on a pavement corner by a Monsieur Marcel or Mademoiselle Louise. They were bizarre people mostly – what are usually called dropouts, misfits, even tramps; and today things are still the same. The one thing Anaïk didn't really know how to do, during all those years, was sell her photos. Maybe she couldn't get the hang of it. All too often her photos provoked displeasure and irritation: why photograph *that*? 'That' was precisely the world right under our noses, which we never see: the frontier world that every one of us finds a bit scary, even very scary. We might realize occasionally that it's our world too, that we might end up there one day. But no – it's impossible, unthinkable. And unbearable. But enough of the sordid underbelly. And what if those frontiers were the frontiers of death? 'Of course they are,' Anaïk would say, 'it's the frontiers of death I was looking for.' And the simpler her photos were, the more they seemed like a challenge to those who saw horror where she had placed tenderness.

Maybe there was also something inside her that said no, that refused at the last moment to hand over her work for publication, to anonymous eyes; after all, you don't show your family album to just anybody.

To make a living from her work, Anaïk took all manner of photos: fashion pictures, film stills, theatre shots; but she could never stay on the show's surface, framing the conventional masks; the actors were not portrayed in a flattering light, maybe because they were mediocre or simply worried, and on their faces you could see the truth reappearing – not of the illusion she was supposed to be magnifying, but of their naked anxiety. It was a cruel thing to do, and that's not what they were paying her for. So Anaïk tried all sorts of jobs, the sort that aren't quite real jobs but frontiers in themselves: artist's model in the City of Paris's studios, short order chef, demonstrator in department stores. And she would sometimes say that it made no sense; that since she couldn't live off her photos, she would have to live without them. But could she?

She went on taking photos. She even started to be published. Was it really by chance that her first big exhibition was in Berlin, the frontier town to end all frontier towns? One day she told François that she didn't understand what was happening, but she could see that in her photos the world kept on opening up, getting wider – and smiling.

At first they had treated the idea as something of a joke. After that, when at friends' the talk turned to more or less distant travel – tourism-business-family-other reasons, tick the appropriate box – François would venture his little wisecrack: 'Well, I'm planning a *really* big journey – I'm going to *do* Line B of the RER.' People laughed, but not as much as he would have hoped; they generally found the joke a bit silly, and snobbish. He was also surprised to discover that a number of Parisians didn't know Line B of the RER. He had to explain that it starts from Roissy, etc. That would jog a few memories: 'Ah yes – the line that's always on strike.'

Then, as the weeks went by, whenever they happened to telephone or see each other, they had talked about it again, and slowly the idea became less farcical: they ended up taking the game seriously, to the point of wanting to define the rules.

12

For a month, then, they would go far away from home, saying goodbye to their families, as you would when setting off for any country you want to visit. He would make notes, she would take photographs. It would be a nonchalant sort of stroll, not an inquiry; they had absolutely no intention of seeing, explaining and understanding everything. The basic rule, which would influence all the others, was to take the RER from station to station and, each time, to stop, find accommodation and have a walk round. They would look at the landscapes, admire or detest them as the case might be, search for traces of the past, visit museums and go to a show if the opportunity arose; they would try to grasp the geography of the places and the people – to see their faces. Who were the people who had lived there? How had they lived, loved, worked and suffered? Who lived there today?

It would be a journey for their enjoyment and education: a cross between Töpffer's *Zig-zag Journeys* and the *Tour de France de deux enfants* from primary school, but without the Swiss accent of the one and the preachy morals of the other. They would go in springtime, in the month of May, because the days are longer then and they had no reason to deprive themselves of the pleasure of the gentle spring air.

What about preparations? They first had to consult the guides, but these proved disappointing; first because modern guides are no longer conceived, as they used to be, on the principle of the itinerary but in alphabetical order. Just as with a digital watch you can no longer see time as a continuity by following the hands, but only as an isolated fraction 'displayed' second after second, which nothing can link to those before or after – time broken into bits and pieces – so in modern guides you can no longer *see* space; gone are the railway journeys, car itineraries and linking threads for the walker; nothing joins together all the unconnected villages, which lie scattered like pawns at the alphabet's mercy – space broken into bits and pieces.

But modern guides to the Paris area are disappointing because they have done away with everything between the important points, which nourished the space covered by the traveller and which, in the old guides, was summed up in a few lines; just one line was sometimes enough to let the reader *understand* his surroundings. Which guide in 1989 still offers descriptions like those in the 1921 Guide Bleu:

The Villers-Cotterêt line forks off from the Saint-Denis line at Plaine Saint-Denis (4 km).
7 km. *Aubervilliers-La Courneuve.* To the S. *Aubervilliers* (trams from *Paris-place de la République* and *Opéra*), 40,180 inhab., once nicknamed Aubervilliers-les-Vertus because of an enduringly famous pilgrimage to Notre-Dame des

> Vertus; is today a highly populated industrial town. . . . To the N. *La Courneuve* (also served by the outer loop Paris railway, p. 211), 56,645 inhab., industrial village on the River Crould. . . .
> 10 km. *Le Bourget-Drancy*, a station serving Le Bourget (1 km N.), Drancy (2 km S.)
> *Le Bourget*, 5,523 inhab. on the Molette brook, was from 28–30 September 1870 the scene of . . . etc.
> The line runs alongside Le Bourget marshalling yard on the right. You cross a vast plain which . . ., *etc.*, *etc.*

Or:

> The vast Plaine de France, which the railway crosses in its NW portion, undulates very slightly with the almost imperceptible valleys of the Rosne and Crould, both slow-running streams; it consists of reasonably fertile arable land and has no forests. The roads running across it are nearly all cobbled. It is unsuitable for tourism in the proper sense of the word, for walks and bicycle or motorcar rides. However, there are interesting monuments to be found in most villages.

Try looking in today's guides, be they blue or green, for Aubervilliers, La Courneuve, or Drancy; and if Le Bourget features, which one will tell you that the Molette flows through the village? Paris's 'Suburbs' and 'Outskirts' are now taken to mean the 'Ile de France' region, and you can read about the latter only in its alphabetically listed monuments and 'curiosities': Saint-Denis (with its basilica), Sceaux (its museum), Versailles (its château). It's tough luck for anyone who wants a few landmarks in the huge gaps in their itinerary; tough luck for the traveller. Now the space exists only in the form of *selected extracts*. Travelling in the Paris area is a thing of the past. People get around, move from A to B. What's in between is the undifferentiated space and time spent in a train or car, a grey continuum that nothing links to the outside world.

So how do you gather information? Fortunately, there are the old guides and itineraries.

And to prepare for a journey in today's suburbs, would they need to immerse themselves in sociology, demography and economy, to study the history of labour migrations, council housing, the Delouvrier Plan and the blueprint for the Paris area? Should they arrange to visit the official authorities and councils, the various offices and administrations? No, to repeat: it was not an inquiry but simply what they saw with their own eyes. Attentive eyes, though, adding that extra something which a friend of François's, Miguel Benasayag, defined in a lovely book about happiness: 'Instead of looking at something, say: *ça me regarde*' – meaning 'it's looking at me' but also 'it's my business'.

14

At one time François had thought of turning the journey into a series of radio programmes, as he had done when he crossed China in winter three years before. In the end they preferred to keep this idea for later: they were afraid of the permanent presence of a tape-recorder – a full-time travelling companion in itself – and of feeling obliged to record come what may, so that when the journey was over there would be tape to edit and broadcast. These things cannot be done by halves. They wanted to keep a certain freedom: they already had to take notes and photographs. François would probably take his pocket Sony as a memory aid, for his own personal use, but they wanted always to be free *not* to make notes and *not* to take photographs if tempted elsewhere by their interests, curiosities and pleasures, and if the sun shone or the wind blew – in short, if their hearts weren't in it. So they decided to see the journey as a kind of reconnaissance mission with a view to possible radio programmes in the future. They would see when they got back.

And if things went well, they would turn it into a book.

They felt that one rule of their railway code was quite unbreakable: they must not pretend. They were what they were and nothing else. In no way were they specialists, but neither were they wide-eyed tourists. They had come from Paris, they might publish a book, or they might not, but they wouldn't cheat, they wouldn't disguise themselves at all. They had no questions to ask on society's great problems, no theories to develop. For that, they had only to read the newspapers or a hundred books, or watch television. They would let the questions come and ask themselves; the questions would be asking for answers. They wouldn't force things, but just be very ordinary. They would let the time pass by, that day-to-day sort of time, and follow the tempo it set. They weren't in the Paris–Dakar race. They weren't looking for anything exceptional. They weren't looking for events.

Shyly they started questioning their friends. They still received a few sardonic smiles, but were surprised to meet with a generally serious, even enthusiastic reaction. They were grateful for literary references: nostalgic souls talked of Cendrars, Doisneau, Prévert, Queneau; others mentioned Céline's *Journey to the End of the Night*; smart alecks inquired: '*In reality*, of course, you'll be doing it by car?'; others with efficient minds talked about sponsorship, and some even pointed out that subsidies were to be had from the Ministry of Culture and from regional councils who, they said, were generous with writers interested in their department. They didn't look into this novel idea of *departmental literature*. Maybe they were wrong.

One question cropped up regularly – and it would follow them throughout their journey: 'It's all very well,' people would say sternly, 'but what exactly have you got *in mind*?' When they tried to explain that they'd got nothing *in mind*, repeating their usual story about a nonchalant journey, a stroll for the pleasure of it, they felt almost suspect – guilty of pretending not to be serious, which was no laughing matter.

They discovered that many Parisians saw the suburbs as a shapeless muddle, a desert containing ten million inhabitants, a series of indistinct grey buildings: a circular purgatory, with Paris as paradise in the middle. The suburbs were something 'all around'. A wasteland. A land for wasting souls. A landscape which had been delivered in bulk, a bit of a wreck forever in the process of reconstruction; and in need of remodelling too. They also learned that there were lots of people who did nothing but remodel the suburbs, and that there was even an Observatory of the Suburbs and Centre for Industrial Development, at Beaubourg; and they felt rather small.

Being Parisians, they themselves had for years watched their bustling *quartiers* being slowly transformed into museum-style shop windows – Anaïk at Montparnasse, François at Saint-Paul near rue Saint-Antoine; they had watched the departure of an entire class of craftsmen, workers and small shopkeepers – all the people who went to make up a Paris street. They themselves had hung on, but saw renovation force out the poorly off, old people, and young couples with their children, who all disappeared as rents rose and flats were sold. Where did they all go? To the outskirts. To the suburbs. Paris had become a business hypermarket and a cultural Disneyland. Where had the life gone? To the suburbs. 'All around' could not, therefore, be a wasteland, but a land full of people and life. Real people and real life. The only wasting souls they knew were those they saw and felt on their city's every street corner. And if Paris had emptied, if it was no more than a ghost town, didn't that mean the true centre was now 'all around'?

So – wasn't it time to go and see where the real life was?

That was probably what they had *in mind*.

They were surprised and happy to be taken very seriously by other friends who lived in the suburbs either because they were exiled there or because, like the youngest ones, they were born there: 'You're going to see different landscapes, different things and people. You'll see – in a single kilometre, you move from one world to another.' For Akim, who was born in Aubervilliers, even neighbouring La Courneuve was a different planet. For Philippe, who had relocated to Massy, the Cité des Ulis estate was 'Injun country'. Others took the chance to relate unsolved curiosities: Yves told them to go and see if it was true that reed-beds had grown on the gasometer site on Plaine Saint-Denis; Anne asked them to inquire after the fate of the workers' allotments.

2

'There's nothing to see.' – Seminar on a motorway.
– The Gaul stands guard at his window. – Some big
invasions. – When Alexandre Dumas raced the mailcoach
over the Plaine de France. – The Aulnay 3000:
crossing the Rose des Vents. – 'This is home.'
– We've seen nothing in Garonor.

TUESDAY 16 MAY, CONTINUED. Where will they sleep tonight? They would be wise not to leave it till the last minute, if only so that they can put their bags down: they're not trudging round with those all day long. Such is the explorer's basic principle: first establish base camp, and only then head off in search of adventure. Well before their departure, they kept telling themselves that for the first night it wouldn't be difficult: hotels proliferate round an airport like Roissy. Maybe, but the hotels at Roissy are more luxury three-star affairs. Staying at the Sheraton, Méridien or Novotel is out of the question. They are ugly, which doesn't matter, and expensive, which rules them out immediately. Right next to Roissy, however, is Garonor, the big haulage depot, the big sorting and warehouse complex where the lorry drivers of Europe rub shoulders. There they are bound to find the hotels they want. Besides, not to visit Garonor and the adjoining Parc des Expositions, the exhibition complex, would make no sense: together with the airport, they are the economic centres for the entire area. But how do you get to Garonor?

At the SNCF station, a concrete block on an asphalt lake surrounded by more concrete blocks, where the nearby jets growl spasmodically and the pervasive smell of aviation fuel fills the air, they consult the destinations shown at the bus stops. A gentleman in a vaguely military cap calls to Anaïk: 'So you're carrying on your journey, then. Where are you off to this time?' 'Garonor.' 'Are you now,' says the man. 'Why Garonor?' 'To have a look round, of course.' 'But there's nothing to see in Garonor – apart from beefy truckers.' (Expression of disgust.)

'He's an old acquaintance,' Anaïk tells François. 'He thinks I'm crazy. You remember that day last March when I decided to do a life-size experiment in real time, out in the field: a reconnaissance mission to see what a trip like ours might be like – the kind of people we'd meet, photos I could take, stuff like that?' 'Yes,' said François, 'and in particular I remember you calling me from a phone-box in Roissy-village – night was falling, and you told me it was bucketing down and you were fed up. You'd been searching for sheep to photograph with planes in the background – or vice versa – because you just *knew* there were *always* sheep at airports because they keep the grass down; but you hadn't found any sheep, and in the end a lady on her front doorstep, practically the only human being you'd come across, explained to you that the sheep were further out, near Gonesse – and there you were in a deserted village, soaking wet and chilled to the bone, waiting for a bus which didn't come. And to cap it all, I told you I'd seen your one original photo on a hundred postcards.' 'Didn't you just,' says Anaïk. 'It didn't exactly cheer me up.' 'But I'd warned you: when you're planning an expedition to Karakoram, you don't pay a flying visit three months before, for an hour or two, just to have a nosey-round. That's cheating.' 'Anyway,' Anaïk goes on, 'that guy thinks I'm crazy. When I got off the bus, he was the one I asked for directions to Roissy-village. He said: what for, there's nothing to do in Roissy-village. I replied: I'm going sightseeing. He said I'd be better going to the airport: you can look round the boutiques. And later on, when I came back dripping wet, he asked me if I'd liked it, and I said I had because I love the countryside in the rain, and he shook his head in disgust, just as he's doing now.'

Meanwhile, a group of gentlemen – some with caps, some without – have gathered and are debating the matter: no, there's nothing to see in Garonor. 'Surely there's a hotel?' asks Anaïk practically. 'A hotel? You've got the Novotel just opposite.' 'A *small* hotel,' stresses Anaïk, believing optimistically that the locals always know the good addresses. 'You know, somewhere nice and quiet.' 'Ah, you'll find nothing like that in Garonor,' pipes up a tubby little chap. 'No, nothing like that,' chimes the chorus. 'But I know just the place,' says Tubby. 'Hôtel des Charmilles at Thillais.' 'You'd be better off visiting Chantilly,' chips in another between two roaring jumbos. And for a moment, a whiff of fresh Chantilly cream and roses mingles with the jet fuel, then drifts away and vanishes far above the control tower.

François deciphers the bus timetables. He discovers that they could head off east. They would turn their backs on the promised suburbs and come upon valleys and forests full of pure air and literature: the LO6, for instance, would take them to Dammartin-en-Goële and Othis. They would meet the gentle ghost of writer Gérard de Nerval, who would himself be searching for the ghosts of Sylvie and the beautiful Adrienne;

a descendant of the Valois royal line who became a nun, Adrienne was also related to the daughters of this misty land who sang romances full of melancholy and tales about princesses. Gérard had this odd habit, when he came out of the theatre at one in the morning, of deciding, on the spur of the moment, whatever the time of year, that he wanted to go for a walk in the country, and he would rush through Les Halles to catch the last mailcoach. At that time, the departure point for mailcoaches heading north and east towards Senlis and Soissons was in passage du Grand Cerf, off rue Saint-Denis. It was 1852, so Gare du Nord was already there, but Gérard wasn't too keen on trains. Don't spare the horses, coachmen and postilions. 'How sad the Flanders road is by night, becoming beautiful only when we reach the forests. Always the same two lines of dreary trees, blurred grimacing forms.' At La Patte d'Oie at Gonesse, the stagecoach forked east and had to go through Roissy, driving between the Plaine de France's 'squares of verdure and ploughed earth', which today are covered by concrete runways and motorways. On Saturdays-Sundays-Bank Holidays, the LO6 would gallop on to Ermenonville, and Gérard would act as their guide on the trail of the fleeting tracks of Jean-Jacques Rousseau: he would take them running in woods still shrouded by the autumn mists (in the middle of May?), which would slowly clear to unveil the sky-blue mirror of the lakes. Before vanishing with the mists, Gérard's ghost would have time to show them, near the island where Rousseau was buried, the rocks covered in poetic inscriptions that people would come upon while tripping through the woods:

> This place is the stage for chases valorous
> That warn the stag of furies amorous.

Still on Saturdays-Sundays-Bank Holidays, the LO6 could also take them to The Sea of Sand, where there are attractions like the Indians and the little train from the Wild West. Would the author of *Sylvie* have disliked that? For a little further away, at Meaux, he himself fell so deeply under the spell of the 'Merino Woman' that he paid twenty-five centimes to admire her hair, 'a magnificent mane of Barbary merino wool', and not just admire it either, because for that price spectators could also 'ensure the wool was authentic to the touch, by checking its bounce and smell' . . ., etc. But *revenons à nos moutons*. François, who has never seen the wonders of The Sea of Sand, has long dreamed of taking his daughter Julia there. But Julia might prefer the Parc Astérix. Another bus could in fact take them north to the Parc Astérix. In the meantime, there is always the LO5, which goes to Saint-Pathus and Saint-Soupplet; François doesn't know what they might find there, but they sound appealing saints nevertheless. The 350, which simply takes people back to Gare de l'Est in Paris, does a more austere line in bus-stop names: they are called Descartes, or Lenin. And Garonor.

They get on the 350. The few people on the bus are silent. 'Don't forget,' shouts Tubby. 'Hôtel des Charmilles at Thillais.' 'And visit Chantilly,' shouts the other. The 350 sets off. It winds round and round the spiral curves surrounding the airport satellites. It's difficult to get your bearings.

Difficult is the word. You have to keep repeating it: there is nothing remotely geographical about the place. It's simply juxtaposed horizontal and vertical divisions which are impossible to take in immediately: between the connecting roads cutting under and over artificial embankments, sometimes with long bends well over 180 degrees, almost circular even – a swing left, a swing right, and you always see the sun just where you're not expecting it – between buildings rearing up here and there and blocking out the view, barely identifiable and almost anonymous cubes and towers, which at first glance, at least, are no use as reliable markers, then there's all the asphalt running over your head, the railway line, and the motorways you keep cutting across, the bridges and tunnels, and all the vehicles pelting along, overtaking, overlapping and separating, watch your left, watch your right, and not a single pedestrian to give the whole thing a scale; no, it's not a space – these are (thank you, Perec) *species of spaces*, pieces of badly stuck together space, always giving you the feeling that a missing piece of puzzle is needed to give the whole thing a sense. But who's asking you to make sense of something that is only for travelling through? And quickly. By car. Even if it means going round and round and round. These are temporary spaces.

The 350, which goes to Gare de l'Est via Garonor, drives past the bottom of the giant Camembert of Terminal 1, far lower than they could ever have imagined, plucks from a quiet little bus shelter three passengers who look like mice coming out of a maze after some strange and mind-boggling odyssey, and finally rejoins the A1 motorway and begins to zoom so fast towards Paris that they can already see themselves at Gare de l'Est, their journey over – oh the shame of it – then it leaves the motorway again, goes round and round for half an hour before dropping them at the gates of Garonor, where they are greeted by an interminable stretch of warehouses, heaps of hoardings advertising famous companies, and rows of lorries sitting high and dry. 'Garonor's a desert,' suggests Anaïk. 'Yes,' says François knowingly, 'but just you wait till dark.'

It is 1 p.m. and there's no one about, the green plants of the local Information Office are behind locked doors, and in a huge cafeteria office workers are having lunch. There's only one bar, the Baronor. They find out that the lorry drivers' hotel is just round the back, but there are only a few rooms and it's full. Is that the only one? No one really knows. What about the Fimotel they saw the poster for? Yes, maybe. It's over there. Or there. They head off in the hot sun through the huge stretches of lorries between the huge warehouses. Their bag-straps are digging into their shoulders. Finally, on the extreme southern edge of the warehouses, down a path where a railway line on its last sleepers has petered out, between more depots and, behind its fence, the A1 motorway where lorries and cars are tearing past tail to tail, which means that once again they have to shout to make themselves heard, so luckily they don't have much to say to each other, finally there's the Fimotel, a small block built almost to human scale smiling at the infernal motorway with every one of the bright red parasols on its terrace. There are a few trees, too, giving it an unexpected rural edge-of-the woods feel. On the other, inaccessible side of the motorway, diggers and skip-trucks are hard at work. The lobby, in matching cream and bright red, is soundproofed and very cool, the welcome is charming. Where have you parked your car? Yes, we have rooms available: they'll only be free tonight because during the day they're used for seminars. It's true, though, about the seminars: there's a notice pinned up on a board. A seminar for executives. From Forsomething: Fordur, Fordum, Fortruc? And there are the executives. In they charge, all dark-suited men except one undeniably feminine creature: such elegance, such charm, such efficiency, a PR exec straight out of the Office Equipment Salon: she herds them along on a tight rein, with an iron hand and a ruthless smile. They sip kir on the motorway terrace, then make a beeline for the dining-room.

And so our two travellers, bushwhacked already but at least relieved of their bags, sit down on the now-empty terrace, turn up their noses at the gastronomic menu for the Forwhatsits and have sandwiches, a Coke and coffee (with glass of water). And they cannot get over their joy at finding such a pleasant haven – now they are free from their secret worries, their sunny terrace is quite marvellous, even though it's only separated from the motorway by a lightly tinted glass partition, for the soundproofing no doubt; yes, they are in seventh heaven under their parasols and start making plans, shouting all the while of course, because the partition proofs very little in the way of sound; and Anaïk takes some photos. Then they head off again on foot between the warehouses towards the bus stop, from where the 350 will take them in the opposite direction towards their decidedly distant destination: Roissy-village.

When the 350 leaves the motorway, it follows a different route between storehouses, office blocks and maybe even buildings where people live, all landscaped with hedges and yellow road signs: rue de la Jeune Fille, route du Noyer du Chat. In chemin du Chapitre, garrulous Africans appear.

Living people at least. Real people, normal living people.

And finally, at 3 p.m., after changing buses under the mocking gaze of the man with the vaguely military cap, who is delighted to see the two nutcases again (so, how did you like the beefy truckers?), here they are in place des Pays de France in Roissy-village – which, they realize, they should in fact call Roissy-ville; they are caught in the midst of a dense mass of background noises in which the planes, curiously, come off second-best against the lorries thundering down the main street and, in high-pitched counterpoint, the birds. In a photo or silent film, it would be a setting of provincial, even rural, calm.

On the map, Roissy seems to lie entirely inside the airport perimeter. But the bus trip, with its disconcerting circuits and detours, was long enough for them to feel a long way away. No planes are flying over the village. Maybe that's it – the legendary calm in the eye of the storm. And there is not a single human being to be seen; just a few four-storey blocks of council flats in rather nice brick, mingling with late-nineteenth-century mansions, trees, flowers and open ground. Shops are scarce: just an antique dealer who, as is often the case, is more of a second-hand clothes dealer, and an ironmonger's store which, alas, is not long for this world.

Near the church, tall, extremely fine black cedars mark the site of the château that belonged (very briefly, as we know, due to bankruptcy) to Mr Law, the Scots economist who advised the Regent during Louis XV's minority.

*

There is a mood of contemplation in the cool, distinctly rural atmosphere of Saint Eloy's church: a square tower set solidly on its buttresses, semicircular vaults on thick capitals. Its 'substructure' (in this case a few stones found at the foot of a pillar) is dated from the fourth century by some archaeologists, from the eighth by others – about the time of good Saint Eloi and good King Dagobert; rebuilt in the sixteenth, renovated in the nineteenth, and finally, in the twentieth century, restored according to prevailing tastes, like everything else; namely scoured, sandblasted and brightened up in such a way that the stone appears and the forms are refined in all their authenticity and simplicity, stripped to the historical bone, all things which have of course never existed in real history, for real history is more about accumulation, mixes, confusion and even bric-a-brac . . . but that's another story. The walls filter the noises outside and sort through the mass of sounds, distancing the roars, enhancing the chirruping of a swift or screeching brakes at the crossroads.

Behind the church they walk down a path lined with lime trees; and

Roissy-ville

behind the graveyard, carrying on down the dirt track would take them across country fields towards Tremblay or Le Mesnil-Amelot. But no: the paths which led to Thillais and Mauregard have been severed; beyond the recently planted trees lies even more airport and the tangled tentacles of the motorway interchanges. On the way to Gonesse, once famous for its exquisite white bread rolls and its lacework, chaos rules on the old farmland, with the national mine-testing centre, warehouses and even a clay pigeon shoot. Does Roissy-en-France have a siege mentality?

As they leave the church, they see a man leaning out of his window doing sentry duty: he's very much Roissy born and bred and has remained faithful to his town, a Frenchman and Gaul who has always stayed on the Plaine, with a great tuft of grey hair poking out from under his shirt. They pass the time of day, take photos. An entire lifetime in Roissy. 'Are many people still born in Roissy?' A bad question. 'No one's born in Roissy any more. They're born at Gonesse.' François really should know that in thousands of French villages the 'births' column in civil registers is empty for good. People get married in Roissy, divorced there, and die there; but they are not born there any more. They are born in the next village, at the hospital or the clinic.

Before the Great War, the man's father had owned a 430-hectare farm with forty horses and forty oxen. And how many people did it take to run all that? It was the time when the carters used to deliver sugar beet to the refinery at Saint-Denis, or straw when there used to be straw fairs. On

23

their way back, they used to collect mud from the Parisian sewers, 'solid waste' for the fields, which made the road particularly slippery and fragrant; halts were frequent, the horses being such old hands that they would stop of their own accord outside their drivers' favourite little cafés. The soil was systematically enriched with Parisian shit, which was usually dried and mixed with rubbish to make *poudrette*: in 1906 one particularly observant traveller, Monsieur Ardouin-Dumazet, described the edges of the Plaine de France as follows: 'There is barely a bush to be seen, but right in the distance stands a row of poplars; dotted about in the dingles are clumps of trees. Myriad pale stars twinkle across fields of vegetables: these are fragments of glass mixed with sludge from Paris, the principal, if not the only, fertilizer used.'

The farm isn't there any more; it was razed to the ground. After being wounded at the front, the father was forced to sell it in 1919. The village honoured their hero by making him mayor – for two years. They inaugurated their monument to the dead, then put heroism in mothballs. Still in Roissy, he started a business, a factory called La Perle de Verre ('The Glass Bead'), with a shop in the XXth arrondissement in Paris. He employed Italians who had learned their trade at Murano. They were a good crowd. He had studied at Collège Stanislaus in Paris: Greek, Latin, there was this blasted rule, a verb you can't write in the plural when the subject's neuter, τα ζοα τρεκει – something like that, anyway; no, he didn't like it really. He used to travel around selling his pearls, but he didn't really have the knack, and there was a competitor – he remembers once in a haberdasher's in Orléans. . . . And then the war came along again, which meant curtains for the Italians, people had it in for them because of Mussolini, a stab in the back it was, as if they had anything to do with it, the poor things, so they had to go back home – it's a shame, because they were settled here. And after the war the glass industry was finished. He went on working with celluloid, and this time the workers were Polish. Then he made stencil plastic – you know, that purple stuff they use for restaurant menus – until he retired.

'Roissy-en-France. . . . When my mother made her yearly visit to Le Bon Marché, the department store in Paris, people asked her: where's that? Nobody'd ever heard of Roissy.'

What about his sons – or grandsons? They're married to Polish girls. His daughter married an American with an Italian name who teaches over there at a university. Has he been to see them? Of course. He's flown round the world. He saw Japan, Alaska, Anchorage, where an enormous (stuffed?) polar bear welcomes you off the plane, Formosa – or Taiwan, as it's called now. He's seen his fair share of airports. But he's never been through Roissy-Charles de Gaulle. No, just Orly. You see how they've got it all wrong.

'The airport landed on our heads, just like that, one fine day in 1964. Roissy's well off today, of course, but everything's artificial. Where's the real life in Roissy? They told us that with the income from the airport, we'd have no more taxes – but we're still paying them. They do spend so much money.'

But his old, low-roofed house is so handsome. . . . From the back of the room, a woman's voice calls the Gaul inside. The window closes and a lace curtain falls.

'They're never happy, old people,' says François.

*

Yes, with its 'restored rural habitat', its 'beautiful old-style country walks' which lead nowhere, choking in the sweet smell of kerosene, its airport police residence and council houses for customs officers, its five primary school classes and three at nursery level (1979 figures), its pool-tennis-village hall complex and everything else, in fact all you need to live and survive, Roissy-the-typical-French-village is artificial, but how, I ask you, do you avoid getting lost inside it? It's so perfect and, yes, so typical, that you wonder where you are, and what is holding the scenery together. But maybe most of France is like the waxworks in the Musée Grévin, waiting to become a cultural Disneyland?

'You know the day I went scouting in Roissy,' says Anaïk, 'when it was raining so hard. . . .' 'Yes, I know – you didn't see a soul.' 'But I *did*, that's just it. After I called you, it finally went dark but it was still bucketing down, and I took refuge in a bus shelter. There was a group of youngsters there. They told me they were there because they had nowhere to get together. They told me that the youth clubs in the area were for the kids from the area, not the Roissy kids; that there was nothing for them in Roissy. That Roissy was boring, dead boring.' 'They're never happy, young people,' says François. 'They told me that if I came back, I'd find them easily – in the bus shelter.' 'You see, they're not there. They were telling you fibs.' 'It's not the right time,' says Anaïk. 'That's all.'

A sign in the shelter reads:

In the function rooms of the Hôtel Ibis
The 'Grey Hair' Association is organizing a
GRAND REVOLUTIONARY BELOTE COMPETITION

Two little West Indian girls are waiting for the bus. The little blocks of brick flats are just ticking over. The antique dealer is outside, soaking up the sun. Photo-time. The bus zooms up.

*

The shape of the *Plaine de France* is very clear on Cassini's map – or rather the *Cassinis'* map, since it needed several generations of the family, from Louis XV's reign to Napoleon I's, to draw up in sections of twenty thousand square toises (about forty square kilometres) the first scientific map of France. The Cassinis' map is a wonder. The Plaine de France appears as a plateau with unusually scattered villages, ringed by forests, by Ermenonville and Montmorency, and gaps such as the one to the south through which the Canal de l'Ourcq flows today. Only one road runs across it in the north, the straight, poplar-lined, cobbled main road to Soissons and Mauberge; it has to go through Roissy after forking off from the Lille road at La Patte d'Oie at Gonesse, where, on 17 August 1783, the terror-stricken inhabitants skewered with forks and pumped buckshot into a frightful monster which, after being sprinkled with holy water and exorcisms by the priest, expired with a diabolical hissing noise, spreading noxious vapours. Which goes to show that there had been no point in belatedly pinning up and bellowing this

WARNING TO THE PEOPLE

A discovery has been made which the government has seen fit to make public in order to warn of the terror that it might occasion among the people. By calculating the difference in weight between air that is *inflammable* and the air of our atmosphere, it has been found that a balloon filled with this inflammable air will rise towards the heavens. . . . A Globe made from taffeta coated with elastic gum, thirty-six feet in circumference, rose above the Champ de Mars into the clouds where it disappeared from view: it was carried north-east by the wind and it is impossible to predict how far it will be carried. It is intended to repeat the experiment with much larger globes. Anyone sighting such globes in the sky, looking like the darkened moon, must be warned that far from being a fearsome phenomenon, they are simply machines made of taffeta, or of lightweight canvas covered in paper, which can do no harm and which, one may presume, will one day be used in applications useful to the needs of society.

Which also goes to show that the emergency landing of Monsieur Charles's and Monsieur Robert's first hydrogen balloon, which fortunately wasn't carrying any passengers, did not tickle an especially aeronautical fancy in the inhabitants of the Plaine de France. Only one thing, perhaps, points to some premonitory interest in air transport: one unusually common Roissy surname is *Pigeon*.

Later, the railway went round the Plaine, turning it into an island pincered between the main lines, and the people of Roissy had to catch the train either at the top of the map, at Goussainville, or the bottom, at Tremblay.

From north to west, the trumpet of war has by no means neglected the

Plaine de France: it would be difficult to count all the hordes, armies, gangs, battalions, crusaders, revolting peasants, Protestants, Catholics and rebels during the Fronde who have plundered it; the Romans, Huns, Franks, Normans, Armagnacs, Burgundians, English, Spaniards and raiders from Lorraine, and so on up to the Cossacks and Prussians. It has always played host to invasions. The most recent were those during the Empire, the Franco–Prussian War and the two world wars. In 1814 no fewer than four enemy armies – under Langeron, Kleist, Blücher and York – crossed the Plaine. In 1815, Grouchy – who had just escaped from Waterloo in the conditions we know about, the mercenary – had at his disposal outside Gonesse the 40,000 men Napoleon waited for in such cruel circumstances, in return for which the people of Roissy saw their village devastated by the Cossacks. In 1870, the retreating French troops were ordered to burn the farms: the villagers managed to put out some of the fires, after which 10,000 Prussian soldiers and 1000 horses camped in the village, fraternally mingled; and as they were hungry and cold, they scoffed all that was scoffable and burned all that was burnable – doors and windows in particular, which didn't seem like a wise move. In 1914, it happened all over again: on 2 September, the population of the village was evacuated on ox-drawn carts in awful conditions – all except nine people, including the priest and the lady tobacconist, who stayed put. The French army regrouped, prepared its defences (in October, Gallieni even set up his HQ in Roissy); then came the Battle of the Marne, and this time they didn't capture Roissy. Even so, Prussian mercenaries were reported at Gonesse, while in its big pivotal manœuvre, part of the French forces crossed the Plaine to reach Meaux and the River Marne. The villagers came home and, wrote one villager, Monsieur Auguste Pigeon: 'Every house had, of course, been looted.' By the French army, mind you. But the tobacconist wasted no time: her wine jumped from ten to fifteen sous a litre. Upon which we learn of the death of the first villager, Henri Pigeon, on the Marne. There are four Pigeons on the monument to Roissy's dead: Eloi, Henri, Jules and Eugène. And thirty-four names, in all, for the 1914–18 war. At the beginning of the century, Roissy numbered 850 inhabitants. In 1916 seventy men were conscripted. If you add on those who had already fallen and those from subsequent call-ups, there must have been more than a hundred men from Roissy at the front. We can say that one man in three – a third of Roissy's workforce, of the young men who had danced at the Bastille Day ball in 1914 – were killed during those four years. Not to mention the wounded; and those scarred for life, in body and soul. Then, finally, came the Second World War: in 1940, Roissy was spared destruction; in 1944 the Germans blew up the crossroads outside the church, the Resistance attacked and the Americans liberated Roissy on 30 August.

In peacetime, Roissy was certainly on the main road, but no one ever stopped there. On 31 July 1830, Alexandre Dumas proved no exception to the rule. High on 'Les Trois Glorieuses', the three glorious days of the July Revolution, he heard rumours that Paris was running out of gunpowder, just as fears grew of a return offensive by the troops of Charles X. He remembered he was the son of a general of the Republic, nicknamed the Horatius Coclès of the Tyrol, resolved to carry out a heroic mission, went before the still-dashing General Lafayette and offered to fetch powder from where he knew there was some, namely the garrison at Soissons – which of course he knew, since he was born a mere stone's throw away at Villers-Cotterêts – and to bring back the powder dead or alive. His escapade has given us a very precise description of the journey from Paris to Soissons across the Plaine de France, a schedule detailing the exact number of post houses, which coincide exactly with those shown on the Cassinis' map. First stop was Le Bourget: the postmaster there, filled with enthusiasm, lent him his personal cabriolet, helped him to sew a big tricolour flag and to attach it fluttering in the wind; he took an hour to race from Le Bourget to the next stop, Le Mesnil-Amelot, on the other side of Roissy, through which he galloped with his carriage and four, at a speed of four leagues or ten miles per hour; and he managed to keep up the same pace between the post houses at Dammartin, Nanteuil and Levignan. He seemed to feel that this was the greatest achievement of his entire jaunt; even so, he was still obliged to point his blunderbuss at the head of a recalcitrant old postilion. To complete the tale, we should explain that Alexandre Dumas was indeed heroic – that he singlehandedly (or almost) took the fort at Soissons by storm, without bloodshed to boot, and brought back the powder. It must be said that when the colonel's wife, who had experienced the revolt led by the black slave Toussaint-Louverture in Saint Dominica, saw the father (-to-be) of *The Three Musketeers* come into her sitting-room, she cried out, 'Oh my God, the niggers are here!' and fainted, which struck a decisive blow to the troops' powers of resistance.

So Roissy and the Plaine de France went unnoticed (and not just by the traders at Le Bon Marché), seemingly off the track beaten by the century's advance. In the end, this state of oblivion went on too long, together with the rural calm it fostered, and made these locations the choice for a brutal introduction to the modern world. It was a 1950s novel which first made Roissy a world-famous – and scandalous – name: a writer needing a location near to Paris but unusually remote was bound to choose Roissy; the book was *The Story of O*. Maybe someone should look for the wall of the house in the village where the Blessed O was chained up and masked, then whipped, sodomized, tongued, infibulated and the rest; after all, they show you Porthos's cave on Belle-Ile and Juliet's balcony in Verona. But there are no signs in Roissy-ville vaunting the local literary glory.

And then, of course, came the airport.

Situated about twenty kilometres from Paris, Roissy had until then lived the life of an essentially rural village. The Plaine was fertile, the farmers were rich – at any rate, the six, working more than a hundred hectares in 1896; as for the twenty-two with less than one hectare, things are less clear. It was an area of wheat and sugar beet, where the women made Chantilly lace. In 1896, the village had its doctor-chemist, a music teacher, nine grocers, three cobblers, a tobacconist and no fewer than fourteen cafés and drinking establishments. This relative wealth declined in the 1920s. In 1950, Roissy's population was stable at around the 950 mark, even falling away slightly. By way of comparison, the figure five kilometres south at Aulnay rose from 680 in 1870 to 50,000 in 1950. In the meantime the local farming proletariat, already on the wane with the quiet beginnings of mechanization, had been drawn into Paris by less thankless jobs; so Roissy's workforce was replaced first by Bretons, then by Poles. Until the day farming no longer needed a workforce.

And in the end there was no more farming at all.

*

They return to the RER station to take the first step of the journey by train: Roissy-Parc des Expositions. It is a huge construction, and seems ready to welcome the high-speed TGV. An impressive number of electronic turnstiles proffer their stumps and little luminous green arrows to the passengers waiting for their tickets. But what is different about a traveller arriving from New York or Cotonou is that he or she will not have any tickets, or local currency with which to buy any. What's more, Roissy is the only station in the whole network with no automatic ticket distributors. And since it is rare to find two counters open at once, muddled queues of unfortunate people form, pulling and pushing their luggage, trying to understand and make themselves understood, which is useless because in any case the 'intercom' renders impossible any attempts at conversation with the ticket clerk. François thinks that sixteen francs twenty for a two-kilometre journey is expensive, considering that on the rest of the line the trip from station to station costs three francs forty, but he has already been carried away in the crush.

At Parc des Expositions they are the only ones to get off on the deserted platform of the brand-new, empty wreck of a station. To the east, the exhibition complex is closed, to open tomorrow or another day for some new trade fair, the 'Shop Local!' promotion or the Breezeblock Show, or indeed the Book Fair. No, this year the Book Fair is at Porte de Versailles.

Which leaves the shopping centre to the west. The station is located on the edge of a plot of land that would like to be a park and gardens. Who said that 'the leisure park and the shopping centre are the two symbols of modernity'? Near the station, concrete buildings seem to hide a cafeteria, and a hotel, invisible from the train, which they discover too late. An empty bus stops outside the empty station: it's the free shuttle; the driver chats up Anaïk, Anaïk calls François, the bus drives round and round in the usual way and dumps them in one of those huge car parks that surround hypermarkets. There is scarcely anyone about, but an ocean of things – Filipino furniture and Walkmans from Singapore, products from 'The Four Dragons', Swedish furniture – and they get out of there as fast as they can; what were they doing there? They knew this journey made no sense, and this time they've got proof. Move on please, there's nothing to see. The bus driver turns on the charm again for Anaïk: all dark shades and flashing smile, like a playboy at the wheel of his convertible. Photo-time. They meet a young Québécoise who lives in Sevran: 'It must make a change from Montreal,' says François, the wise old bird. 'Not really,' says she.

On to the next station, Villepinte, which is just as modern, empty and dirty. This station is special in the sense that it is located far from any populated place and, among others, from Villepinte, in the middle of a large desert which, on the maps, takes the form of a green area bordered on all sides by motorways and urban speedways, and crossed by vague dotted lines. They come out into the sunny car park, where endless rows of cars lie sleeping. Stretching down a very long shelterless pavement, orange and red signs indicate the stops of a multi-numbered bus line which are difficult for the unaccustomed traveller to understand. Still, in off-peak hours there are no buses or passengers, but you feel that it just needs the cameras to start rolling for everything to come alive in sound and pictures, for crowds to gather, buses to zoom about and cars to form traffic jams. There is an almost dizzying feeling of suspended time and incomplete space.

A black child goes into the station, walls daubed with tarry intertwining tags; he comes back out and shouts to his mother in disgust: 'There's *nothing* in there.'

They had seen on the map that by turning their backs on Villepinte, which is to the east on the far side of the tracks, and walking in the direction of the distant blocks of flats on the horizon, which fence off a bumpy expanse of parched fallow land where a pack of bulldozers are on the roam, they could, by walking alongside the motorway, get back to Garonor and their hotel. Why give in to the law of the distant suburbs: waiting, always waiting?

A few solitary walkers head off down the maze of new roads leaving the station, or scatter into the bushes. Why not do the same? Direction westwards, then, towards the sinking sun, so no need for a compass; the signposts are not much help. This area has a name: Parc Départemental du Sausset (the Sausset is – was, rather – a brook that babbled across the Plaine de France). But for the moment, the only name to describe this place is *no-man's-land*.

Here, one day, there will be a lake, hillocks, trees, banks and who knows what else. There will be a landscape. One day, will there be human beings too? In the meantime there are just white concrete barriers enclosing nothing, rows of dwarf poplars, an entire nursery of scrawny trees, and concrete pillars sticking up here and there which have to support floodlights and hoardings, lots of hoardings:

MY DEPARTMENT IS FILLING ITS LUNGS

Parc du Sausset is, they say, one of the big operations of 'Suburbs 89', a great idea from Roland Castro, the President's urban planner. In his distant youth, Roland was a great Maoist leader. He used to say that imagination should be empowered.

They come to a complicated crossroads and tack right. Walking in front of them is an African with a suitcase on his head. He leaves the road and heads off over the rough ground. Further along, a woman and her children come out of the scrub. There are places like that at the end of the world, where you sometimes see people spring out on to the road and head off towards improbable destinations.

Cars go by with – theoretically – people inside. The asphalt path they are following is named after Camille Pissarro. They walk alongside a high rusty fence dotted with notices:

NO HUNTING

They pass thickets of unripe brambles and, by their feet, a dead rabbit.

Reaching the far side of the park, they come to a two-lane road shaking with lorries which they take to be a motorway but which is none other than the shorn and grandiose avenue Henri Matisse. They move from painters to discoverers, from Renoir to Bougainville, and end up in the Milky Way.

They arrive on a big housing estate. Without realizing it, they have reached the northern limits of Aulnay-sous-Bois. There are long lines of five-storey 'walls' of housing (a sixth floor would require lifts) but few high-rises. They are tinted pink and pretty, seen from a distance. The grass is bare, the trees are sickly-looking. Squares of soil and cement mark the site of dead trees. Walls are dirty. They walk along the avenue between straight façades of buildings. On one second-floor balcony, a man is watering a profusion of plants and flowers in the quiet evening air. Anaïk wants to photograph him. He refuses aggressively and, in reply to their compliments, says that this year his plants aren't doing very well: it's the neighbours' fault. The doors of the blocks of flats are cramped, as though making them narrow cost less. The one in front of them bears the scars of a recent fire. An advertising sign sings the praises of cleanliness: under the tangled scribblings covering the sign's plastic cover, which aren't even tags, or anything, you can make out that *the street isn't a dustbin* and *cleanliness leaves no traces.*

ILE D'OLÉRON, THE ISLAND OF LIGHT

announces a sticker on a rusty car.

It is the time of day when children are out playing, their mothers come home from shopping and the men tinker with their cars. The children stand by the sign: photo-time. On the other side of the avenue, from something half resembling an abandoned sports ground, half a public garden, with a few concrete benches and beams, two girls call them over. One of them has a child in a pushchair, the other a husky dog: her face is very pale, and she is holding a slightly faded rose which, she says, comes from her garden. She used to live just above the burned door. She's waiting for her fiancé. She'd like to do what they're doing: have a walk round, take photographs. Of people, and things. Be free. Earn a living like that. Do you work for *Oxygène*? It's the local newspaper. They read it. This is a really bad area. The Rose des Vents. The Aulnay 3000 estate: haven't you heard of it? But it's famous. It's got a bad reputation. Rapes. Muggings. Drugs especially. You should see the needles they find in the gutters. A boy died from an overdose not long ago. It was in the papers. They've set up a committee named after him: the Rodrigo Committee. But this is home. Anaïk takes photos. Of them; the child; the dog. Then of them, the child and the dog.

'But this is home. At least there's fresh air. And space. You can breathe. Do you come from Paris? Paris is suffocating. How do people live in Paris? You're right to go and have a look round: there are some beautiful things to see round here. Do you know the Vieux Pays? It's difficult to describe, but it's nice. It's special, it's in the country. And Parc du Sausset? If you're heading towards Garonor, go and see Parc Ballanger – there are geese and goats. What would they do if they had the choice? One would like to live in Châteauneuf-sur-Loire: she's been there for her holidays. The other fancies the Charente. Down there you can trust people

Parc du Sausset

Aulnay: the Rose des Vents

and they trust you. A house of her own. Will you send us the photos? Anaïk always sends the photos.

They go back to the foot of the 'walls'. Anaïk asks a lady if she may photograph her; dressed in a long, glinting silk tunic, her head covered by a scarf, she's holding a pigtailed little girl by the hand, waiting for her husband to finish unloading the car. Madame Zineb has gaps between her teeth, the sort called *dents du bonheur*, 'good luck teeth', and a vertical blue line on her forehead. She has lived in Aulnay for twenty-one years. She was born in Tlemcen, Algeria. She has nine children. Two of her daughters are there, just home from work, and ask the travellers what they do. Do you work for *Oxygène*? Madame Zineb smiles: 'It warms my heart, you asking to take my photograph.' She's feeling down. She looks at them: 'You have the same eyes.' Blue eyes, faraway eyes. She invites them up for a cup of tea. Anaïk hesitates. François refuses because time's getting on, it's turned seven and they still have some way to go. Or, as Anaïk later complained, because he was embarrassed. They'll send the photos. They'll come back and see her. They swop addresses and telephone numbers. Madame Zineb has a sad smile.

(*October 1989*: return to the 3000. Anaïk took Madame Zineb her photos, and this time they all had tea together. Madame Zineb talked about her husband, who used to be a builder and was unemployed. About

34

her children, all born in France, some of whom lived at home: a son who had studied classical guitar and piano for seven years; a daughter who worked in a ministry in Paris and who would so like to have a job where she was free, like photography; another daughter, who was out of work but wanted to be a receptionist, a tourist guide or an interpreter. About the joy of her trip with her husband to Mecca. And about the hard times today, and the drugs taking hold of the young people. She'd like the government to clamp down more. Drugs are the new plague.

Anaïk took the opportunity of this second visit to the 3000 to photograph the monster tag that the chemist, weary of seeing any old person scrawling any old thing on his iron shutter, had commissioned from the Rose des Vents' top tagger. She went to look for the artist, a teenage boy. She would have liked to congratulate him.)

*

They had heard about the 3000. A friend who worked at Aulnay Hospital had told them what she had learned over the years. Through the families. Through rumours. Through her work. The 3000 was out of the way, with no train or metro. Far from the rest of Aulnay and everything else. The motorway cut it off like a ditch from nearby neighbourhoods, from nearby estates, from the rest of the world. And it was bang next to another motorway too, with just one access road. The estate was built there early in 1970, because right next door was the big new Citroën factory. It's called the Rose des Vents ('The Compass'), the 3000 or 'The Liner'. Why?

Is the architecture to blame? Where are the bridges and gangways? And who would dare to mention the word 'architecture' anyway? Loneliness on the high seas is to blame, more likely. It's a liner, their friend had said, on which the passengers embarked on long motionless journeys but always remained in transit. They had come from Paris or elsewhere, from hostels and furnished hotel rooms, and found their first flat there. After a few years, those who could tried to find something better, nearer a town centre, nearer a metro station. Those who, being out of work and in debt, could no longer meet their repayments also ended up moving further away in a new migration. But where did they go? They were lost beyond the department's frontiers, beyond the Ile de France, towards even more deprived estates, even further from everything, like those at Creil, Compiègne, Dreux. She had talked about sixty different ethnic groups living on the estate. About conflicts. About social workers breaking under the strain; workers for whom polygamous fathers and 'following wives' were a headache and a nightmare. About the youths running an extortion racket outside the school, and a certain nearby tunnel which was best avoided. And about the needles in the gutters.

But this friend lived in Paris. 'The awful thing,' she said, 'about working in the suburbs is that I never really live there for more than a few hours. There's nothing – no quiet bistro, nowhere to relax for an hour or two. No place to go for a stroll. I know a policeman from Aulnay who works in Paris. In my own neighbourhood. He tells me about my own streets and shopkeepers. He likes it there. But what can I tell him about Aulnay?'

Later they would find out more and realize that the 3000's first problem, its original curse, wasn't drugs, delinquency, intolerance, illiteracy or racism. The 3000's real problem was called Citroën. The estate was born in a state of euphoria in 1971: Citroën was opening a factory and needed workers – unskilled workers, the last of whom were mostly North Africans or Turks, who had been recruited specially to plug the local labour shortage and needed housing. The matter was entrusted to the public housing body and put in the hands of a town planner whose career notes say that he was interested only in aerial photos: viewed from a plane, problems of different ethnic groups living in overcrowded conditions; waterproofing; lack of soundproofing; and the quality of building materials obviously become hazy: only large masses matter. The planners thought big: 16,000 inhabitants were expected. The Communist town council, for its part, must certainly have dreamed of a radiantly happy proletariat living on a happy estate. One must also remember the background to the story: the shantytown period was barely over. There was a feeling of making a huge and praiseworthy effort to provide decent accommodation for all; not long before, the French bourgeoisie was still explaining that in any case, what was the point, the working classes still kept their coal in the bath – so you can imagine what the Turks are like. But it was time to think of applying widespread housing remedies that were less precarious, less shameful and ultimately more rational than shabby digs and shantytowns. These people were to get a home of their own. Bright apartments with everything that had been admired in previous decades in the name of 'modern comfort'. There was work nearby: 11,000 new jobs, 8500 of them at Citroën alone. Garonor was being built, and many other industrial zones were sprouting between the motorway and the airport. To separate the estate from the factory, they designed the Parc municipal de la Rose des Vents: it must all have looked pretty, seen from a plane. There was no need to provide transport to go job-hunting further afield. The birth of the 3000 on beet fields was particular in that, unlike other estates such as Sarcelles, no mixing of different social classes was intended. Apart from executives from neighbouring firms who had accommodation there, people stayed put. All the necessary social environment could be found on the estate: crèches, schools, community clinics, sports halls. A real little paradise.

Barely had the estate seen the light of day when crisis struck. As early as 1975, Citroën started laying people off. So did everyone else: Ideal Standard's Aulnay plant closed down, making 2960 workers redundant in one go. In 1978–79 Citroën shed 1132 jobs, and more were to follow. How could people live on 'The Liner'? They had to get work elsewhere. A long, long way away, which required hours of travelling. Unemployment followed. Were they helped to pay the air fare home? They were now surplus to requirements. And as people were starting to talk a lot about tolerance thresholds, and housing departments and town councils everywhere were starting, more or less openly, to apply quota policies by refusing more than a certain percentage of foreigners or coloured people, an estate like the 3000, where the limit had been exceeded from the word go, served as a natural overflow for those refused elsewhere, whom socio-politico-administrative linguists, who never seem short of a verbal brainwave, describe as 'marginalized'. For many, the question was no longer how to leave the 3000 but how to stay. In Aulnay this year, 1989, 180 tenants have been evicted and 400 cases are under examination. It's not as if the authorities are stony-hearted: eviction is considered only when all makeshift remedies using social, humanitarian and charitable welfare have been exhausted.

Meanwhile, in an effort to defuse the situation, and also to keep different ethnic groups apart, the housing services blocked off 600 empty flats. Did they give up the profits for all that? No, because the operation was financed by the *FAS*, the welfare action fund. But from exactly which part of the *FAS*'s budget was the money taken? From the part for immigrant housing. So who financed it? The immigrants themselves, would you believe. But this story of empty flats turned sour: squatters moved in. Arrivals included exiles from the notoriously poor Châlon area who had already squatted in housing condemned by the renovation round Gare de Lyon, the drug-dealers' mecca. Smart operators set up parallel flat-renting networks: Africans, for the most part, got swindled with fake contracts and receipts corresponding to flats that were in fact only squats.

What was to be done? In 1979, under Giscard's presidency, a big operation to renovate the estate was launched. It was barely eight years old.... The prefabs were defabricating and the prestressed concrete was destressing. They renovated. They repainted. It's crazy what gets painted in the Parisian suburbs. While they're at it, why not give everyone rose-tinted glasses? With the billions swallowed up, say the realists – are they optimists or pessimists? – there would have been enough to knock everything down and build *pavillons* for all. The Communist council tilted at windmills with *Opération HVS*, an initiative to improve living conditions; the 3000 hasn't noticeably changed, but it's easy enough to say – who knows what would have happened if nothing had been done....? The council launched another, even huger operation in late 1979: *VIA* ('Living in Aulnay') involved a big campaign of airing views and taking part in local life; there was even *Radio-VIA*. With the arrival of Mitterrand in 1981, efforts were stepped up. The 3000 was declared a 'sensitive zone' and a *ZEP*, an 'education priority zone': today there are ten school support groups for the children of the estate. Never again will Citroën create unskilled jobs; nor will anyone else. But there are openings in the service sector, so if the children get good qualifications.... Meanwhile, at least an entire generation has lost its way: the youngsters who have been in limbo, and still are, who have never known what it is to have a real job. They are now twenty, twenty-five years old. They have missed the boat. But is it their fault if the boat never sailed their way? They're getting older. They have learned to live some other way, and badly. But they've learned. French-born Arabs or not, they are all in the same boat. Some tell the social worker: 'I'll never scrape a scabby living Arab-style.' What's involved is not 'race' but the image of the father who has given all his strength, all his life, and finds himself unemployed, crushed, defeated. The sons want to be stronger than the rest. They also tell the social worker: 'You're a silly cow working for 6000 francs a month.' Because there is easier money to be had, sums that take away any desire to earn an 'honest' living through jobs which most of the time make no more sense, and for which you have to beg. Yes, there's easier money.

Even if they don't get it themselves, they see others getting it, through break-ins or drugs. Drugs? The word's on everyone's lips. To fight the problem, there's this Rodrigo Committee made up of young people, named after their friend who died from an overdose. Is the problem really that widespread? The council did a count-up of the notorious needles found in the gutters. The result – twenty a month for 12–13,000 people – is worrying, though maybe not the huge wave talked about. But people are frightened. What do the elderly think? It's true, they say, it's no joke coming across a gang of youths hanging around on your way home. And what's the 3000's reputation like? Try going out of the estate when its reputation clings to you. Southern Aulnay is getting high on security fantasies. So things always come back to the 3000. They stay entrenched behind the motorway barriers. On the far bank of the Sausset. Cut off. On Sundays, you can go to the African market and find everything from over there cheaper than it is over there, including the tooth-extractor's magic universal remedy.

In the 3000, a large part of the population don't have the vote, because they don't have French citizenship. But another part is making itself heard. In the 1988 presidential elections, the Communist Party realized that on some working-class estates the Front National had picked up 38 per cent of the vote.

Today the new local council is right-wing. As in Villepinte. Are there other solutions? No one has any solutions. Except trying to hang on, trying to stop things exploding. But how long can it last? And building Parc du Sausset will only confirm the isolation of the Rose des Vents.

It's true that with its marshes, the park will offer a precious haven of rest to migrating birds. And as everyone knows, Paris needs *lungs*.

They met and would meet people who knew Robert Ballanger, the Communist senator-mayor after whom the Rose des Vents' municipal park is named. He was quite a character, of that very particular species of old-style French Communist which, in this neck of the woods, was a blend of staunch radical socialism and Stalinism. Ballanger believed in the 3000. He had experienced poverty and unemployment, he had fought for the Front Populaire in the thirties. He didn't see those flats as holes, as human kennels: he saw that, finally, here was something that offered modern comfort, light, crèches and public services, and he was proud of having had them built. You have to hand it to Robert Ballanger: he lived in the 3000. He died there. And his Party named the park after him as a tribute; after, mind you, dismissing him from his duties: they said he was senile. Ah! The Rose des Vents must have been so pretty the spring Citroën was taking on workers.

Near the sign saying the street isn't a dustbin, Anaïk photographs

some black children playing. They pose for pictures. They're beautiful, the children of the Plaine de France. There are few places in the world where the children look so healthy, so free and spontaneous in their clothes, bodies, movements, expressions. Also near the sign, a car is listing to starboard; it too is spray-painted with some indecipherable scrawl. The owner, say the children, is from Senegal. How many horsepower is it? Seven? There's a problem with the engine. Now is the moment, decides François, to recite Desnos's sad little song:

> With a horse
> Or a camel
> You can go to Senegal
> With seven horsepower
> 'Cross mountain or through bower
> You can go to hospital
> You can go to the grave
> But the best thing's that
> You get a parking ticket.

Seen from a distance, and even from quite close up, tinted pastel shades by the sun's oblique caress, the Rose des Vents in the evening seems a peaceful place. Not even grey or drab. Simply old before its time. But the girls had said: 'This is home.' 'Do you think they love the 3000?' wonders Anaïk. They would certainly like to. At least not seem to disown it, in any case. Because nobody can take that away from them: whatever happens, this is their home.

But what use are all the splashes of colour and sticking plaster when the wound runs so deep? What's missing is not benches, or trees, or patches of grass, even if they could be preserved and looked after. What's missing is far more serious: from the outset, the people who designed the place forgot, or left out, an entire dimension. The vertical lines are the walls. The horizontal lines are the ground. But where's the third dimension? Did they really think it would appear, just like that, at the intersection of two flat surfaces? The third dimension costs too much. You walk alongside high walls: a door, windows, a door, no windows. There's the occasional shop – with a flat window. But what's behind all that? There's no depth to it. Where are the courtyards, the recesses, the shop hidden in a shaded doorway, the patch of sky where you can see the clouds sailing by and the tail of the concierge's cat, the lazy café terrace and its awning soaking the customers in orange light? These estates are blind.

They still have a long walk to Garonor. Is François also gripped by security worries? He doesn't like the fact that all the time they were talking to the two young women, three or four idle youths had been

circling them and discussing something. He doesn't like the fact that these boys have followed them, and even walked in front of them at times, right down the avenue; that they watched Anaïk taking photos; that they called others over. Nor does he like the way Anaïk always leaves her large bag wide open. 'Maybe,' she says, 'they want me to take their photo but daren't ask?' Maybe. François would like to get back to Garonor before dark. 'Even so,' repeats Anaïk, 'we really should have had tea with Madame Zineb.'

To reach Garonor, they have to walk through the 3000: they go down rue Paul Gauguin, walk past Parc Robert Ballanger and the low-roofed, detached-style flats, more well-to-do and enclosed, lining rue Michel-Ange, where they pass a few pale, sullen faces being tugged along by large dogs; then they come out on to boulevard Georges Braque, a dual carriageway where they again find the lorries and a lack of human beings. That walk wasn't designed to be done on foot. On the other side, an industrial estate. Then they come to boulevard André Citroën, a huge roundabout and the bridge crossing the A3 motorway, which at this level is split in two. There follows a lonely walk over the rush of traffic where all they pass is other lone people in a hurry, looking straight ahead. Once over the motorway, the mass of Garonor can be made out on the right. But there is no way in from that side: they will have to walk along the fencing, maybe for several miles. To the left, behind another set of railings, a complicated forbidden landscape stretches out in the fading light: a little valley with, at the bottom, what must be a water-treatment plant, like a dried-up lake, surrounded by wild flowers, lofty trees, rocks, and, further away, tall ruins: maybe an abandoned farm, factory or warehouses. And still further away, on the other side of the valley, a smooth wall of eight-storey metal-and-glass buildings: the Paris-Nord Business Centre. They cross a building site, and a sign informs them that here is the location of the Bonaparte office development:

BONAPARTE: THE INTELLIGENT CHOICE

proclaims the voice in the desert. And out of the desert staggers a black woman who asks them the way to the bus. So there's a bus!

And just when, feeling quite exhausted, they declare themselves lost, just after they have passed a cemetery and lofty outlines of 'walls' come into distant view, the Fimotel looms up on the outermost edge of Garonor, at long last, as the A1 motorway comes within earshot once more; with its unusual, friendly plume of trees, approached from behind like that, it almost comes as a surprise. The driver of a coachload of English tourists watches them arrive with the sort of menacing stare usually reserved for prowlers.

At the Fimotel the Fordum execs, or whatever their name is, have finished stuffing their faces and are piling into cars under their elephant driver's command. Their next stop? With Paris twenty minutes away, a club crawl perhaps? Another coach arrives, and out of it step Dutch pensioners for their evening stop: they are having a nice tour round the motels of Europe.

They must now go out and see Garonor by night, as the place comes into its own. They head off again into the darkness creeping up on the still-deserted warehouses. And at the end of this latest walk, the doors they find are all closed. Except at the Baronor, which closes at 9 p.m.: it's 9 p.m. already. But you can stay till eleven, says the lady proprietor – no one will disturb you. In the cafeteria, dry chicken is the only thing left. They are the last customers. They put down their trays at the back of the room, where there seems to be a bit of activity. Some men are playing cards. François follows the game: poker, poker-rummy? The bidding is high: 100, 200 francs. Rather big bucks. 'We don't like nosey spectators,' remarks one. 'Cool it,' says another. 'You know we're only playing whist.' 'You're not journalists, at least?' No, they're not journalists.

On their way back, they stumble along in the dark patches beneath the high floodlights, at times blinded like rabbits or hedgehogs as they are caught in the beam of an HGV out for a spin; and again they say that they've seen nothing in Garonor.

Garonor

3

Such a pretty little beach. – Villepinte: the edifying
story of a sanatorium. – Tremblay Vieux Pays:
a walk to the end of the world. – A jumbo and a lark.
– The rip-off. – Crocodiles in the canal. – Monsieur Salomon
'acts girlie'.

WEDNESDAY 17 MAY 1989. The night has been fine and balmy. The roar from the motorway would have kept them awake were they not lucky enough to be travelling in a country where the air-conditioning neither breaks down nor makes hellish rumbling noises, and allows the windows to be kept closed.

In the morning they return to their cherished sun-soaked terrace. Speeding past just a few metres away behind the glass screen, the stream of HGVs is still dizzying. The Fordum execs have disappeared. 'I feel a long, long way away,' says François. 'It even took me a fair while to realize it wasn't normal to pay forty-five francs for a phone call to Paris.' 'This hotel,' says Anaïk, 'is by the motorway as others are by the sea. The terrace is the beach. The roar of the cars is the ocean. This blue sky even seems to contain a shade of Atlantic grey. And the traffic fumes sting your eyes like seaspray.'

According to their schedule, they should catch the train from Villepinte to the next station down the line, Sevran-Beaudottes. But they have not visited Villepinte; they even turned their backs on it.

Their method needs reviewing. Yesterday proved: (1) that there are not necessarily any hotels near stations, so they will sometimes have to look for them a long way off, making their expedition a great deal more complicated; (2) that stations do not necessarily take you to the localities whose names they bear; (3) that to discover a little of the surrounding area they must therefore count the daily RER hops as only a minute fraction of total distances to be covered. The various districts are remarkably interwoven, which can leave our travellers quite by accident, as in Aulnay the previous evening, in a town they were only due to reach several days later.

In short, they will stick to the rule of a one-stop ride per day, but make it less rigid and allow themselves to skip, bounce, and go back on their tracks. To start with, they will stay in Villepinte tonight. They are bound to find a hotel in the centre of the village, where the map shows the town hall, a church and a sanatorium.

But nobody can tell them how to get from Garonor to Villepinte. Retracing yesterday's steps, with their luggage, is out of the question. The only thing for it is to head back to Roissy; wait half an hour for the bus that goes along an empty road behind the hotel; change at Roissy SNCF station; walk past the increasingly curled lips of the inspectors in their peaked caps; queue in front of the talk-screen (this time the crowd is Japanese); and pay sixteen francs forty again: 'Airport tax,' shouts the employee obligingly. It's gone 11 a.m. when they finally set foot on the platform of Villepinte station, which is still as deserted as ever.

Anaïk photographs the empty station. Its concrete, tags and torn posters would have had Raymond Hains drooling: in times gone by, François used to come across him in Paris at night looking for torn posters to peel off fences; those sublime works of art are now at the Pompidou Centre. She photographs the squalid green-tiled subway. The Roissy–Aulnay branch of the line was built at the same time as the airport: the stations are modern, designed by real architects applying a well-tempered technique – elegant curves, aerial struts, suspended roofs, clean lines, in a noble blend of concrete, glass and wood. Everything has been spoiled.

Outside, under the blazing sun, nothing has changed. The car park is as vast and silent as ever, with its banks of scraggy tamarisks and thorny bushes with white flowers (they don't know the name – perhaps a variety of eglantine? – since they haven't brought a plant guide) and a line of bus stops. Waiting in the open on a cold and rainy winter's night must be awful. The Villepinte bus is number 648.

A man of Indian appearance (from Mauritius?) looks even more lost than our travellers. They would like to help him, but conversation reveals that he knows his way around the area quite well. He's not in a daze, just very, very tired. He has been up since 4.30 a.m. He comes from Stains. He used to be a roadmender, he's still getting 80 per cent of his salary in benefit, but it isn't enough. So he got up that early to go to a hiring session, but he wasn't taken on. Instead of going home to bed he went to see a friend in Villepinte who might be able to find him work. . . . And this friend sent him to see another friend at the Aulnay 3000 who might possibly. . . . He's tried calling him several times from a phone-box. Should he go and see him anyway? He just doesn't know. He talks. He needs to talk. Fifteen, twenty minutes. Then his bus arrives and he runs to his stop at the other end of the pavement. He had only come to the 648 stop for a chat.

47

At last the 648 turns up empty, drives past them without stopping, does a big loop, then goes and hides behind a copse of trees. A young girl coming out of the station reassures them: 'It'll be back at 11.07.' Two crooked old ladies also greet each other and converse about their solicitor and 'The Wheel of Fortune'. The young girl makes shy stabs at conversation. 'Ah, so you're sightseeing, then?' She's not surprised. 'There are some lovely things to see around here.' The old ladies chip in: the Vieux Pays. The Village. The Canal. The girl lives at the next stop, La Haie Bertrand, a new development of *pavillons* of which half were put up by owner-builders. Her parents are from Paris, from the XIth arrondissement. They moved first to a council flat in Aulnay, but the girl has always lived here. She's happy: it's the country, and she doesn't fancy living anywhere else later on. Certainly not in Paris. She'd suffocate. She knows Paris well: she goes to Lycée Racine, she's studying to be a PA. No, it's not what she really wants to do, but she doesn't have much choice. She goes by bus *and* RER *and* metro. It's OK – things really get tough when you travel between suburbs: a girlfriend of hers lives in Villepinte and works in Bondy, which isn't that far away, but takes an hour and a half each way. What about hobbies? Oh, she's shy, so she likes staying at home. On Sundays she takes her dogs out. No, she's never frightened, but of course she doesn't go on the RER late at night.

The bus returns to take its handful of passengers on to the Plaine de France. To the north are trees, and through them you can see Roissy and the greenish shape of an Ibis hotel with portholes for windows. The girl gets off at her stop: attractive shiny brick *pavillons*, sensibly ringed by a fence. The next stop is old Villepinte, the village, where they get off. The trip from Garonor has taken three hours. By car it would have taken ten to fifteen minutes. Maybe there was a cross-country bus. The RATP has tried very hard to create intersuburban lines, but how can a stranger locate them? Advice for the traveller: (1) Don't rely on the large and expensive book *Banlieue de Paris, Plans, Rues-sens-uniques, Autobus* ('Paris's Suburbs: Maps, One-way Streets, Buses') published by Éditions de l'Indispensable: the 1989 edition, for example, mentions nothing about buses in Villepinte. (2) It is hopeless and, what's more, risky to make local inquiries. Villagers asked either never use the bus, know only *their* bus, or – most frequently – have no idea of the whereabouts of the destination given them, for the good reason that most of the time they are not locals. The only reasonable way to sightsee is by car. Anything else belongs to the days of sailing boats and oil-lamps.

'Talking of sailing,' says François, 'here's an aphorism that fits our situation perfectly: "Sailing is the slowest, most impractical, tiring and costly way of getting from one place to another place where one has absolutely nothing to do."'

Villepinte

Villepinte was once a farming village like Roissy. Midday on a deserted place de la Mairie. Just an electronic noticeboard. 'Messages' appear: the day's menu in the school canteens; then

MOTHER'S DAY
A poem for Mum
The prizewinning poems will be
displayed in the electronic newspaper.

There were farms here once. All that's left is the church, now unlit and closed, built on to the dark outbuildings of the sanatorium, now a hospital. The latter is a large edifice, a nineteenth-century brick château with turret. In the courtyard are some black nurses in white coats; open doors reveal big laundries. On the other side of the road, in another park, is the Saint Mary Centre for handicapped people. It is all extremely peaceful. Two nuns walk past. Anaïk refuses to photograph them. 'I don't like nuns.' 'Don't tell me you only photograph what you like,' says François. 'Yes,' she says. Not a hotel in sight.

*

Villa picta: Villepinte, the 'painted town', probably dates from Roman times. It was once an out-of-the-way farming village between Gonesse and Tremblay, in the middle of a broad expanse of farmland running roughly north–south. Three kilometres south of the town, this land stopped at the edge of Bondy Forest; then, after it had been dug, at the banks of the Canal de l'Ourcq. The first railway line, to Soissons, was built alongside the canal, followed in the 1920s by the first housing developments, and then, after lengthy protests, the opening of Le Vert Galant station. Urbanization crept towards the old village to form an urban fabric of variable density. Today the original nucleus is no more than an outpost in the northernmost reaches of the village, which becomes more built-up as it drops down towards the canal. Only a few years ago the rural village was still alive, with its large farms and mansions set amongst trees. To the south was a proletarian village for workers displaced from Paris, thanks to canny developers who put down a vague grid of cinder tracks and then split up and sold off the plots of land. The plots had no running water (each new arrival had to dig his own well), lighting or drains. During the first winters, the 'pioneers'' land was flooded with water and mud. Many people's houses were just wooden huts. So the village had its worthies and its poor people long before it became the town of 20,000 inhabitants it is today.

In 1899 the village teacher, Monsieur Bidet, wrote:

Some families are certainly not systematically hostile to education; some of the most well-to-do even give their assistance to the teacher, who need not call on their authority as a last resort. But the workers, who are out of the house from five o'clock in the morning until six or seven o'clock in the evening, are revoltingly indifferent to the idea. In reply to the observations of the schoolmaster who brought up the majority of them, they say that 'they have absolutely no time to look after their children, and that they are relying on him to educate them'.

This task should, of course, fall to the mother; yet her very nature means that she lacks the necessary energy, and the child takes advantage of her weakness . . .

On leaving school, the boys become farm workers and the girls dressmakers, or rather laundresses. As far as the old people can remember, things have always been that way, and I believe it will be a long time before things change.

At the time there were forty-five pupils at Villepinte school. As custom had it, the schoolteacher acted as clerk to the town council, and he bemoaned the extra workload this responsibility entailed: 'The many bereavements supplied to him by the phthisical hospital alone take up all his time . . .'

The 'phthisicals' were that flock of pale, consumptive young women clad in black who haunted Villepinte for years. A hundred years ago, there came to settle in the château what was first the Charity for tubercular young ladies, then Villepinte Asylum, and in the 1880s, when Koch's bacillus was discovered, Villepinte Sanatorium, the oldest in France. We owe its creation to the sisters of Succouring Mary in rue de Mauberge in Paris, whose special field was the care of bodies and the saving of souls. A devotional book tells how heaven dictated the idea from a child's mouth:

> One night in Coulanges Ward, a young patient was dying. As she lay sleeping, she suddenly woke up, her eyes aflame, and called the sister. 'What is it, my child?' said the sister. 'Oh Mother, I dreamed I saw a beautiful big house in green countryside, where crowds of consumptive young girls were being received by the sisters: some were cured and the others died, but they all had radiant faces! I offer my life in sacrifice so that Jesus may make this dream come true.' The child passed away at the first light of day.

The people of Villepinte do not seem to have taken kindly to the asylum's creation. A decision by the town council shows that there were grumbles about the number of people dying there; the villagers themselves were not ill, they died normally, so they didn't see why they should foot the bill for a cemetery extension:

The townspeople will never agree to the remains of bodies buried in the first half of the cemetery being taken out to be replaced by foreign women of all nationalities.... Moreover, the sisters of rue de Mauberge send their patients here a few days before they die in order to avoid the responsibility and cost of burials which would be more difficult to escape in Paris than in Villepinte.

The nuns stood accused of singularly sordid motives. But the people of Villepinte felt invaded, and it was always from Paris, it seemed, that people came to lay down the law. The city was forever getting rid of its excess and waste in every corner of the Departments of Seine and Seine-et-Oise: gasometers, factories, rubbish dumps, sewage farms, cemeteries, homes for the old and the poor. And now they had been landed with the 'phthisicals'. The schoolteacher and council felt that what Paris exported to them and set up in their midst was foreign, and in its most intolerable form, that of illness: and with this foreignness came death itself. The people of Villepinte weren't being spiteful, far from it: they brought to the sanatorium generous quantities of produce from their gardens and hunting trips.

The affair rumbled on. Between 1881 and 1890 nearly 8000 people were treated. New buildings went up. There were dormitories, strict timetables, discipline and virtuous distractions. All patients, little girls and grown-ups alike, wore a uniform – a black smock with a white collar. Postcards of the time show sad and terrible pictures, even if they try to be so devout and reassuring: sewing room, 'air therapy', walks. *Le Figaro* led a campaign to collect funds from high society. In 1931, the fiftieth anniversary celebrations were presided over by the Duchess d'Uzès and blessed by Cardinal Verdier. Amongst those present were the Marquise de Montaigu, the Comtesse de La Rochefoucauld, the Marquis de Rochambeau and Monsieur Panhard, 'the devoted Chairman of the Board of Governors'. A young patient recited congratulations and presented a rose, a famous Villepinte rose:

> Barely opened floweret, to those who care for you
> Say: Thank you!
> And you, little bud who wants to keep on growing,
> Smile to the future and, facing the dawn,
> Say: Thank you!

Moreover, up until 1950, when the widespread use of antibiotics rendered the system obsolete, Villepinte Sanatorium was at the forefront of progress and research in the fight against tuberculosis. A bacteriology laboratory was installed in 1897, and it was there that innovative methods such as 'air therapy' were experimented with. Nowadays, the sanatorium does research in different fields, particularly cancer; the number of beds has fallen, and some buildings have been demolished.

*

Not a hotel in sight, but there's a café. François can remember the time when he used to go off for long walks through the fields and woods around Paris. Every village had its café-grocer's where you could also take a room. In the middle of winter it wasn't often heated, but you slept well. Here, the woman at the bar eyes them suspiciously, and her husband says there are no hotels nearby. Isn't there one near Le Vert Galant station? Maybe, he's not from round here. He's only been here two years, so you see why he's not had time to have a look round. (That probably explains why he doesn't know the Hôtel Ibis, sticking up like a horrible great pudding barely a kilometre away.) No, it's not bad round here, and he can't complain about the clientele. 'Except a few of them, if you see what I mean.' No, they don't see. The café acts as a tobacconist and newsagent. It doesn't have *Le Monde*; but there at the ready is *Présent*, the Front National newspaper. But *Présent* is on sale in most of the area's watering holes.

The owner agrees to look after their bags for an hour or two. His wife remains surly: maybe they're trying to bomb Villepinte, you never know. They head off again in the sunshine towards Tremblay Vieux Pays. Keeping to the road will take them past the animals' cemetery – a must.

The road is straight and relatively free of cars; two cyclists in racing kit pedal by, heads down, without seeing them. And here is the graveyard where, as they had read in a booklet, 'lie dogs, cats, monkeys, birds, rabbits, etc.'. They would like to have known a bit more about the *etceteras*. The caretaker barks through the gate: 'We close at twelve. Come back at two. You'll have to go and see the human cemetery instead. It's just over the road and it's free.'

The road cuts through large fields. Sweet peas are in flower, wheat and maize grow densely. 'I know that smell,' says Anaïk, 'it's the smell of my childhood.' The smell of last winter's rotten beet rising persistently from the earth. 'It's a dirty smell,' adds Anaïk, 'the smell of death.' At the end of the road, the silhouettes of farms two or three kilometres away stretch out among tall trees; visible over the treetops are shiny noses and tail sections of jumbos crawling towards their takeoff points. Visible, but audible more than anything, with their blasts of infernal roaring. By the side of the road they find dead little red-black snakes crushed in the ground, almost encrusted in it: in fact they are plaits of an African woman's hair.

And at the end of the road, Tremblay Vieux Pays. Now that they're close up, the farms turn out to be no more than ruins. The houses are

bricked up. They walk into the village, coming out on to the church square. There's a restaurant sporting innumerable credit card stickers, with expensive cars parked outside; a delicatessen proposing a 'superb value' meal, which makes them suspicious; set back from the road, a fire station made of metal and turquoise panels; and a few new houses. The airport perimeter is a short walk to the north, behind two or three plush-looking houses and tall trees. There are also two farms with huge, deserted square courtyards whose peeling buildings are already starting to look like Gallo-Roman ruins; rusty tractors, washing on the line. Jet engines roaring at full thrust obliterate everything, and during the moments of respite, hundreds of birds begin to sing: are they the *song thrushes* so vaunted in the Parc du Sausset brochure? Seeming quite strange in this deserted world's end, a deckchair and parasol await him who would come and rest his weary feet. In front of the medieval church, whose doors are closed, the soldier on the war memorial proffers into thin air greenish-yellow laurel branches tinted blood orange. They go behind the church and collapse on to dirty grass under the lime trees. A few steps away, some Turks are picnicking by the open door of their old car. Anaïk gets to work with her lens-brush: 'I don't understand why there's so much dust round here.'

A few steps along the main road bring them closer still to the runways: a clearing in the trees, a pile of rubbish, and they come to the edge of a field; sticking up at the far end is the top of the control tower. They look for a 'Château Bleu' shown on the maps, can't find it, but meet Madame Agnieszka, who has few teeth and less French. '*Dzien dobry*,' says François politely. '*Dzien dobry panu*,' replies Madame Agnieszka, but the Polish of the one is even more limited than the French of the other. Even so, it emerges from the conversation that she arrived from Poland in 1947, has always worked on the local farms and doesn't know the 'Château Bleu'. And that's that: she's the only person whose voice they'll hear in the Vieux Pays.

They turn their backs on the village to return to Villepinte by a path which cuts across fields. They turn their backs on the stream of planes preparing for takeoff, but others fly very low overhead. They turn their backs on the world's end.

The Vieux Pays is like land's end. Behind it is the fence, and behind the fence are the planes taking off for other lands. But what lies beyond the planes? Is there another hinterworld? After the runways can there really be another fence, can there really be more fields, villages, roads, towns, and so on, up to the globe's northernmost point? Is it possible to meet more people? In Tremblay Vieux Pays, a landscape which has been shelled from the front line, life seems suspended, precarious, like a bivouac amid litter-strewn ruins, close to being abandoned for ever: isn't

Tremblay Vieux Pays

this the last port before the end of the world, and isn't Madame Agnieszka the last human being? *Finis Terrae*, Finisterre, lands from another world where you sense that you've arrived at the place where everything stops; as in the outer reaches of Labrador, for instance, when the last road stops dead at a blueberry bush before an endless landscape dotted with dwarf pines, and you know that from that point on there is nothing but thousands of kilometres where nobody lives and where you will find only a few seasonal huts for sheltering the Indian hunters and, maybe, a long long way away, on the edge of the Baffin Sea, as far as the ice floes, towards the North Pole, some mythical Inuits. It was on the shores of that world's end, one summer's evening when the sun just kept on setting, that François met a friendly whale.

They're perspiring, they're hungry, they talk about the sandwiches waiting for them at the café in Villepinte. Larks fly away from the green wheatfields towards the sun, and their strident song grows fainter. They disturb a partridge and find rabbit droppings among the broom, the blue flowers, the buttercups, and the puffball dandelions with which, blowing softly, you can play 'She loves me, she loves me not ...'. Down below, towards the main road, a sign announces a forthcoming 'caravan site for people of the road' marked by a concrete surface: it would have been hard to find anywhere more remote than this godforsaken place. They plunge into a wood through which the dark and muddy Sausset brook flows; two little girls are paddling. They pass under the arch of a neglected bridge, a near-ancient relic of a railway line which was never put into service – electoral pledges were made and petitions signed! Back to the café, then, but the café can't provide anything to eat. Not even a sandwich: 'The baker's closed. He opens at three.' But isn't it well past three? 'Yes, but it depends – if he's gone for his vegetables it'll be later. I wouldn't wait.'

They go with their bags to the RATP bus stop near the church. The church is still closed. The bus drives right through Villepinte and drops them outside Le Vert Galant station, on the other branch of the RER. There's a hotel, another Ibis, but it's full up. And a second one, a two-star with lift, telephone and TV in the rooms, and even Canal Plus, the subscription channel. An affable gentleman sympathizes and expresses his regrets, but today's the start of the Salon for . . . (a word ending in '-tex'?). 'The clients book a year in advance – here, take a look in my diary. Believe me, I don't usually leave people in a tight fix, I normally phone round my colleagues, but this time I *know* it's hopeless: *everywhere*'s booked up as far as Paris.' The prospect of a return to Gare du Nord looms. But this man is a kindly soul. As it happens, he can rescue them. He does have a room: it's a bit unusual, but still. He likes to help out. If they'd care to take a look. They take a look. Is it their trek in the dazzling sunshine of the

Plaine, or the heat of the road? François peels his eyes and sees nothing out of the ordinary, just two beds and a basin in the bedroom – dark but comfortable. There's a table to work at, and that's the important thing: François wants to bring his notes up to date. Anaïk says nothing. They go back down, clic-clac goes the credit card, 350 francs, confidence reigns, and there they are back in *their* bedroom. François flops on to his bed. Only then is his eye caught by a large thing against his feet, an enormous, monstrous thing which suddenly seems to fill the whole room. 'What's that?' 'That,' replies Anaïk, tight-lipped, 'is the bog.' What's more, the thing is adorned with a notice that leaves no doubt as to its use:

This device is intended
EXCLUSIVELY
for faeces.

Try as they might, it's impossible to move around the room without bumping into the thronal thing. 'There's no telephone,' notices Anaïk. 'And no television,' realizes François. So long, Canal Plus. They were too tired, in any case. 'And if all the hotels are full, what will we do tomorrow?' 'In the street, I saw a poster for a hotel in Sevran-Beaudottes.' 'Well done,' sniggers François, 'but since everywhere's full up ...' 'I phoned from a call-box,' says Anaïk. 'We've got two rooms for tomorrow.' Life suddenly seems brighter, under the big black eye of the gaping bog.

Let's fight back, let's get out of this hole, let's get back into the sunshine. Behind the station is the canal, thick green water stagnating lazily amid tall trees. On the other side are an embankment and a wood, the remains of Bondy Forest, the forest park in Sevran which once sheltered the national explosives factory. It's a balmy late afternoon. They walk for three kilometres along the old towpath, which is milling with bike fanatics, jogging freaks and people walking dogs. *Big* dogs. And the fashionable animal this year is definitely the husky. The anglers tell them about the crocodile found in the canal the previous month: 'It's true, there was a photo in the paper. In *Dialogue*. You can check if you like.' (Yes, it's true. They found the photo. It shows the man who saw the crocodile showing where he saw the crocodile. They also found the photo of *le monstre d'Aubervilliers* hooked a little further up Canal Saint-Denis:'It is a strange type of turtle whose mouth, coincidentally, is reminiscent of a crocodile's, except that it lengthens into a sort of snout.'

Coming out of the wood before reaching the lock at Sevran, they encounter Monsieur Salomon taking the air in a camp chair outside his house. He's in shorts and a low-cut vest. He's 'acting girlie', he says, along with his dog Mickey. He's reading the free newspaper *93*. The small ads

Canal de l'Ourcq

Canal de l'Ourcq

Le Vert Galant station

help to pass the time. He used to be a farm worker in the Aisne region, it was a terrible time, and then he came here to be a mason. He's retired now, and happy. He'd be even happier if his wife wasn't in hospital all the time. His house has been mortgaged to pay the medical bills. So he'll just have to wait – what's the use in worrying? – up until the day they lay him out on the *quai des allongés*, ready for the great departure. But now it's time to go and make himself some tuck. A photo? He'd like to, but he's wary. 'How much will it cost me?'

The canal looks beautiful, and up above the dense and leafy treetops mesh together. Ivy hanging from a footbridge reaches down to the water's surface. Not a single boat. They walk as far as Freinville, to the Westinghouse factory complex, past the lock and to the Kodak factories, then come back along the opposite bank. At Villepinte, the only restaurant they had located, *Le Bar des amis, chez Zézette et Coco*, whose name Anaïk liked so much, is closed. There's always the one at the hotel, with its white tablecloths and dainty lights: the exhibitors for the '???-tex' Show have arrived and are sampling the *mousseline de saumon aux petits légumes*. Andiamos, let's go and see what's on offer in Aulnay – a real town. On the RER.

Night is falling on Aulnay; there's a pizzeria in the square and further on, at the end of a street, a Chinese restaurant sign and some tables outside under a bower. Chicken with citronella, a spicy dish from Szechuan and some wine: sheer bliss. And the Chinese restaurant is also a hotel. A Chinese hotel? Yes, and there'll be two rooms free in two days. It's a deal. Life is smiling on them.

A nighttime return trip on the RER. The night is hot and very African. Girls at the end of the carriage are dancing and shouting at the top of their voices. At Le Vert Galant, Anaïk catches up with them in the square: 'I love the way your hair's done.' Photo-time. 'We had a fight on the train,' they say. And they laugh.

4

THURSDAY 18 MAY. Sleep is hard to come by: electric signs spasmodically flood the room, and goods trains shriek in the night. In the morning, François decides to work: since he has the much-hoped-for table, why not make the most of it? He makes space for himself in the room, which remains dark even though it's bright sunshine outside. He has to turn on the lamp. The lamp isn't plugged in, so he has to pull out another plug taking up the only socket. Right. And since the gargantuan, gaping-jawed sanitary pan is still there, why not make the most of that too? Right. And so to flush. But what's happening? Everything that was previously inside the contraption is rising up from the floor and washing over the foam mat. Then it clicks: the plug he pulled out to be able to see properly was the lead for the evil machine's GRINDER. Get out while you can, wading across the booby-trapped room.

Away, let us away to more salubrious climes. To the RER, then: they must change at Aulnay to go back up the line to Sevran-Beaudottes, their third port of call. And there they are.

Les Beaudottes station is underground. Seen from the train, it looks brand new. Close up, the concrete is virtually rotten. The walls are formed by alternating vertical concrete and metallic orange ridges, which deters bill-stickers but has provided an irresistible challenge for some prodigious graffiti wizards. Les Beaudottes station has a bad reputation, especially as a major drug-pushing centre. The fact that it's underground must fan the rumours even more. A new town that has shot up out of nothing has no history and therefore no secrets: and where better to make secrets than underground?

In winter the station is like a great blast of icy air, but unlike Villepinte there are real bus shelters outside, with metallic blue arches which you get

Sevran-Beaudottes

to through Plexiglas tunnels. Our travellers come out into the already dazzling morning light on to a huge and unfinished leafy forum, more a campus, lined with only moderately tall new blocks of flats. At the far end stands a façade of more traditional buildings, but the part of Les Beaudottes backing on to the station has been built to look like a real town: terraces, varying levels, columns, pedestrian streets opening on to large courtyards where children can play without their mothers losing sight of them from their kitchen, balconies at unexpected angles and even, on the top floor, a row of vaguely Moorish concrete arches, fine and slender. Façades are pink, ochre, or white earthenware – everything suggests that the planners wanted to break things up, to fight against monotony. But despite everything, what is it that gives the place its incomplete, temporary feeling, when in fact everything should be finished and permanent? Is it simply because this new town has no history and its inhabitants arrived here without really having chosen to come, with their own stories and too many problems to take the time to mix their own tale with other people's? Is there no history or joint project? Is this a pioneer town or a transit camp? Les Beaudottes is one of the places where the entire region's most recent immigrants end up.

The hotel is in rue Gagarine – they've got a thing about cosmonauts round here. Just a few white storeys, blue wooden shutters and, like everything else, brand new. Our travellers' bedrooms are on the ground floor: clean, light and functional, like boat cabins. The windows look out on to a sunlit strip of parking spaces, a faded lawn and, on the other side of an avenue, some high-rises. And best of all, for the first time they find some peace and quiet. After two days slogging round the Plaine with the heat and incessant roar, they are already starting to sag.

Les Beaudottes also means Beau Sevran, with the square mass of the Euromarché hypermarket behind it. Beau Sevran is a huge shopping centre, just up from and next to the station. Throughout their walks, they have come across tricolour posters:

BEAU SEVRAN's
having a revolution
Races with tricolour rosettes for the winners
Revolutionary
prices and bargains
from 16 to 27 May on your Republican calendar
125 shops, 10 restaurants, 5 cinemas

A high Italianate gallery boasts Piranese-style perspectives; the shoppers under the slim ceramic pillars and green aerial arches don't get squashed along with the prices. In any case, on a midweek morning like this one, the crowd is scattered. Relaxed. The shops are the same as they are everywhere, whether in the Montparnasse Tower or the Forum des Halles, and they are drowned by the same indescribable music.

In the middle of the gallery, where it opens out into a rotunda, they eat a pizza. 'I've done market research here,' says Anaïk. 'For cat food. It was a Saturday and we rounded everyone up – nobody escaped.' Anaïk has vast experience of hypermarkets. On the wrong, not the right, side.

'My first job was as a photographer at Carrefour in Gennevilliers. It was eight years ago. I'd been recruited for a show called "A photographer a day" – every day for a week there was a different photographer and a photo exhibition on the way in. I suppose the idea behind it was something like "we at Carrefour know about culture too", but no one really explained the idea, and it stayed a bit hazy.'

'How did you find it?'

'Horrendous.'

'I mean – how did you get the job?'

'Through a friend who was in charge of recruiting the photographers, of course. He's a concept photographer. In fact there was nothing but concept photographers. It was antirealism, the poetry of shapes. People didn't exist – at least, no more than the shapes. They too were just features, spots, passing shadows. A tribute to tinned food. The supermarket ambience is all about music, friendly voices coming out of the loudspeakers, colours and lights, signs with exclamation marks, a party atmosphere – but it's a sad party, and distrust reigns.

'The saddest thing is the people who go just for something to do, to kill boredom. To be with other people for a while. The old people who come every day when once a week would do. And then there are the youngsters who have no money and wander around inside the monster's belly between mountains of food dripping off the shelves. I always get pangs of anxiety before going in. All around is a desert, and when I go in I feel as if the monster's swallowed me. When I come out, it's such a relief – I haven't been eaten!

'Actually I soon went behind the scenes – to the bakeries, and where they prepare the delicatessen dishes and ready-cooked meals. It's a real food machine in there, with no natural light. I got a warm welcome from people who do a really tough job, working like robots on the production line, an existence that's been completely integrated into the sausage machine, or the box-squashing machine, considering the time you're attached to it. It's the opposite of all those modern bosses' speeches about autonomy at work. My photos were never exhibited.

'Later I worked as a demonstrator. You can be sent to the provinces.

The first time I sold revolutionary Maggi soups: exotic, country-style, etc. I had the Maggi outfit – yellow trousers and a red top. Luckily you couldn't taste them. The trouble was, because it was at Etampes, most people told me they had vegetables in the garden, and it was spring, so soups. . . . Buying three sachets entitled you to a refund voucher for five francs ninety; five packets got you a ten-franc voucher. You have to send them off along with your bank account number. I'm sure no one can be bothered to do that.'

'Yes they can,' says François. 'I did. For tins of sauerkraut.'

'I've also sold *îles flottantes* (custard and whipped egg whites in a plastic sachet) and packs of Fischer beer – enormous they were, a special bumper size for nostalgic old colonels to drown their sorrows. For the *îles flottantes* I was dressed as a milkmaid – everyone was worried because it was a new product, but they went like a bomb and I was congratulated.'

'The backroom chefs' team spirit always amazes me. The lowest-paid staff really get policed. They say it's a lot worse than fifteen years ago, but they're resigned to it. There's an obsession with shoplifting: when they leave work, they have to open their bags for the security guards. To eat, they go in small groups to the big rest room: it's got a paying coffee machine, tables and sometimes a microwave to heat up what you've brought in. There are no canteens. Funnily enough, the only place where I found a true feeling of solidarity between the staff was at the Inno in posh Passy. I think it's because of the clientele – they're such a pain that everyone closes ranks. It has to be said that the staff at Inno-Passy come from the suburbs, a long way away.'

*

Near the hotel are two roadsweepers. One of them, aged about forty, was born in Asturias. He worked for fifteen years at a big printworks in the XXth arrondissement. That was demolished, so he emigrated to Neuilly-Plaisance, then Aulnay, and finally Sevran. The other is North African and slightly younger. He arrived in France in 1956, when he was three. His father was a metalworker at Vaujours, five kilometres from here. He himself worked in a dye factory at Le Bourget. But that factory was demolished too. He lives in another Sevran housing scheme further south, in a three-roomed flat costing 2016 francs a month: how do you manage, with a salary around the 5000 franc mark? He's found a second job. Does he go back to Algeria? Not since 1976, it's too expensive. What he'd like is to have his own *pavillon*. In Sevran? No, somewhere else. Neither of them cares for Les Beaudottes. They know what they're talking about: they're the ones who pick up the needles. It's a dodgy neighbourhood. Be careful in the evenings – round the station it's *bad news*. Lots of thefts.

Cars get broken into for the radios. But, they say, if you really want to know how people live in Les Beaudottes, go over the road. It's the Paul Bert Social Action Centre.

They receive a cordial welcome. The director is thirty-five; he used to be an organizer at Sevran's council centre, where he arranged work experience for young people and ran retraining courses for the unemployed. The Paul Bert Centre is a country mansion which opened in 1984, when Les Beaudottes received its first inhabitants. Its activities revolve around the problems of finding a job and those of 'people in difficulties'. Of course the director doesn't find youths a job as such, but he helps them to draw up a professional and a personal programme. For example, a computing course has been scheduled: besides providing work training, the staff organize what are basically leisure activities – photography, making videos – which seek to raise self-esteem and help young people to avoid the vicious circle leading to drugs and delinquency. The centre is running a literacy initiative for thirty to forty women four afternoons a week, and a weekly one for forty men and women. And evening classes for between eighty and a hundred. Who are these people? Asians, North Africans, black Africans – Malians, Mauritanians, Senegalese – Mauritians, Indians, Poles. . . . A *baby-college* gives beginners' courses in English to 160 children aged six to nine. Add to that workshops, gymnastics for teenagers and the elderly, yoga, dance, theatre, musical theory. . . .

The director lives not in Sevran but in Joinville-le-Pont: he needs to keep a distance from his work.

And what about drugs? People always make such a thing of it. It's not as widespread as all that. Drugs aren't the real problem. The real problem is redundancies: in 1987, Westinghouse alone laid off 300 employees out of 800.

They depart equipped with the latest edition of *Dialogue Sevran*, the monthly newspaper produced by the council, which is still Communist: it won re-election in 1989 with 51.62 per cent of the left-wing vote, a 43 per cent abstention rate and, what's more, a score of 24.1 per cent for the Front National. A very close call, but the Paul Bert Centre can carry on.

*

This evening they have arranged to meet a Parisian friend. In the meantime, Anaïk carries on walking round Les Beaudottes alone. François lectures her on security measures. Don't leave your bag open, brimming with lenses. Don't this. . . . Don't that. . . . What should he do? He returns to the calm of his hotel room to continue writing up the notes interrupted by the Villepinte tidal wave. Or he might have a nap. He is meeting Anaïk at 6 p.m.

But Anaïk isn't there at 6 p.m. Or 7 p.m. The friend is due at Aulnay station at 7.30, which leaves François just long enough to rush into the RER station. He leaves Anaïk a message: he's waiting for her at Aulnay. He is overcome by his security obsessions: Anaïk has got lost, been kidnapped, raped. No, he knows full well that she hasn't got lost, been kidnapped or raped. So where *is* she?

It's the rush hour at Les Beaudottes station, and François has to fight against the underground tide. Lurking behind the turnstiles, a veritable pack of ticket inspectors is scanning and sorting through the flood of arriving passengers. In Aulnay station concourse there is a pitiful monument to de Gaulle, who deserved better than some kind of photoengraving on a narrow, tomb-like standing-stone: it is enough to put everyone to shame – sculptor, spectator, and de Gaulle. The friend steps off the train from Paris. François pours out his anxiety. An hour later, Anaïk finally shows up. Things are said. She got the time wrong. And anyhow, she'd walked so far that she had to get a bus back to Les Beaudottes, and you know what the buses are like. . . . Plain irresponsible, repeats François. Anaïk airs her view on intellectuals who can see the world without leaving their hotel bedroom.

*

Even at midnight the last train from Paris is full of people, but silence reigns, a silence heavy with absent minds and weariness. At moments like these, anyone raising his voice even slightly only adds to the leaden atmosphere. It's embarrassing, unseemly, almost obscene. And at moments like these, signs come to mind:

CONVERSATION TAKES PLACE AT THE PASSENGER'S OWN RISK.
THE SNCF ACCEPTS NO RESPONSIBILITY.
USING WORDS
IS PROHIBITED WHILE THE TRAIN IS IN THE STATION.
WARNING: ONE PASSENGER MAY HIDE ANOTHER.
MY NEIGHBOUR WON'T GET PAST ME.
TALKING CAN SERIOUSLY DAMAGE YOUR BRAIN.
SILENCE!

Les Beaudottes station has recovered its gloomy solitude: people walk, almost run, towards the exit in tightly packed groups, and still not a word. Knots of people race after the pacemaker towards the stairs. No one lags behind; they all come out together on to the deserted central concourse. They set off head down on to the housing estate to just the sound of hurrying feet, and the pack breaks up only at the last moment.

Les Beaudottes by night is serene and sad.

On the late news, the Chinese students are demonstrating in Tienan-men Square. Is China going to plunge into chaos? President Mitterrand said today that there is still much to be done in the fight against unacceptable poverty in France.

*

FRIDAY 19 MAY. A refreshing night's sleep. The breakfast for dynamic executives is substantial: a self-service buffet of cereals and orange juice. And still the splendid sunshine beats down on the yellowed grass and the grey-and-pink mass of Beau Sevran. On the empty, unfinished terrace, the demons of the night have vanished. Spring is charming the concrete.

They walk south-west towards the centre of Sevran. Beyond the modern estate, in the trees, are other flats on more traditional lines. Winding footpaths cut between short hedges. A few women go past weighed down with shopping: African women in boubous, two gaunt-looking young mothers pushing prams, and dogs, always dogs. Stored on balconies, supplies covered with canvas sheeting; in one fourth-floor flat, two supermarket trollies are piled high, but with what?

Then come several hectares of cultivated land. In the middle is a mound crawling with machines and lorries, and further on, blocking out the view, are the tall silhouettes of enormous blocks of flats trembling slightly in the heat haze, which gives them faintly fantastic shapes: giant battleship gun turrets or science-fiction fortresses, jagged jutting battlements, the ruins of some abandoned galactic space station with ramparts, prows, gangways, antennae and rockets. Like an uncertain floating apparition from one of those invisible towns which, according to Italo Calvino, Marco Polo recounted to the Great Khan:

> Four aluminium towers rise from its walls flanking seven gates with spring-operated drawbridges that span the moat whose water feeds four green canals which cross the city, dividing it into nine quarters, each with three hundred houses and seven hundred chimneys . . .

They follow schoolchildren down a path behind a rusty fence (No entry, beware of the dog), and there they are on a dirt path running alongside a grove of willow trees. Further on, the Cité du Parc du Montceleux is being built; with so much earth being dug over, it's hard to tell where the natural mound was and what resulted from excavations made to let the RER through. This field is probably being farmed for the last time, and it is the last field on the last farm in Sevran. Paris is eleven kilometres away as the crow flies.

Earlier they had walked across the deserted sports field, where anything

Sevran: Butte de Montceleaux

so much as emerging from the ground is daubed with tags (but the cinder surface is immaculate and the pitch freshly marked in white); alongside some schools; and then two young mixed-race girls walked past with tennis rackets. On their left they have passed some attractive two- and three-storey flats and brand-new breezeblock houses, each with its own garage, interwoven with tiny garden courtyards:

THE 'ROSEGARDEN' IS TAKING SHAPE
67 RESIDENCES AVAILABLE FOR PURCHASE

There really are roses; and a parasol in a little garden, with an Argentinian bandoleon melody floating through a window.

On the far side of the fields, they come to Montceleux farm: the large courtyard is empty, the shed no more than a skeleton, like the rusty metal nave of a church with its caved-in chancel open to the Plaine, to the flats bordering it in the distance, to the sky. Who lives and works here? The enormous dog without a lead chases after them, and the Arab grocer over the way doesn't know.

Place de la Mairie. Lots of old *pavillons* are occupied by the council services, giving an impression of considerable social activity.

SEVRAN'S PUTTING THE OPEN SPACES FIRST
160 M^2 PER PERSON

It's gone midday, the children are coming out of school, groups go past supervised by their teachers, and François says again that nowhere in the world has he seen such joyful children. Such beautiful children. Not even in Cuba, where everybody exudes spontaneity and natural grace, but where the children walk in line and wear uniform. Some people find uniforms dignified and cheerful things. And what about the children of Shanghai, poor children but child kings, who, for the benefit of the visiting journalist, stiffened into ranks, lost their smiles and tensely recited slogans incomprehensible to everybody, not least themselves? Sevran's children have no uniform, and are perhaps the most variously coloured children in the world. They do not recite slogans. They are tremendously varied and relaxed, naturally free. Providing it lasts. If only they could still be the same, fifteen years from now. But that's another story.

Another story? No. Our story. The story of these years, of those children, those young people, facing up to life after leaving school. When François still had his own imprint, he published, with his friend Gérard Althabe, who had worked in the urban development zones in Nantes and

74

Sevran

elsewhere, a book compiled by two Gennevilliers teachers, a collective book of words spoken and written by the teenagers from their technical college. It was the sort of book François liked to publish, in a collection called 'Luttes Sociales' ('Social Struggles'), because Althabe and he thought that books like that, books quite unlike all the rest, which hadn't come out of the heads of professionals such as journalists and sociologists but were useful to these people as well, books without any demagogy or preaching or short cuts, could help to change things, a very little something. Of course the book wasn't a success, it was actually a total flop – except for the teenagers in Gennevilliers, who have now been grown-up for a long time: what are they doing, where are they now? They had wanted to break the silence, address other people, adults – and the adults had no reply. In this book there were testimonies and stories, drawings and poems. Its title was *On n'a pas honte de le dire* ('We're not ashamed to say so'), and the poems were signed Anne-Marie, Ben Saïd, Dalila, Mouloud, Pascal, Patrick, Sylvie and Yahia. This poem by Patrick served as a conclusion – proof that the children of Gennevilliers didn't have many illusions:

> Boîte de graines Boîte à œufs
> Boîte à oxygène Boîtes naïves
> Boîtes à lait
> Pour l'enfance!
> Boîtes à savoir ce qu'il faut savoir
> Boîtes de vitesses Boîtes à images
> Boîtes conditionées
> Contre les rêves.
> Boîtes à idées Boîtes à questions
> L'angoisse!
> Boîtes adaptées Boîtes engrenages . . .
> Boîte à lettres Boîte-désir
> Pour communiquer.
> Boîtes de nuit
> Boîtes à roulettes Boîtes à tuer
> Boîtes de fous!
> C'est ton oppression.
> Boîte-urne Boîte d'alliance
> Boîte de reproduction
> Pour un citoyen normalisé!
> Boîtes HLM Boîtes de sardines
> Boîtes à outil Boîtes-machines
> Métro Boulot Dodo
> Boîtes de conserve Boîtes à café-tabac
> Boîtes à oublis Boîtes à jeu

Boîtes à espoirs Boîtes à sous Boîtes à huissiers
La triste merde!
Boîtes à retraite Boîte à boîte
La dernière boîte!
. . . Quelques boîtes te disent:
NE FERME PAS TA BOÎTE![2]

In the square, gardeners are watering a two-metre-tall clump of greenery shaped like the Bastille. They've been working on it for three months, says an Algerian.

All over the walls of ten-storey blocks of flats, cube-shaped urban human storage units from the 1970s, the tags are re-emerging through recent whitewash; and they are signed (when it's possible to decipher them): Vicious Sharks, *TBD, Tager black, Sink, Ruse, Cash 1, Foxy Bo, Kurt, Black Dragon*. They stop off in the shaded gardens of the Louis Armand Cultural Centre, an old country mansion where the farm has been given over to musical activities. Overwhelmed by the heat, they contemplate the blackbirds and ducks.

Back to the hotel via avenue Delattre de Tassigny. Flowers round the recent *pavillons* are in marvellous bloom. Every property has, by the road, a cherry tree far older than itself, probably rescued from a field. Cherries are in season, and there are some Montmorency cherries, red, dark, plump, shiny – and inaccessible. This is thirsty work.

*

So farewell Les Beaudottes. Four minutes on the RER and they are in Aulnay, to drop off their bags at the Chinese hotel. Then they make for Pavillons-sous-Bois, where they are meeting Gilles.

Gilles is a postman. An employee of the PTT, the French post office. He is also a geographer. Even if he objects to the title, as he would object to all titles, he is the author of a monumental Master's thesis written in 1984, presented in 1986, entitled *The geography of the north-east suburbs of Paris*. He knows its landscape well, since he was born here, lives here, and now surveys it daily from one letterbox to the next. He researched his thesis '46% on foot, 45% by bike, 5% by train, 3% by bus and 1% by car'. It basically consists of about a hundred pictures and original maps, and a text with which he was not satisfied until it was reduced to a few pages. For Gilles is wary of discourse in general, and geographical discourse in particular. He prefers drawing maps, though he doesn't hide the fact that maps too are themselves full of traps, that their subjectivity, and therefore their bias, is already present from the moment the geographer decides to draw them. What he really wants is to ask questions, all kinds of questions. Like these:

Gilles

CAUSE:
what does this word mean?
SPACE:
what does this word mean?
SPATIAL CAUSALITY:
Do these words have a meaning?

We should point out that Gilles, who is twenty-eight, studied at Saint-Denis University with Yves Lacoste, the author of *La Géographie ça sert d'abord à faire la guerre* ('Geography is first of all for fighting wars'), who had told François that Gilles was the most competent, clued-up person on the north-eastern suburbs, and that he simply had to meet him. We should also point out that if Gilles is a postman, not a geographer, it is because, as a reader of Kant, he applies the imperative of *acting so as to treat humanity as well in your own person as in all other people's* and that, considering what he thinks and says about geographical discourse, he is consistent with himself by refusing to nourish it. You have to admire him for it. And finally, we should point out that Gilles, who is somewhat uncouth and not always clean-shaven (except on the day Anaïk wanted to snap him in his peaked cap, delivering the mail), is the sort of fellow to reconcile you with mankind.

But Gilles, our uncouth Kantian, had had his suspicions. When François first called him to explain his project and ask if he could meet him, Gilles, who reads the revue *Hérodote* and had noticed that for the past six years it has no longer been published by Éditions François Maspero – for the very good reason that Éditions François Maspero no longer exists and has been replaced by others – Gilles categorically told François where to get off, informing him that the hoax was not appreciated: 'You can't be François Maspero. Maspero's dead. Goodbye.' François requested, pleaded and begged Gilles to take his word for it. But Maspero was dead, and Gilles wasn't in favour of reviving him. He was so convinced that he became convincing, and after he had hung up, François, who sometimes suffers from identity crises, started to have doubts himself. As it happened, this altercation was the exact opposite of one of François's recent experiences: as part of a series of interviews for a programme entitled 'Profils perdus' ('Forgotten Faces'), with testimonies on the life of Pascal Pia, one contributor had frostily replied to François from deep in his distant retirement: 'No, Monsieur. I am dead, Monsieur. Goodbye, Monsieur.' Upon which, with great vitality, he had hung up.

But in the end the misunderstanding was cleared up. And a good thing too, for what would they have done without Gilles and his intelligent thoughts about landscapes and people?

*

To get to Pavillons-sous-Bois, they catch the train on the Aulnay–Bondy line, which links the northern and eastern networks. Finding any sign of this train on the electronic departure boards in Aulnay station is impossible. A long search is required before they discover, stuck on the wall near a closed ticket counter, a piece of paper with the line's timetable written by hand. The train leaves from some remote platform. The white-hot carriage is like a stifling solar oven. There is something deprived about the Aulnay–Bondy line. Incidents are frequent, and the passengers have christened it the 'cowboy line'. For part of the way – the section Monsieur Gargan opened at the turn of the century to serve his factory – the line is single-track. The train goes very slowly – so slowly as to recall the time, not so long ago, when steam traction engines, with their gloomy carriages and wooden seats, worked the suburban lines: the entire journey was one long groan. Gilles is waiting for them at Livry station, which is of course part of the *commune* of Pavillons. He wants them to meet his uncle, who is the senior deputy mayor and comes from an old local family.

An old local family? There are a good fifty of them. The first inhabitants of Pavillons-sous-Bois arrived at the turn of the century. They were workers from the northern arrondissements of Paris who came to live on the developments in what was then Bondy Forest, fallow land with a camp of rag-and-bone men in its furthest extremities; across the canal was 'La Poudrette', the capital's sewage farm, as well as the former Bondy basins earmarked under the Second Empire as Paris's waste outlet, a system described in 1867 as follows:

> These necessary yet inconvenient depots have been transferred to Bondy Forest. Every night, after harvesting their foul crop, waste carts come and unload it at La Villette sewage works, from where a steam-driven machine propels the liquid part to the Bondy basins, while the solid part is stored, then dispatched into well-fastened barrels for the needs of agriculture.

The great-uncle was just a child when he arrived, in 1894, with his family on the La Colonie development by the Canal de l'Ourcq. Yes, says the uncle, they were true pioneers. As on other developments of the time, they first had to struggle against the elements – the mud and floods of the first winter – then fight tooth and nail to extract each basic 'commodity' – drains, water, a school, down to the smallest mailbox; and struggle against the negligence and cynicism of some developers. The expression *mal loti* (meaning badly off, from *lot*, a plot of land) dates from that time. They had to wait for the 1928 Loucheur Law to see any real improvement in the status of working-class home-owners.

The Aulnay–Bondy line

The *commune* was born out of developing this fallow land. It covers only 380 hectares, and its 17,000 inhabitants have mostly continued to live in *pavillons*. The *commune* is slowly gentrifying with age, and in his town hall the uncle regrets that many people know nothing about where they live: 'They only know three routes – from their house to the station, supermarket and school. And they don't know the street names.'

But for many, being from Pavillons is, by all accounts, something they hold dear. Gilles's family all live less than 700 or 800 metres apart.

They walk past the *pavillons* of Pavillons-sous-Bois. Of the oldest, the most well-to-do are built of millstone, the noble stone of the Paris area: ochre, rough and pitted like a rotten old Parmesan cheese. Gilles likes millstone. Carved on each house is a little piece of a dream. You can dream about those dreams. Some are happy, others less so. A number of houses have been bought by gypsies, who park their caravans there and play host to their large families.

*

Aulnay station in the late-afternoon heat. The crowd are wading through a flood in the underground passage. Finding *Le Monde* is impossible: the distributors are on strike. On the television news, the students are still flocking to Tienanmen Square and getting organized: the wind of freedom is blowing across China.

François thinks about the students he met over there; about those young people who, if you take the time to ask questions that look beyond the first stereotyped answers, hoped for so many changes. Yes, they hoped for so many changes, but at the same time they expressed great doubts about their coming about. There was even, it seemed, a serious sense of resignation: reedy-voiced young girls, hesitating over each French word, murmuring into the microphone that they would so like to choose a profession they enjoyed but it wasn't up to them, that they would so like to visit foreign countries but it wasn't up to them, that they would so like to marry for love but it wasn't up to them.... He remembers the dormitories where they lived in a space of six or eight square metres without running water, the jostling for a rice ration in the canteen, and young people eating from their bowl with their one personal spoon, walking all the while because there was no room in the refectory. He remembers the young Chinese girl, her voice even reedier, even more of a murmur than the rest, who asked him: 'You've asked us many questions: now it's our turn. Is it true there is waste in Europe? Can you give us details about waste in France?' And in her wise voice she had concluded: 'We in China can't afford to waste things.' He remembers their exasperation in the face of the inequalities created by the opening

Sevran

of the free market, the Party's brutal encouragement of racketeering while the professions the students were being prepared for found themselves materially and morally devalued. He remembers the old medical professor whom he asked whether he had suffered a lot during the Cultural Revolution: yes, he had suffered a lot, from harassment, insults, months spent sweeping the hospital yard, forever being made to restart his confessions. And where did it all happen? Right here in the hospital yard. And who was insulting him? Everyone, look, everyone who's here now, *the same people.*

At the Chinese hotel in Aulnay-sous-Bois, you pay up front. The bedrooms are large, clean and sad – and coming apart at the seams. Madame Bernadette, who rules the roost – which means that she slaves away from morning till night doing the accounts, cleaning and laundry – is affectionate, almost maternal, with her dimpled smile and chubby cheeks. She remembers when the hotel belonged to a lady whose life story alone would have taken up the entire book if François had written it all down – but all he can remember is that they nicknamed her Goldengob and that she had taken early retirement, which, alas, Madame Bernadette cannot do. 'This,' she says, 'is Hôtel des Trois Canards', the Three Ducks Hotel. A song from the 1940s went:

Have you heard of the Three Ducks Hotel?
The mice there scamper all over the floors.
Luckily, to put an end to their spell,
A fat cat can squeeze under the doors.

There was also something about finding tadpoles in the soup. But this evening they will dine on yoghurt and fruit bought in boulevard Strasbourg in Aulnay. They have planned a long walk for tomorrow, and bought pears to combat thirst. And even a peeler. It's time they got a bit organized.

At the end of the street with the Chinese hotel, the Hôtel Moderne has a menu pinned up including couscous and Sidi-Brahim wine. It's full up. A reggae song floats through the night air.

5

Rules of conduct for walks in the suburbs. – The trans-Villepinte trek. – Aulnay-nostalgia, Aulnay-'red' suburb. – A tower called Alice. – An African hostel. – A lesson in dignity. – Sunday at Café de l'Écluse. – La Poudrette. – Mixed conclusions.

SATURDAY 20 MAY. At 8 a.m. in the tobacconist's next door, *Mamy Blue* is playing over and over again in the background – after all, it's only twenty-five years old – and some Belgians off to Parc des Expositions are discussing the day's gameplan. A woman is wading through bundles of paper strips: betting slips or pools coupons. The weather is set fair, and already the heat is building up.

They reach the canal to go up to Sevran lock, where they are to meet Gilles, who is walking there from Pavillons. In the southern part of Aulnay, their progress is dogged by animals leaping up unexpectedly behind gates and walls. In these suburbs, you must walk in a particular way. Rule 1: steer clear of the gates – all too often Anaïk forgets and is always surprised when barking suddenly erupts, making her shout and leap into the air. Sometimes the beast sticks its muzzle through the bars; you can imagine it grabbing a sleeve. Other times it leaps so high that the fence seems dangerously low. These doggies are ferocious, frothy-jawed things, accompanying the passer-by to the limits of their territory and then just as suddenly falling quiet. Until another one takes over. They've got it in only for pedestrians; cars can drive on past, the beasts know they're inoffensive. At night the soloists sometimes join forces to perform a rousing canine cantata: everyone for miles around thus knows that a stranger, an intruder, is walking through the estate – this time he will feel distinctly guilty. With a bit more imagination he will be able to hear a rifle being cocked behind closed shutters. Can you be guilty of walking down the street?

Gilles is already there, in basketball pumps and tracksuit. The plan is to walk on to Villepinte, then head north through the estates they glimpsed all too briefly from the bus the other day: there is an almost century-old pile-up of successive housing ideas in there. Going through

87

Aulnay-sous-Bois

Villepinte is like cutting into geological stratifications. But these rocks are alive.

Lots of cyclists on the canal bank: on Saturdays and Sundays, Parisians can hire bikes at Bobigny-Picasso metro station and cycle as far as Meaux. Also more joggers and dog-walkers. And children with their teacher carrying plastic buckets: 'We're going to look for tadpoles.' Anaïk photographs them, and photographs Victor the dog and his master, both perfectly turned out. But for what?

At Villepinte bridge, a sign depicts a dog's head attentively – even anxiously – watching the raised index finger of an authoritative hand without a body, his master's hand:

VAL D'OURCQ CANINE OBEDIENCE CLASSES

They leave the shade and waterside cool, and walk past the front of Le Vert Galant station, wondering about a cryptic poster:

At the COSEC in Villepinte
MUSCLE's 30th party
3rd ANNIVERSARY OF CSMV

Opposite the station is a stone slab bearing the names of the fourteen hostages shot nearby on 14 June 1940. The previous night, a German detachment about to cross the little bridge over the canal had run into machine-gun fire from the 24th Infantry. The combat proved deadly. The Germans accused the civilian population of being involved. Early next morning, they shot fifteen people living nearby in retaliation. One of them, an Italian with only a stomach wound, played dead, crawled away and, nursed by the good sisters of the sanatorium, pulled through. About ten other civilians were requisitioned to dig tombs and threatened with being shot as well, while the villagers were rounded up in the square in front of the station. The German detachment was then replaced by other units, and the safe hostages were released.

The monument to the hostages is besieged by cars parked at an angle, and gives the impression of being topped and squashed by an enormous poster for Franprix supermarket, as well as by this slogan in giant letters:

TO SEE LIFE IN STEREO

They walk back up avenue Karl Marx. The modern church on the right is open: cream-coloured concrete ribs, a central aisle covered with kitchen tiles, and a finely tuned sound system. On the way in, they decipher a cryptogram:

L	G	W
E	E	I
T	T	T
Y	R	H
O	E	G
U	C	O
R	O	D
S	N	
E	C	
L	I	
V	L	
E	E	
S	D	

and read this parish notice:

WANTED

Name: Liturgist   *Necessary qualities*: goodwill
                                          good humour

Age: no object   *Standard*: anyone can do it

Description: give a little of your time once a month

REWARD:
the pleasure of fellowship and serving the community.

It's amazing to think that in times like these, some priests are just larking about. Gilles thinks religion is making a comeback. Not that any more people are going to Mass or worship, but he's struck by the number of homes where the family regularly reads the Bible, Torah or Koran. Outside the church, a poster around an unfurled tricolour flag announces a gala evening in honour of the Bicentenary: 'M'b Soul Company – with entertainment by the *Show Chaud*'. And further on, on a hoarding stuck in the grass, next to the one for *Beautiful Revolutionary Sevran*, a lion-woman lies waiting for them:

Call DOMINA
on 36-15
the first magazine
of secret charms

But they're all over the place.

Moving north, there is a change from old *pavillons* to more recent urbanization. In his thesis, Gilles distinguished several types of dwelling: the old blocks of flats built between the late nineteenth century and the early 1920s (especially noticeable closer to Paris, round Aubervilliers); *pavillons* (individual ones or in developments); the estates nearly all constructed after the Second World War, mostly council blocks in prefabricated concrete slabs or concrete or steel girders covered with compressed panels (as at the Aulnay 3000, La Courneuve's 4000, or Sarcelles); and finally what he calls 'the new estates with different ideologies' which appeared at the end of the seventies, of which we can suppose that Les Beaudottes is a good example. Practically all these styles are represented on the Villepinte plateau.

At La Fontaine Mallet, large blocks have been renovated, resulting in broad sweeps of ochre and green on a cream background coating the sections of each 'wall'. Next come clusters of *pavillons* which gradually give way to flats built about ten years ago. By the side of the road are tiny pink-and-grey houses huddled together, with sharp-angled gables and minuscule gardens containing white plastic seats and parasols. 'Doll's houses,' says Gilles. 'All in a line like beach cabins,' says Anaïk. A mother walks by with her children; they are in striped swimsuits and carrying buckets and spades. 'See, they're off to the seaside.' In this estate, where the streets are almost bare, they come across a West Indian wedding.

They make a detour to the left to walk past the solar-powered houses – a little street of white homes with large, blue-framed glass roof panels, small windows and balconies protected by thickset walls. They are dazzlingly white, like a small Greek port. A family at their window kindly explain that there are thirty-two homes and that the occupiers are nearly all town hall employees; that it's lots better than living in Paris, where they've come from; and that the father takes over an hour to get to work, but he's not complaining. The solar panels provide hot water and the electricity supply is computerized, as is the heating in winter. The trouble is that electricity is the most expensive type of power. To return to avenue Karl Marx they walk back past old brick and millstone houses; again they discuss the nobility of millstone. Yellow acacias are in flower; Anaïk talks about frying the blossom with raspberry petals. A West Indian lady on her doorstep shows them her cats Comma and Sangor (or Senghor?). The latter is black and white and enormous: 'It looks like a panda,' says Gilles. She is growing large poppies in her garden: Gilles and François have a long and confused discussion about the chances of gathering opium in the Paris area.

Still further north, wedged between the wide, two-lane avenue Robert

Villepinte

Ballanger and the A104 motorway which you cross by bridge and which, down in its embankment, makes virtually no mark on the landscape, they come to Cité du Parc de la Noue with its 'walls' and high-rises, and the shopping centre with its bank and Chinese restaurant. Here renovation means trompe-l'œil slates adorning the walls. Over the road, a vast public sports complex stretches out next to the school. They cross the motorway, and here they are amid the white and grey concrete of the Parc des Pyramides. The surroundings and atmosphere have changed: the build-ings are low and layered like Mexican pyramids, with long leafy terraces, steps, long paved pathways: you feel as though you are in a huge Mediterranean rock garden. The place is smothered by green, red and grey trees, and there's a smell of resin in the air. Here you really feel close to the sea. It is one of the finest architectural achievements in the Paris area, and not just anyone can live here, that's for sure. The motorway sliproad is right nearby and if you hop in the car, maybe this place is nearer to Paris than everything surrounding it. But they see nobody in the oasis to ask about the art of living at Les Pyramides. And for the first time since this morning in such a deserted place, there are no dogs barking.

And then, just before they arrive at the sanatorium and the old village, Cité des Mousseaux brings them back down to earth with a bump: blocks made from a metal structure in which the gaps are filled alternately by compressed panels and windows. The notorious modern human shoe-boxes. Gilles says it was probably the population of Les Mousseaux that made the café owner the other day say, in a slightly raised voice: 'You see what I mean.' They talk about humanizing the estates, Gilles goes on, but he has his own idea about it: 'They kick out anyone who's not white' – Gilles thinks it's council housing policy, and won't be convinced otherwise. He's well-placed to say, knowing mankind as he does by his letterboxes – a surefire way of telling. What he has noticed on his rounds is that little by little African and Arab names are disappearing: at Saint-Denis on Cité des Francs Moisons, at Les Courtillières in Aubervilliers – or here.

In the old part of Villepinte, the café where they would have liked to have a cool drink won't serve them. 'It's midday, and at midday on Saturday we close. Weekends are sacred.' And to think that in some countries hospitality is sacred! Never mind. They go as far as the La Haie Bertrand development. Gilles wants to show them a farm that was still being worked the last time he was here. It has been turned into a tennis club. They eat their bananas and pears. Slightly further on, where everything comes to a stop with the indistinct landscape stretching up to Roissy, a small new shopping complex lies dead and ruined. A huge sign informs them that the new mayor has announced new plans for this very

Crossing Villepinte

place in the very near future – but what plans? The sign is already falling to bits. It's very hot. They wait an age for the bus back to Villepinte. And then on to Sevran. At 2 p.m. they are at Café de l'Écluse. The owner makes them enormous Camembert sandwiches. Anaïk photographs the small family of regulars. They feel tired. They feel happy.

*

SUNDAY 21 MAY. Once in Aulnay, the geography changes: the Plaine gets hemmed in between the forests of Montmorency to the west and the hillocks of what used to be Bondy Forest, about fifteen kilometres away to the east. The geographer Jean Brunhes called it 'a human strait', which shrinks still further as it nears Paris to squeeze between the slopes of Montmartre and Chaumont, and which for centuries has been the one and only route for anyone walking from the north towards the Seine. Roads towards Flanders, Germany and England chose this path, as did the canal and railway lines after them.

It also marked the beginning of the military presence around Paris. Defence was difficult on flat terrain, but now it became possible – and necessary. Last-ditch battles were fought there. The encounter on Villepinte bridge in 1940 was just one (there were others in 1944) in a long line of massacres. In the seventeenth century, for example, the Fronde in these parts was not a half-hearted affair. When the royalist troops of Mazarin and Anne of Austria finally overcame Condé's, *The General Account of Poverty in the Countryside and of the needs of the poor on the outskirts of Paris* noted in October 1652:

> ... For all the surrounding districts, Le Bourget, Villiers-le-Bel, Aulnay, Sevran, Bondy and other villages that troops have lately marched through ...
> Localities, villages and hamlets empty and without priests.
> The streets and vicinities infected with rotting carcasses, smells, and exposed dead bodies.
> Houses without doors, windows, partitions, and several without roofs; and all reduced to cesspits and unsafe in structure.
> All the women and young girls fled and the remaining inhabitants were without furniture, utensils, provisions, and bereft of all relief. Some have lived on water and grasses for two weeks and others on fennel leaves and roots, which has exhausted their strength ...
> And finally the largest number is consumed by new kinds of death: hunger, their own infection, or that of the dead having expired close by them ...

And through all this spread an epidemic: the plague, some said; typhoid, said others.

Aulnay was more an area than a village, made up of several hamlets –

Pays d'Aulnoy, Pays d'Aunai and Pays des aulnes. In 1920 it was still, with 7000 inhabitants, a semi-rural, semi-industrial town. The transformation was a slow one. The Marquis de Gourges were rulers there for a long time: one of them was guillotined in 1794, but his descendants did not, for all that, supply any fewer mayors under the First and Second Empires. In the late twenties, the council became left-wing, Socialist, then Communist: Aulnay became a 'red' suburb. Up until recently, that is, when the Communists lost control to the Right after being disqualified for electoral fraud.

The 1921 Guide Bleu notes that 'the woods that once made this locality a pleasant place to stay have now disappeared'; but with nostalgia still being what it used to be, this did not prevent an old Aulnay lady from saying in 1980: 'For several years in the early twenties, Aulnay was a very pretty town with its acacias, poplars, fields, rivers . . .' In 2030, will people write about how nice it was living in Aulnay in the late 1980s? And what will have disappeared by then which lends it its charm today?

In 1920 Aulnay still had its municipal wash-house (which was very busy, since running water was a rarity) supplied by the Sausset and the Morée; and, in the latter stream's 'very clean and pure' waters, a watercress bed.

Must we shed a crocodile tear over the pretty wash-house, the pure stream and the washerwomen's merry banter? Or think instead of the weighty piles of wet washing that the women pushed in wheelbarrows, of the long sessions kneeling down by the tubs – one for washing, the other for rinsing – and the duckboards offering scant protection from the icy water and aches, chilblains and chapped skin?

As Aulnay's working-class population increased, many societies were formed: *The Mutual Help Society* in 1904, *French Providence*, *The Future of the Proletariat*, *The Gymnast Friends* in 1907, *The Aulnay Walking Association*, *The Musical Association* reinforced by *The Child Kazoos of the Sands* and *The Gallic Gaiety*, and in 1930, even *The 'Couldn't Give a Damn' Society*.

Today Aulnay numbers 80,000 people living either side of the station. On the fields of the old farms to the north are the new estates, like the Rose des Vents: that's the new working-class Aulnay. To the south, where the first factories were built near the canal – the first made radiators, then came the Westinghouse and Kodak plants – and where *pavillons* were built which, like those in Freinville (nicknamed *le petit septième* after Paris's expensive VIIth arrondissement), have become gentrified, is the part of Aulnay where white, right-thinking people live protected by their fences and ferocious doggies, stuck between the Paris they see as a monster and the unknown and evil estates to the north. This Aulnay, which has its traditions and old families – in short, a history – has taken decades to model and remodel itself on top of the old compost; and it will remodel itself again in the future. It is in marked contrast with the other Aulnay, which has no history, which has suddenly sprouted on the Plaine, built on a past that was levelled, destroyed and denied. Lastly, and more secret, is the shameful Aulnay, the poverty-stricken Aulnay, as exemplified by Cité d'Emmaüs.

*

It is still very hot. This morning the news gave top billing to two big events. Will there or won't there be a confrontation in Tienanmen Square? Everyone's still waiting. And yesterday on the Aulnay–Bondy line, the cowboy line, three inspectors were savagely attacked by a gang of youths: a strike was immediately declared on all eastern suburban lines.

François slept badly because, from his window open on to the street, the goods trains rattling past nearby gave him railway nightmares. Anaïk slept badly because rising up through her open courtyard window came the thick stench of cold Chinese cooking. What's more, both of them must face up to a problem that has been brewing for two days: blisters. Why didn't they follow the judicious advice of every guidebook in the *entire* world: 'You are recommended to equip yourself with a pair of solid, comfortable walking shoes'? Anaïk's case is worrying because she refuses to wear anything but a kind of grey leather sandal with not especially high heels, her excuse being that they were a present from a gypsy woman from Porte de Vanves; and a gypsy should know about walking, shouldn't she? They have trekked between sixty and eighty kilometres in the last five days, and not just any old kilometres: so that's what it's all about, travelling by RER. And now a strike is looming ...

*

This morning they are meeting a postman friend of Gilles who lives at Cité de Rougemont in Sevran, on the border with Aulnay. They go down rue Louise Michel. For the first working-class councillors in working-class towns, naming streets after outcasts – like Blanqui – or Communards – Louise Michel, Varlin – was revenge on official history, a challenge to the worthies who had gone before. And the worthies found it hard to stomach. When, in 1939, Aulnay town council was dissolved after the Communist Party was outlawed, the special commission that replaced it hastily dechristened huge numbers of streets: this meant curtains for places Camélinat and Henri Barbusse, rues Jules Vallès, Robespierre, Roger Salengro and twenty more. Rue Louise Michel turned into avenue de Soissons, rue Romain Rolland into avenue de Gourgues, and rue Degeyter into rue Brunetière. The cake was iced in 1941: place de la

République became place du Maréchal Pétain. A heck of a time to be a postman.

These were no petty village feuds. When the Communist mayor and deputy of Aulnay-sous-Bois were arrested in 1939, they were deported to Algeria; freed in 1943, they returned to France in 1944, which at least allowed them to avoid the fate of two town councillors who, following their arrest in October 1940, had a taste of the French prisons before being handed over to the Nazis and dying in a German concentration camp. And the same story was repeated with all the Communist councils.

Benoît, our postman, lives in a high-rise called Alice. But how, in this big collection of tower blocks, do you find Alice? Here's Béatrice: a group of teenagers is hanging around outside. They don't know the names of the blocks. Theirs is called Béatrice, they know that, but the others.... 'Try the one opposite – if it's marked Alice, then that's the one.' Thanks for the tip. As luck would have it, Alice it is.

Benoît is Vietnamese, and Chinese on his mother's side; his uncle was a Southern general at the time of Diem. He studied law at the Université de Paris II. He is far from being the only PTT employee to have gone on to higher education. (When you apply for a job there, said Gilles, you must take one basic precaution: don't mention studies and degrees.) He works as a *brigadier*, the lowest rank: above *brigadier* is the *rouleur*, and above him the *titulaire*. He acts as cover for five towns around Aulnay: he's kept pretty busy, because postmen – and they should know – are always in short supply at the PTT.

Benoît has a principle, a Chinese proverb that says the river must adapt itself to its bed. If you come to live in France you adopt the French way of life, it goes without saying. Look at the Chinese in the XIIIth arrondissement: everyone recognizes their qualities, they're discreet and hard-working. He can't understand why people don't try to live intelligently: he's forever clashing with people who turn a deaf ear, who behave like barbarians. It shows a lack of respect for other people, whether they're white, black, yellow or purple. It's not a question of colour, it's about responsibility. Why do so many people in this country have no sense of responsibility? The worst example he's seen is Les Beaudottes: there used to be a time on his rounds when he would literally find shit outside the doors. Today Les Beaudottes is sorting itself out. He thinks that owning their own home would make the inhabitants more responsible. Others, on the contrary, feel that it makes people more withdrawn, indifferent or, worse, aggressive. But for him the tenant is someone who has nothing to defend but himself. Especially with the huge rent rises at the moment, which are creating even more unbearable tensions. Things can go downhill so quickly. But what can be done to stop the slide? And how can order be restored? Benoît says the evil must be attacked at the root. He talks about viruses, about eradicating the evil. He knows that at Montfermeil they are planning to blow up whole 'walls', as at La Courneuve's 4000. It had to be done: the lifts over there are stuck, the entrances burned, the letterboxes torn off the walls. But is that really attacking the evil at the root? What is it that's so rotten about this country, although there are all the conditions necessary to satisfy the need for peace, order and reason which he feels so strongly and which should be at the heart of every human being?

Benoît even has problems in his own block. Yet he has all he needs to be happy; the neighbourhood and his block have been renovated, he's among the trees, and his two-room 52-metres-square flat belongs to him: 'It's like Versailles here. The great thing about the suburbs is the space.' But the soundproofing is terrible. And the neighbours upstairs – Blacks, Africans or West Indians, he doesn't know, he doesn't know them, it's impossible to talk to them – they make an unbearable noise, day and night. Again there's this lack of respect for other people. It's absolute hell.

And yet he's happy. He doesn't feel the need to go to Paris. He finds everything he needs right here: at Sevran there's the Conservatory, and he goes to the library; and the Canal de l'Ourcq with its superb cycle path.

Yes, really, *without that* he could be perfectly happy. One of the big financial problems is the rates – it's a struggle paying them, they're at least five times higher than in Paris. For him, that's one of the reasons why a lot of people voted right-wing at the last elections. As for the far Right, the Front National polled 24 per cent at Sevran, its fourth-highest result nationally. Yes, it's worrying, but, he wonders, isn't it the result of many immigrants' lack of responsibility and respect for other people?

*

They leave Alice at noon. Out in the sunshine they dream of the idle life: of returning to the cool canal, the green flow. They cross a deserted bridge over the RER tracks, walk between blocks of flats. Outside one of them, under some trees, is a stall of exotic fruit, mangos, tubers; Africans in boubous sit idly around, and someone is playing the tomtoms. To one side, some North Africans. They walk past a courtyard: by the entry to a cellar, men squat round a fire talking. Then things get out of hand: mechanically, Anaïk gets out her camera and, from a long way off, takes a photo. Commotion ensues. One man breaks away from the group and calls to them. Anaïk immediately looks his way and walks up to him. 'Not wishing to order you about, and with all due respect, but what did you just do?' They have gone into a courtyard, and a group has formed around them. The men are all impeccably dressed, shirts freshly ironed. The discussion lasts a good half hour. They are polite. Very polite. And very firm. A lesson is delivered on morals and dignity, with the theme: when you take someone's photo, you ask his permission first. The theme is elevated to a principle for life: respect comes first. 'If you had asked me first,' says the first one to speak, a big green-shirted Malian, 'I would have been flattered.' 'And if I asked you now?' replies Anaïk. 'It's too late. Not this time. Some other time maybe.' The big Malian used to be a student. He introduces his brother. And another brother. Another, older man, who has just arrived, inquires in his own language and takes François to one side to repeat the lesson even more severely and politely than before. He would like to think they are not police or journalists, they could even be friends, but friends don't behave like that. 'There are lots of Malians here,' says the former student, who works in Paris. 'In Mali, people have always respected France. But France today isn't what it was – there's no respect for other people. Yet my father fought for France. There are journalists who come to Mali and take photos and then do disgusting reports.' 'Not wishing to be indiscreet, what are you doing round here?' They explain that they're from Paris, that they've just been to see a friend at Rougemont and are walking towards the canal. Just for pleasure. 'And still not wishing to be indiscreet, what do you do for a living?' Anaïk replies that she's a demonstrator in supermarkets. 'You don't surprise me – just by looking at the way you smile and walk. You're a very attractive woman.' François chooses to state his job as a translator. Otherwise try explaining, in the heat of the moment, the difference between writer and journalist. The professions given are accepted politely, like everything else. With smiles. 'So,' insists Anaïk, 'now we've explained ourselves, still no photo?' No. But one day, he promises, perhaps if they meet in Paris. The circle breaks up. They shake hands. The big Malian puts his hand on his heart. 'May God go with you,' he says to Anaïk.

They arrive on the banks of the canal. 'I don't know what came over me,' says Anaïk. 'You know spy photos aren't my style, that I like to take time to talk first, to get to know people, yet with all the long-distance photos I've taken since the journey started, I feel as if I'm becoming a robot. It's stupid – the photo was of no interest anyway, taken from so far away.'

They would spot that family again later that day on the canal banks. Keeping to themselves. Away from everyone else.

At Café de l'Écluse, the customers don't fight shy of the portrait session. 'You're journalists, aren't you? Then you must work for the town hall. For *Dialogue*, isn't it? I'm sure I've already seen you at the town hall.' Our travellers will later return faithfully with the developed prints.

Canal de l'Ourcq

Everyone here is a regular: they all feel at home. The café sells fishing lines, which makes for plenty of coming and going. What's more, the fishing society's president is there, with his glass of red wine. They are all long-time inhabitants of Sevran and Aulnay. It's not like the 'good old days' when the farms were still there: like the one at Rougemont with its pond where people went fishing for frogs – today all that's left is the poplar tree near the high-rises, didn't you see it? It's got one foot in the grave. Montceleux Farm, the last one left, isn't long for this world, and the chap who farms the land doesn't live there, he comes from further away, we don't know where, he just stores his machines there. And the canal's dead: there's no more barge traffic, just a few pleasure craft. They remember the time when barges were towed; some can even recall horses tugging them.

At the café, where they're amongst friends, where they're happy, the general opinion is that Les Beaudottes is Zulu country: 'I'm not racist, but ...' Watch out for the thefts, says one, with an expressive conjuror's mime. But opinions are mixed about Beau Sevran: 'First of all, Beau Sevran isn't Les Beaudottes,' states an optimist. 'You're telling me,' says another. 'Beau Sevran's different, anyway. You can go for a quiet walk there.'

Some of them tell their life story. Whole chunks pour out, and it's difficult to piece them together. There's no need to ask questions, prompt, say the wrong thing. A piece of existence just streams out, unfolds. The day the Germans blew up Freinville bridge, I ...; no, not the Germans – the French. And when I was a concierge in Paris.... There's this desire momentarily to flesh out images and colours; as though there's treasure buried, scattered in the memory, and it's just too unfair. Then the time so briefly conjured up by a few words dies away. You've heard the same thing a hundred times: 'You could write a book about my life.' And no one ever adds: 'How about you?' They're just monologues – as if, to recite one, two's company.

The owner tells our travellers how hard it is keeping the business going. She would like to go and live in a *pavillon*, like the old days, and live the peaceful life. She stands them their drinks.

Sailing through the lock is the Meaux-bound launch on a cruise from Port de l'Arsenal in Paris, near Bastille. With the return trip by coach. Or vice versa. It's pretty, but it must drag on a bit, sitting behind the windows – just another coach trip, really. The passengers have the slightly lifeless look of people being moved around and no longer really knowing if it's for their pleasure, or for what exactly? It's for taking photos, of course. They wait for the lock to change, sipping fizzy drinks.

Work on the canal began in 1808. It is no longer operated by the

highways department but belongs to the City of Paris, which it supplies with water. Even before it was navigable, it brought water to Paris: 'On 15 August, Emperor's Day, its waters were introduced for the first time throughout the city's mains, and flowed in large waves into the Fontaine des Innocents before the astonished gaze of a public that had never seen the slightest trickle of water in Paris's fountains.' The canal skirted around Bondy Forest. Terrible Bondy Forest, where highwaymen had their dens: in 1743 the Marquis de Gourgues was murdered there. Sorrowful Bondy Forest: Gilles told them that at Montfermeil they show you the spring where Victor Hugo's Jean Valjean met Cosette, the Thenardiers' slave.

On the other bank, going up towards Villepinte, are the workers' allotments: vegetables for the pot, absolute whoppers, flowers, and raspberry and blackberry bushes sagging with scarlet clusters. But they are out of reach behind the fence's high bars, the entrance gate is locked, and inside, each plot is fenced off and padlocked too. The gardeners and their doggies are nice and relaxed in the shade of the tool sheds. A forbidden paradise. Further off is the forest park, on the site of what was once Sevran national explosives factory; a factory, but an entrenched camp too. Beyond the park, past Freinville, is Livry, where Madame de Sévigné spent her childhood. But it's a long way away, and who knows what remains of the abbey belonging to her uncle, the Abbé de Coulanges, which was destroyed in the Revolution and damaged again in 1870, as the old Guide Bleu explains so nicely?

And on the banks of the canal itself, towards Aulnay, neither is there any trace of the *guingettes* of fifty years ago, open-air cafés for drinking and dancing: The Sautéed Rabbit, The Fishing Cat, The Danube, The Robinson, and The Ducklet, where you could eat fried gudgeon and mussels; not forgetting *Le Jardin perdu-lillois*, with its big orchestra and privet mazes for lovers in search of hiding-places. No trace at all. Just shady strips of ground.

Later they will continue their walk as far as La Poudrette. The *poudrettes*, where fertilizer was made from ground rubbish mixed with the product of the Parisian sewers, were once located all around the outskirts of Paris. This one is within the boundaries of Pavillons, by the canal, like a hidden recess between Aulnay and Bondy. During the last war they tried to create subsistence plots there, but it was a failure: there was infertile waste fifteen metres deep. On the site today stand dilapidated warehouses. A few families live there in caravans. They meet Monsieur Pierrot emerging from piles of rusty debris. He's a Breton, he says, and lives on a nearby estate. It seems to be the emergency estate built in 1956 at the time of the Abbé Pierre's big campaign for the homeless. It was called a transit

Pavillons: La Poudrette

camp, but it's a long time since anyone passed through: the departmental housing office has filled it with people who have exhausted all resources and survive on council welfare support. In northern Aulnay there is also Cité d'Emmaüs, a poverty-ridden estate which receives help from the Fondation de l'Abbé Pierre: 700 flats for more than 2500 people, many of whom aren't even above the poverty line, where you find cases of malnutrition (a word meaning 'hunger' in socio-administrative language) and diseases thought exceptional in modern society, like diphtheria or typhoid.

*

Our travellers feel weary. Lying under the lime trees, they review the first week. Conclusions are mixed.

'That's what we said – not a sociological inquiry, not a report. Just a journey, for the pleasure of walking around and finding out things. And all of a sudden everything throws us off balance, all this life tangled up in inextricable knots. How can we take it all in?'

'I've never taken photographs so quickly,' says Anaïk. 'The Africans at the hostel were right: you must take your time and show respect for

others. I don't want to end up like those snap-happy tourists who are in too much of a rush to see what they're snapping. They only look afterwards, when their interest's sparked off by the developed photos. At night I dream that all these people – in the RER, the estates, the high-rises – come and cling on to my bed and keep tugging at me. But where do they want to take me?'

'We shouldn't linger,' says François, 'but for every question there's a flood of answers we haven't got time to look for, and which always prompt other questions. To talk properly about Les Beaudottes, for example, we'd need to stay there a long time – dwelling on the facts about the job market, the creation of new businesses, the service industries, as always, and the unemployment rate; and on the pitfalls of home-owning. So I take notes, and more notes, and soon I'll have no more time to look around me.'

'Even so, don't tell me you intend to write your own *State of the Suburbs?*'

No, he doesn't intend to write a *State of the Suburbs*. They'll have to keep walking on by. Just walking on by and not looking back. Building up a stock of memories, as you do on a real journey.

But he would at least like to know how to describe the balmy late-afternoon air under the lime trees by the canal's slow green water.

Swimming just below the surface, its nose barely poking out of the water, a coypu scurries silently from one hole in the bank to another, as if there were nothing in the whole world except him and his mysterious little affairs. Families laze on the dirty grass. Our travellers close their eyes against the orange light: with the heat and isolated snatches of conversation, all that's missing is the faintest murmur of rolling pebbles and they could be on the beach at Saint-Eugène in Algiers, how many tens of years ago? Behind them, two bare-breasted women sit near a bush doing singing exercises, their faces raised in ecstasy towards the sun. On the other bank, just opposite, the anglers are out in force: one eye on the float, the other on the breasts. Lots of cyclists ride past on the path just a metre away. It feels faintly like a weekend at the time of the Front Populaire. It's Sunday. They eat apples and yoghurts.

PART II

Petite Couronne

In these parts, the name of the towns and villages is written on the weather vanes instead of being carved on the milestones.... You follow the arrow, but the wind blows and you're lost once again. It's as though the towns were running away. You can't lay a hand on them.

JACQUES PRÉVERT, *Spectacle*

6

Blanc-Mesnil, the last people's democracy. – Le Bourget:
four-wheeled hell. – Return to Les Beaudottes. – Solitude of
the Air Museum. – They died in 1870: the press irregulars.
– Bondy and disaster. – RER strike.

MONDAY 22 MAY. They have left their bags at Hôtel des Trois Canards.
In the phone book they have located two hotels in the *commune* of Blanc-
Mesnil, their next port of call: first they will go and see what they're like,
choose, then come back to collect their bags.

10.07 a.m. The journey from Aulnay station to the one at Blanc-Mesnil
takes two minutes. The latter station is located right at the beginning of
the big Le Bourget marshalling yard, which stretches out for several
kilometres towards Paris. The tracks are on a lower level, straddled by a
concrete bridge and, slightly further along, by the bridge of the A3
motorway with the deafening skull-splitting roar of its two-way snail's-
pace procession of lorries: a separate world of perpetual motion, living its
own prison life.

Rereading François's notes is often a source of surprise. About Blanc-
Mesnil station they say: 'The most defaced we've seen.' As if they haven't
said that about every single one so far. It is built against the containing
wall, the piles that support it rising up from the platform; it resembles
a crenellated pillbox. As usual at this time of day, human beings are
scarce. A few people are waiting to use the telephone, and the piped music
playing is *Nos ancêtres les Gaulois*:

> You've got to laugh, got to laugh
> To stop the sky falling down

– a tune which remains associated in François's mind with the picture
jukeboxes – the *scopitones*, Anaïk clarifies – in rue Saint-Denis in the
1960s: for the time the forty-five played, you were allowed to watch a
colour screen showing Henri Salvador disguised as a Gallic cannibal
running between straw huts. The sky isn't likely to fall down today, the

weather is still set fair, but fortunately the heat is tempered by a few gentle gusts of wind. On the embankment, a riot of field flowers *à la Sisley* – poppies, cornflowers and dandelions, and some spindly acacias. The European election campaign is under way: sickening, undifferentiated posters pronounce, by and large, that to assure the children of France a bright future, they (the future and the children) must be European. Peeling off them, some comforting stickers:

> VOTE FOR THE ROTTEN PARTY
> APPROVED BY: THE CANDIDATE

Pavillons stretch away to the north-west, with high-rises beyond. There's a car park, a standard no-man's-land, and on the left, turning your back on the sun to walk towards Blanc-Mesnil town centre, about two kilometres away, a site of undeniably daring constructions rub shoulders: two- and three-storey houses with light wood exteriors, sides cut at surprising angles, diamond-shaped windows; off-white roofs, pale ochre walls, red window-frames. How can one put it: the place has a certain *je ne sais quoi*. Gables point skywards like ships' prows and some of the roofs swoop down to the ground to let narrow passages through. 'They look like Viking longships,' says Anaïk. Inside there must be lots of strange nooks and crannies and potential for pretty cupboards.

> Attractive surroundings for all in Seine-Saint-Denis
> Mayor Robert Fregossy
> his council team
> and SODEDAT 93
> are working to brighten up your town.

Another sign explains that the development consists of 88 council houses 'with an experimental wooden structure'.

In rue Pierre Semard stand magnificent specimens of *urban property*: an information board on forget-me-not blue plastic posts announces:

> This evening
> M.R. Fregossy, mayor and general councillor
> Youri Nara, soprano
> will sing works by N'guyen Tim Dao
> at the Erik Satie Centre

(also listed are other artists, songs from India, etc.). On the other side is a diaphanous red, white and blue cloud:

The blue
The white
The red
17 artists are exhibiting at the Town Hall

(It's on a white background: the blue is written in *blue*; the white, of course, in *black*; and the red, in *red*. On reflection, the white having to be in black isn't quite right.)

They walk among the cherry trees (still out of reach, the cherries) and a profusion of roses, admire a *colonne Morris*, an old-fashioned pillar-shaped billboard also in tricolour plastic; a Buddhist monastery, GETAVANA VIHERA, in a tiny house with a turret and a swing; and they are caught in the usual canine chorus. And then suddenly, behind roses and a fence its owner is painting yellow and beige, a truly sublime vision on a lawn. Here is a succinct inventory:

- bright red giant's boots filled with aloes and succulents, each placed on a tree trunk,
- a wrought-iron Bambi carrying two plants in pots, *idem*,
- a white plaster donkey carrying two baskets of plants, *idem*,
- a miniature plaster well with a red-tiled canopy, hanging from which is a begonia-bedecked bucket

. . . etc.

We should note that an industrious electric-sign salesman has worked wonders in the area: everywhere, flashing outside the most modest house used as a shop, are illuminated words thought up by little sign-writers on which each owner – insurance men, vets, dry-cleaners – announces his personal message, and occasionally, being a devoted servant of the public good, relays the exact air temperature.

As you near the church steeple, the housing grows denser. Avenue de la République is a thoroughfare with heavy traffic. Outside École Mixte Jules Verne–Léo Delibes Hostel, a hand-written poster:

DANGER! CATCHMENT AREAS ARE CHANGING
Without consulting parents or teachers
the Town Hall
is imposing catchment area changes on some children
without thinking about:
– the daily home-to-school journey
– the children's safety
As dissatisfied parents, we must act quickly
e.g.: a child living in rue Éboué will have to attend

École Curie
and must therefore *cross* the big carrefour de la Poste.

And seeing the big crossroads looming up in the distance, so wide and heaving with traffic, François, who knows a thing or two about journeys to school, would not under any circumstances like Julia to have to cross it two or four times a day.

Turning left at carrefour de la Poste, a street drops down towards a flat stretch of land: rising up from it are metal structures – railway signals? – and, in the far distance, big groups of buildings: it is La Courneuve industrial estate, which backs on to Cité des 4000. To the right, past the police station, church, health centre and the Blanc-Mesnil Boulodrome and Sporting Star Club, is the town hall, built in 1964. It's superb: volumes of well-proportioned, dazzling white concrete. There's nothing monumental or massive about it. The reference books say that the man responsible, André Lurçat, had been disappointed by the Stalinist art of the 1930s. He was a Communist, and in the difficult years when civic architecture, Stalinist or otherwise, lapsed into gigantic dimensions, he tried to conceive of forms and volumes that wouldn't necessarily make people associate the words 'popular' and 'masses'. After the war, André Lurçat was the first architect to organize consultations to try and gain a precise understanding of future inhabitants' specific needs.

By way of a belfry is a sort of crow's nest, twenty metres high and very slender, on which have been temporarily stuck what look like musical staves, their notes apparently cut-out characters; the whole thing is adorned by a tricolour rainbow, obviously representing an artistic contribution by Blanc-Mesnil to the bicentenary celebrations. On either side of this mizzenmast, the main entrance steps lead up to a big ceramic decoration curiously similar to a tapestry, which ceases to amaze when one sees the signature of Saint-Saëns, written in 1967: 'The same high blue wave carries the day for every man.'

To the left, a cockerel and some starfish on an ochre, gold and orange background. To the right, on a grey background, an anvil, a hammer, orange-lined tongs, ears of wheat on a yellow background (a sickle?), a man's head and flames emerging from a forge (or is it a lyre?), and stars, lots of stars.

The industrious present and the radiant future: we've already seen that somewhere.

They visit the exhibition of tricolour painting in the foyer, watch a video of the council's activities, admire a window-case of respectful souvenirs from foreign delegations, nearly all from the Eastern bloc: a samovar, dolls, a pennant from East Germany – real collector's items. The town hall is buzzing like an efficient beehive. You get the impression that the council that built this town hall nearly thirty years ago was quietly confident of being in power for ever. They haven't been proved wrong to this day.

On the town hall lawns, some roses, including the

RESURRECTION ROSE
Created for the 30th anniversary of the release of prisoners
from the death camps
Never forget

'I know that rose,' says François. 'It was launched by Vilmorin or Truffaut, I forget which. My mother bought one, like all her old campmates – it's what you call a *captive market*. It died right away, I'm afraid.'

The hotel they are looking for is in avenue Charles Floquet, but this goes on and on. They admire in passing Blanc-Mesnil's public convenience: it's a DOUBLE and it's FREE as well! Chirac and his measly City of Paris single-seater pay cubicles just aren't in the same league. They pass estates of strictly cubic blocks painted in tonal harmonies – light grey on dark grey, cream beige on milky-coffee beige. At the entrance to Cité Victor Hugo, whose population seem darker-skinned, is a parked police car. And here is the infant school, the Irène and Frédéric Joliot-Curie school complex, with a funny circle of three stone baby chimpanzees; the Erik Satie National Music School; and the immaculate stadium wall opposite a rampart formed by one unbroken estate 150 metres long, extended on the inside by other walls; six storeys, small windows, a bit of grey, some trees – sheer utilitarianism. The Jean Bouin Stadium is magnificent, like the town hall, with its monumental double flight of steps and its own crow's nest being erected. And it's all white.

All white? 'Don't you get the impression that since we arrived in Blanc-Mesnil something's been missing?' And all of a sudden – hell's bells, that's it. But of course: there's not a single tag in the entire *commune*. Everything's whitewashed, double and triple whitewashed. '*C'est clean*,' says Anaïk.

But avenue Charles Floquet has run out of numbers, and they are now on La Molette industrial estate with its blank brick walls, ancient factories converted into warehouses, masses of lorries, Benhydro, Liquid Air, stretching for hundreds of metres, kilometres, under the skull-splitting midday sun. Not to mention the blisters on their feet. A giant sign says:

With a bit of common sense
The Caribbean is within your reach
CARAÏBOS – the exotic fruit nectar

What gets them isn't so much the message as the picture: a carafe with an arrow showing which way to unscrew the top, and the carafe is *trickling with icy droplets*.

They come upon an abandoned goods train, and then there it is, Auberge le Castel, *Bar-Restaurant*, and behind it a rather rickety building, Hôtel du Parc, but where can the bedrooms be? Think of all that traffic on the cobbled road: No, let's be serious, says Anaïk, the lorries will split our heads open. So on they go.

After passing some attractive industrial buildings for executives in attractive parks which have been converted into attractive car parks, they arrive in rue de la Défense in Le Bourget: they can't be far from the airport, and there they will find a cool resting-place, and hotels, but first they must cross the A1 motorway, and so find the bridge that straddles it, which is itself a dual carriageway (it's far more dangerous than coming out of École Jules Ferry), but at last they cross over on to the Nationale 2, next to the airport perimeter and hangars, and they can't hear themselves speak, it's hell, hell, hell – just lorries, brakes, revving engines, lorries, screeching, roaring.

Opposite the airport, on their side of the main road, a row of old run-down flats and a row of restaurants and hotels: the Air-Hôtel (ramshackle but superb, with its two 1920s cement columns), Le Parisien, a gastronomic hostelry, Le Méhari, for couscous, Le Palais du Bourget, for a Chinese, Le Tabac du Port, Le Looping, Le Bar de l'Aviation, Le Café du Nord. It's most unusual to see a town come right up to the very doorstep of an airport. This façade of houses and bistros is more reminiscent of transport cafés than of the splendour and great adventure of the first airline companies: the Grands Express Aériens from 1923, the Compagnie Franco-Roumaine – which linked Paris by a Caudron tri-prop to Strasbourg, Prague, Vienna, Warsaw and Bucharest – Latécoère, Air-Afrique and Aéropostale.

They cross the main road. Everything is vibrating and shuddering. They walk to the central building, a very well-proportioned neoclassical construction dating from 1937. François recalls the airport he knew twenty years ago: it was so pretty, with people milling around, at once austere and gracious – along the high pillars in the interior concourse ran elegant gangways with guardrails painted a nice shade of green (at least he remembers them being that colour) – with its statues in the style of Bourdelle (or are they simply by Bourdelle himself?). The airport is still there, but no longer in use. It houses the Air Museum. A 'monument' marks the entrance: three real Fouga-Magisters from the French Patrol, one blue, one white, one red, attached to huge tubes, giving the rather failed impression that they are soaring towards the sky and going to explode like the grand climax of a firework display. The Air Museum is closed on Mondays. They will have to come back.

They eat *aeroburgers* amid the deafening noise, and are themselves transformed into noise, with the impression that they are nothing but giant ears without a head. 'It's no worse than boulevard Magenta,' says the owner of the Lighthouse Bar, or is it the Port Lighthouse, they can't remember. She's a comfort to them because she knows what it's like to have sore feet. They've walked for two and a half hours to get to this sea of lorries. 'We must be mad to do this,' says Anaïk.

The hotel they were looking for, the Blue Airport Restaurant, a *café-hôtel*, is certainly passable, but they are put off by the prospect of the noise and dust which, in spite of the heat, would mean having to keep the windows closed. Further back from the road, in Cité de la Justice, Hôtel du Soleil Levant looks calmer, but inquiries reveal that its rooms are furnished and rented by the month. Their attention is caught by roadside signs announcing a Novotel, an Ibis and other air-conditioned wonders: turn right at third traffic lights, one kilometre. Is the hotel or the lights one kilometre away? They certainly won't be going to find out.

*

After the lunchtime hurly-burly has died down, when the workers have returned to their offices, the packers to their warehouses, and the lorry drivers to their HGVs, there is barely a soul left on the pavement, one bank of the motorized river. Just a few elegant young women in boubous. One of them wears one in indigo blue over a sky-blue dress. Anaïk, who knows all there is to know about wearing pareos, says she can deduce the country of origin: indigo blue is the most traditional and most expensive; and women from the Congo, in particular, wear two like that, one over the other.

They've got to get out of there. Apparently there are no buses going to Blanc-Mesnil station. Does the 152 give its destination as Blanc-Mesnil? After making inquiries, they discover that Blanc-Mesnil is right here, they're on the boundary, and that Le Bourget is over the main road. Of course they know the 350, which goes up to Roissy. Or down to Paris. In the end, they walk back the way they came, towards the centre and town hall. A few dozen metres from the main road and airport, a shady brick house bears a ceramic name plaque above its door: *Mon rêve – 1939*. In the five years after they christened it, the owners must have dreamed some funny old dreams.

Back they tramp across Blanc-Mesnil. The National Circus announces for today an evening at Cité Victor Hugo with

AN AFRICAN HIPPOPOTAMUS

but they will definitely not be in Blanc-Mesnil tonight.

Fresh explosions of roses, and a villa with exotic trees: a gingko, magnolias mingling with Japanese flowering cherries and pale European maples. Then the Louis Daquin Municipal Cinema, which is showing Joris Ivens' *Une histoire de vent*; a school with children playing under the trees; the other side of Jean Bouin Stadium, where youngsters are playing tennis; the Yuri Gagarin Municipal Youth Centre, where you can use videos and computers, and make miniature rockets. Strolling round like that on the surface of things and people, you might easily conclude that there are worse purgatories than the suburbs of Paris.

Behind its four rows of lime trees, here once again is the town hall, and just opposite: 'Police Station'. They get the vague impression that the station's missing something. Then it clicks: it's the only public edifice in Blanc-Mesnil with no name. Even so, 'Sacco and Vanzetti Police Station' would have done quite nicely.

A good look at the map, and Drancy station seems closer than the one at Blanc-Mesnil. Off they go. At 5 p.m. they are outside the station: people are heading in both directions, hurrying home, hurrying not to miss their train. A hotel opposite the station catches their eye: like a storm-beaten concrete spur it overhangs the bridge and marshalling yard, which here reaches its widest point. Restaurant Hôtel NN**, oriental cuisine, shellfish, weddings, banquets, conventions, couscous, paella. The entrance, below the café on the corner, is closed, but in fact it's not the way into the hotel but leads to the private *Enchantement-Club*: there's no one there, and with the trains roaring past just underneath, they haven't the heart to persist. They will not be booking rooms at the Hôtel NN. What does it mean anyway, the NN you always see on hotels? They ought to know. Everyone else seems to. They must make inquiries one day. François knows only that in Latin N is short for *Nemo*, nobody: the Nobody Nobody Hotel?

At Aulnay they ask if they can have their rooms back. Too late. Madame Bernadette is terribly sorry. They can have them tomorrow, if they like. Oh yes, they would. Anaïk phones the hotel in Les Beaudottes with a last-gasp inquiry. Yes, they have room, and as night falls they go aboard their quiet, welcoming boat cabins. They have moved forward one space and gone back two.

*

TUESDAY 23 MAY. In Le Bourget cemetery, in the same dazzling sunshine, Anaïk photographs the tombs of the soldiers killed in 1914 (mostly in the

119

Sevran-Beaudottes

early battles, near the River Marne): neat rows of uniform tombs. The man carrying the small watering can walks up and tells them that two of his brothers are buried there. He is tall, straight-backed, athletic-looking: he is eighty-four years old. He has come to tend the flowers on his wife's tomb – he comes nearly every day, and he can't really see the point in living any more. He was born at Meudon. Yes, it was lovely in those days, with the riverside *guingettes* and the funicular: what, you don't know the funicular? It started from the banks of the Seine. But there was poverty too. His father was a crystal-worker at Sèvres. His mother took the boat once a week to go to Les Halles in Paris to do her shopping; they had to economize – there were eight children. They had a small vegetable garden and some rabbits. Luckily, everyone kept rabbits in those days, because the meat. . . . And when they came here, to the workers' flats, the poverty was still there. Yes, he knows all about poverty, that's for sure. Afterwards he made his way in the world, and today he can't complain.

Those flats were on the edge of what today is the airport: they looked out on to courtyards, they were sad – they've been destroyed, of course, and he wasn't sorry to see them go. He remembers the first plane to put down, in a field in August 1914: he can even remember it was a red Blériot. Everyone scattered because they thought it was a Kraut. It took off again, and the airfield came later. But what have you come to see here?

The reminders of the 1870 war? There's a chapel, the vault called *le caveau de 70*, and Major Roland's tomb. Of course the vault was moved when they extended the airport and carved out avenue Kennedy. The fighting went on round the church – you see the tower, that's where they all fell, Baroche, Brasseur, Roland, and the streets nearby are named after them. Yes, it was a real bloodbath, the poor creatures. You must see the paintings in the church, but it only opens on Sundays, for Mass.

He talks about the fighting in 1870 as if it were part of his life. When he arrived here in 1910 – some thirty-five years later – eyewitnesses were still alive: it was a lot nearer than the Second World War is for us today. The story permeated his childhood; for the children of Le Bourget it wasn't just another story, it was their story.

He goes and hangs up his watering can on a wall by the cemetery gate. He bids good day to an old man coming in, and walks off, still very straight-backed, because, he says, you mustn't stay outside too long with a bare head in such a hot sun.

They hadn't approached him. They hadn't asked him any questions. He had started talking of his own accord. He looked so dignified, that Anaïk didn't even dare ask to take his photo.

The little cellar-chapel in the trees, 'The burial place of the brave men who died for their country', bears the names of the battalions and their men: they were mostly in mobile units. Not regular soldiers but hastily conscripted Parisians; and many of the dead were from the battalion of press irregulars. The names have recently been re-engraved, but time had worn away many of them, so those spaces now stand empty. Further into the cemetery is a pyramid to the memory of the soldiers of the Third Grenadiers of 'Königin Elizabeth'.

There were two battles at Le Bourget. The first was fought between 27 and 30 October 1870. On the 27th, Bazaine capitulated at Metz, which brought the Parisians' anger to boiling point. The Germans had been occupying the capital since late September. The government of national defence was at Tours, Trochu was commanding Paris, the people of Paris were demanding a mass evacuation, and Monsieur Thiers, a Paris deputy, was preparing to offer an armistice to Mr von Bismarck at Versailles. The French troops were deployed to the north-east of Paris outside the forts of Saint-Denis, Aubervilliers and Romainville, and at La Courneuve and Drancy. At Le Bourget, whose plateau dominating the Plaine was considered a strategic position, the population was all but gone and the village occupied by the Germans.

It was the leader of the press irregulars' battalion, a career officer named Roland, who submitted to General de Bellemare the plan for a surprise counterattack on Le Bourget. It seems that he even forced his hand. The battalion numbered some 300 men. They were mostly typesetters, from a milieu where, more than the rest of the Parisian proletariat, the workers were socialist and pro-Blanqui. The attack took place at night in rain and fog. The village was recaptured. The people of Paris greeted the news as a great victory, but finally the counterattack came. The press irregulars were joined much later by mobile units, including those under Major Baroche, and by Major Brasseur's infantry. In the two days that followed, these men, drenched to the bone by the rain, went without food and sleep: they were exhausted. No relief troops or reinforcements were sent. When, on the night of the 29th, 20,000 Germans counterattacked, only 1600 soldiers were defending Le Bourget. General de Bellemare had 25000 men at his disposal, but the reinforcements he finally released got lost or arrived too late; others were held in reserve and took no part in the battle. For several days the general had been demanding troops and artillery from Trochu; he had even tried to see him the night before, but was unable to do so and obtained nothing – 'no orders, no directives, no promises'. He was even accused of dragging his feet in Paris until the small hours, and returning only when the Prussians were already attacking.

The fort's artillery fired little or badly. On the morning of the 30th, then, the great barricade of cobblestones blocking the Imperial advance was bombarded by forty Prussian cannon. It was located beyond the crossroads of the roads to Dugny and Blanc-Mesnil, next to today's airport perimeter – about the stretch where there is now a service station. By nine o'clock they were fighting with knives, the barricade had been cleared and the mobile units had withdrawn from the houses on either side of the road that forms Le Bourget's main street, as wide then as it is today. The Germans stormed the shell-torn church, using ladders to climb through the windows; men were shooting each other and fighting hand to hand around the confessional: Brasseur and the survivors surrendered. But Baroche, who was not a career soldier but chosen as an officer by his men in the XIVth arrondissement, even though he was a *grand bourgeois*, a wealthy landowner and son of Napoleon III's Minister of Justice, died in a suicidal gesture advancing without cover towards the Germans to unload his revolver one last time. Nearly all the remaining press irregulars died. (We should point out that a number of them, disgusted by events, had gone home.) Major Roland, on the other hand, was safe: when Le Bourget had been captured two days earlier he had, for reasons unknown, left his command or been relieved. Years later, having become a tax inspector, he presented his glorious sword to the municipality. So the old man in the cemetery was wrong in lumping together those soldiers whose names feature on the street signs; as if, in the imagery of memory, it took death to consecrate the true heroes.

With the cobblestones from *'la grande barricade'*, the Bavarian grenadiers built this pyramid to the memory of their 2000 comrades who had
fallen there: the monument is reminiscent of the pyramids of skulls that
Bulgars and Turks built on their battlefields near the Iron Gates.

On the afternoon of 30 October, when everything was over, Parisians
living in the northern *quartiers* could see long columns of reinforcements
and artillery trooping past their windows. It's true that Trochu had other
problems, and that for him the enemy was first and foremost inside the
city walls: he knew that the news of Bazaine's capitulation, which had
been made official at last, would cause trouble in the capital, where
already the watchword on people's lips was a *Paris Commune*, modelled on
the one of 1792, to take control of defence and national security. Trochu
had anticipated well: the very day after the bloodbath at Le Bourget,
twenty-three furious battalions of the national guard marched on the
town hall, declared a committee for national security, and took prisoner
the government's representatives – Trochu, Jules Ferry, Jules Simon, Jules
Fabre – who, in the end, were saved only by the intervention of Breton
mobile units, whom they would have been ill-advised to send to fight the
Prussians. And if their exploits hadn't left them bloodied and bowed, the
press irregulars would doubtless have played an important role in this first
attempt at a new Paris Commune.

Le Bourget's second bout of fighting took place in December. This
time the town didn't just lend a helping hand, for the clashes came into
the scheme of a large-scale battle, namely the sortie that aimed to join up
with the Northern Army commanded by Faidherbe. And again it ended
in carnage. It was bitterly cold, the temperature dropping as low as minus
18° centigrade at night. While the right flank's advance was checked –
the bridge planned for crossing the Marne, whose frozen surface had
broken during a brief thaw, was too short – French marines and Prussians
were killing each other at point-blank range in Le Bourget, and breaches
were being made from house to house without the French managing to
get decisively across the road. The Prussian-held church was once again
the scene of fierce fighting, and just to wreck everything, the 138th
Infantry was massacred by a French artillery bombardment. And once
again, the reserves – 200,000 men in all were deployed at intervals
between Le Bourget and Paris – did not come to back up the thousand
men who had succeeded in entering Le Bourget.

Six months later Eugène Pottier, a Parisian *chansonnier* who had
survived the Paris Commune, wrote some couplets which could be sung
to *La Marseillaise* and subsequently became famous. One of them, though
certainly not the most frequently sung at meetings, goes: 'S'ils s'obstinent
ces cannibales à faire de nous des héros, ils sauront bien que nos balles sont

pour nos propres généraux.' ('If those cannibals go on making heroes out of us, they'll soon know our bullets are for our own generals.')

*

The Nationale 2, the old Flanders road which starts from Porte de la Chapelle, runs through Le Bourget: the flow of lorries is so dense that to cross it you have to use uninviting underground passages or walk alongside until some dipped headlights allow you to wade across the river. This road, with its market gardens on either side, has always been Le Bourget's pulse. The village has never been turned in on itself. *Pavillons* went up here before the working class arrived, and they were well-to-do houses: at the end of the last century, the Northern Railway Company complained that it was difficult lodging the workers from the marshalling yard because rents were much higher than they were in Drancy or La Courneuve.

Since the Middle Ages the road had favoured the opening of many hostelries and even more alehouses. They did a roaring trade until 1840, when the railway was built. The post house was the true focal point of the village. At the Revolution, Le Bourget's postmaster employed sixty people and owned 140 horses. It was a responsibility and a privilege that could be worth 300,000 francs. The one who helped Alexandre Dumas to fix a tricolour banner to his carriage on 31 July 1830 was called Musnier and came from one of the area's wealthiest families.

We get an idea of what the Flanders road must have been like on its way through Le Bourget from Arthur Young. This Englishman travelled around France in 1787 and 1789, and painted an irreplaceable and meticulous picture – through a love of agronomy, say some; because he was desperate to escape a shrewish woman, say others – and stopped several times at Le Bourget: he came to visit Cretté de Palluel, a renowned agronomist, who owned land at Dugny and Le Bourget and whose brother, incidentally, was the village postmaster. Arthur Young was not a fan of the French post, which he deemed 'worse and more expensive than in England'. The horses were old nags, and from inside the windowless carriages he could see nothing of the landscape: 'I would much prefer to make the entire journey blindfold on a donkey.' He also found French roads, and particularly those on the outskirts of Paris, unusually empty. Arriving by the Flanders road in 1787 – and so changing horses at Le Bourget – he wrote: 'For the last twelve miles, I expected to find the crowd of carriages which stops the traveller at the gates of London. There was no such thing; right up to the city walls, the road was a perfect desert.' His conclusion: 'The French are the most sedentary people on earth.'

Le Bourget

If Arthur Young were here on this day in 1989, on the same Flanders road, he would be reassured to see what had become of that perfect desert.

*

The Air Museum is open, and is as empty as the Flanders road was two hundred years ago. The young man in uniform behind the ticket counter is bored: he thought it would be fun to do his national service in the air force, but it's not. Was he posted there by chance? Not exactly. Family connections. His father knows the general who runs the Air Museum. But if he had known, he would have tried to get invalided out.

The concourse of the former airport is entirely devoted to the early days of aviation up to the end of the First World War. First there are the new life-size reconstructions of old – even legendary – contraptions such as Leonardo da Vinci's; and even, in some cases, genuine creations built from plans which were never executed. A perfectly painted hot-air balloon (to a scale of 1:16) rises and falls in time to blasts of hot air. You can admire Francesco Lana's airship (1670), a wooden skiff suspended from four copper spheres, propelled by a sail and oars; and nearer our own time, Cayley's heliplane (1843), a huge spring equipped with propellers and rotors; or Charles Renault's ten-wing glider. Then come the first machines that actually dragged themselves off the ground: Count Massia's glider, which, with blinding logic, equipped man with what he lacked – two wings and a tail; those by Lilienthal and the Wright brothers; and, of course, Clément Ader's plane. The accompanying notes tell us that Clément Ader – who would have thought it? – was a victim of the Dreyfus Affair: 'The Dreyfus Affair erupted in 1894, complicated by sluggish finances, a situation whose fatal consequences Ader failed to recognize.' Ader, as we know, got airborne for a few metres of runway at Satory camp, though he failed to convince the assembled military. But it wasn't the bad weather, or the weight of his steam machine, or of course the dull-witted army brass which caused him to crash: if he fell to earth, Dreyfus was to blame.

The Air Museum is a marvel. You could spend hours there dreaming. They spend hours there. There is the same sheer quiet you get at high altitude. Hanging from the ceiling, the Morane, Spad, Caudron, Bréguet, Fokker and De Havilland are as dazzling as the day they were born. And there's a nacelle of the first Zeppelin: it's all cramped, it's the one with the engine. François would so like to see inside the nacelle of a 1930s Zeppelin, the one which flew its passengers from Hamburg to New York, and where, as legend has it, piano recitals were given on board.

Parked in adjacent halls are more recent planes. François would have liked to see again the fabulous airships of his childhood, from the time when air transport was a byword for unimaginable luxury. One was the

Latécoère 631, 'the biggest hydroplane in the world'. He remembers religiously exploring the cabin of one of them (or was it simply a life-size model?) at the 1937 Paris Exhibition: he was only five years old at the time, and it was one of his most magnificent memories of that brief but fabulous prewar period; what has stuck in his mind – and who knows if it is somehow linked to reality? – is that it had several bridges, an interior staircase and cabins with bunk beds, like a boat. And maybe there was a lounge, and a bar? And a piano? When, as a grown-up, he had to catch a plane for the first time – it must have been a Languedoc or a DC4 – everything seemed very cramped, as if progress had come to a halt with the war and could from then on offer human beings only small and utilitarian things. Later still, he rediscovered that feeling of vastness and interior luxury on board a six-engine, twelve-prop Aeroflot Tupolev: this aircraft was flying a route for which it had probably not been intended, and to ease the length of the journey (a nonstop, seventeen-hour flight), half the seats had been taken out: there was room to play dominoes (double-dozen dominoes!) on real tables, and chat in small groups. From the corny chandeliers hanging from the high ceiling, and the curtains, down to the mysterious staircase adorned with a copper balustrade descending goodness knows where, everything seemed straight out of a Jules Verne story, a *Nautilus* where no one had spring-cleaned for years, or like the Czar's saloon carriage as it appears in old issues of *Illustration*. But you could tell it was a Soviet plane: there was no toilet paper. The Latécoère, though, came to a sorry end. During the war, the individual parts were hidden by patriotic engineers. After the Liberation, it was seen as a desirable symbol of rediscovered French greatness. In the eyes of the world it was supposed to be the Concorde of its time. In 1948 its inaugural flight made the front page of all the newspapers. The next chapter was cruel indeed: somewhere over the Caribbean it started to fall apart. A propeller came off, sliced through the fuselage and severed a journalist's arm – oh, the shame of it! The Latécoère 631 was heard of no more.

He would also have liked to see the 1950s clippers again, the last planes you could still say looked like 'large birds', such as the Superconstellation, with its slim, curved cockpit and three fins; that was in the days when the air hostesses used to offer you sweets because sucking them was supposed to unblock your ears. Or a good old DC3, like ones you still find on airfields in Africa and Latin America, whose nuts were tightened after the stops; through the portholes you could see the wings beating in thin air.

Mostly there are the planes he saw in the 1940s gleaming and raking their machine-gun fire, and sometimes nose-diving with long trails of smoke. Spitfires and Lightnings, bearers of death and yet messengers of freedom. It could have been the exhilarating sight of so many planes skimming through the clouds, despite all the bombs and exploding ground-to-air shells which for two years rained down on his head, or maybe the fairy-tale memory of the Latécoère, but at the age of thirteen François felt a strong aeronautical calling. Every Thursday he would drag his cousins along to 'The Small Wings of the French Air Club' to construct wooden model gliders (ah, the CB32, with its triangular fuselage!), which they never managed to assemble completely because all the parts were missing and the glue was duff. This vocation went into tailspin in the third form after he had founded and presided over the *Avionnet' Club*, whose aim was to promote paper arrows and planes in all their forms, but which met with no sympathy from the school's senior authorities, the teachers and headmaster, and thus became the first of his ventures to be scuppered by the disapproval of serious people. But today one of his cousins is a colonel in the air force, and François remains convinced (even if no one else is) that he was behind this fine career.

Might this explain why the first jet planes, in a different hall, are more sinister, more directly threatening and cruel? Great metal bodies devoid of a sense of speed and space-conquering freedom, leaving just the faintest reflection of cold-blooded murder on their grey riveted forms. Like a gloomy pets' cemetery, calling to mind the birds of prey at the Botanical Gardens. The place has the atmosphere of a port's backstreets where retired test pilots go to dream nostalgic dreams, bald gentlemen trying to explain to their grandsons how they climbed in there to storm the skies, trying to tell them that in those cockpits they experienced moments of brief and intense happiness which, as they sadly realize once more, are impossible to convey.

Outside in the sun on the old runway, a Concorde and a Caravelle display rotten entrails inside their fuselages, their sides flaking off with a vengeance. A state of total decay. It seems there should be other big planes here, but apparently they are being repaired for the air show next door, preparations for which are well under way. Under a wing of the Concorde, a gentleman complains that no one's interested in aviation any more. There's been an exhibition, he says, at the Grand Palais, which got only 300 visitors per day, and next door some painter or other, 'Degas, I think it was', was pulling in 9000: it's not right.

No, it's not right.

A worried-looking individual appears from between two hangars and questions them in an improbable language. After several attempts, it transpires that he knows a few words of German and is looking for the way out. François suggests that the best way to get out might well be where he came in, but all of a sudden the man seems freed from worry and

anxiety, utters *'unmöglich'* a few times and hurries off towards the barriers behind which the air show is being prepared. They conclude that he's a spy. Bulgarian, decides François.

Should one talk about Le Bourget's finest hours? On one side of the airport car park is a statue of a woman taking to the skies, a monument to Nungesser and Coli, and Lindbergh: 'In honour of all those who tried and he who succeeded.'

There is no monument celebrating the stirring words Daladier is supposed to have uttered here on his return from Munich in September 1938, when – having gained nothing, since he had ventured nothing – he discovered that the massed crowds had come not to lynch him but to give him an ovation.

*

At the Three (lacquered) Ducks Hotel, Madame Bernadette has saved her best rooms for them; Anaïk's has no lock, but a padlock does the trick; apparently the proprietor is coming to repair it some day.

Late in the evening, after the restaurant has closed, all the hotel staff, including the recently arrived young waiters who speak no French other than the words on the menu opposite the Chinese characters, follow the latest news from Beijing in the dark.

'Hardliners lose battle for Beijing,' announces *Le Monde*: 'Outright defeat for Prime Minister Li Peng.' The soldiers sent to the capital have refused to fight. 'The army loves the people, the people loves the army,' proclaim the demonstrators' placards. Everything seems to indicate that the regime 'was looking to announce in late afternoon wide-ranging changes demonstrating Mr Ziao's victory'.

*

WEDNESDAY 24 MAY. François thinks about the advice friends gave him about bringing not only books but some work, such as the translation he's working on, *for the quiet moments*. But there are no quiet moments. They have had to cancel meeting people who live and work around Villepinte and Sevran, friends or friends of friends. They will see them later. After the journey. For the moment they have to keep going.

*

Today at 1 p.m. they are meeting a friend who works in Bondy. It's a joy discovering the warmth of a familiar smile, talking about the journey with someone who is both observer and accomplice, and also, most of all, chatting about everything and nothing. The Bondy line is still out of action, and the strike has spread to the northern network. Should they take the bus? They'll never get there in time. So it's the ultimate disgrace: Taxi! A ten-minute ride and they're in place de l'Église in Bondy, where the bar apparently serves coffee with teaspoons with holes. Some claim that it's an anti-drug precaution, so the teaspoons aren't used to melt heroin in the toilets. Others, who have less imagination and who, in particular, know all about old firm canteens, know that it's the routine precaution to put off teaspoon thieves. Because such things as teaspoon thieves exist: there are even lightning conductor thieves. Which goes to show how, when a faintly unusual detail is mentioned, someone will soon bring up drugs.

Karin's smile is waiting for them. Karin lives in Paris and works in a child psychology consultancy unit at Bondy Hospital. Apart from the café, where they will not be going to check if the teaspoons really have holes, and the *Bric-à-Brac*, a bring-and-buy open to all – a sort of hospital focal point and place for making friends and contacts, one of the links in a chain of charitable associations (created by 'the 1901 Law') – and a few other stopping-off places like the godforsaken transport café where she takes them to eat ham and chips, she has never had the time really to get to know Bondy, though she'd like to. 'I've always told myself that one day I'd do a tour of Bondy. Go round the schools, for example, to see the children somewhere else than in consultation.' What she knows about Bondy is that the town's split in two by the canal: to the north are the working-class estates, the council blocks; to the south it's still the village. A familiar tale. But in fact there's only one true centre, even if it's not a geographical one: the supermarket. Karin thinks that there are as many poor French people as poor immigrants. She can't see any difference on that score. What causes problems with immigrants, in practical terms, is the family structures: with the North Africans it's always the father who presents himself as the only spokesman, the sole authority, giving his final categorical word; and in an African family, it's extremely difficult to get your bearings. She has experience of Africa: she knows that an African family seems complex to a European, but over there she managed to work things out, with patience, and to construct real family trees – namely who was related to whom. Here everything's dislocated, unsettled; she has no markers, no compass. She's just completely disorientated.

What do the people of Bondy dream of? It's crazy, says Karin, how many people want a *pavillon*. So they work like mad, see even less of their family, and the family comes apart even more. . . .

Karin finds the travellers sad and worn out. She thinks they should go for a walk, it would take their mind off things. In Bondy Forest, say. That way they'd know if it really exists. She lends them her car. They should just bring it back at 5 p.m. to the Montreuil surgery, where she has to rush off to now.

The car ride is awful. For a start they haven't brought their map, so they begin by taking the motorway in the wrong direction, then miss an exit, and in next to no time find themselves in Paris, at Porte de Bagnolet. Once they're heading the right way, it's traffic jam time, then they exit on to the Nationale 3 and do the long drive through Pavillons and Livry. They can't get their bearings pinned in this box; time, space and distance take on a different meaning: the signposts, for example, tell them that if they turn left Sevran lock is nearby, but they can't recognize anything, they're in another world, the world of car-driving reactions, of traffic fits and starts and the landscape flying past before they've had time to grasp and understand it. When they finally escape from the flow of the urban trunk road, when they're finally driving down a road winding between scattered trees which must be Bondy Forest, it's too late to stop and go for a stroll in the woods. The undulating ground and mounds blocking out the horizon give them the fleeting impression of being deep in the countryside. Once past the strategic road leading to the fort at Vaujours, they came to Coubron, which seems like a real village, but they've no real way of knowing, they're driving past too quickly, they've got to rejoin the Nationale and motorway if they want to return the car to its owner, who needs it.

When they meet up again with Karin, they don't really know where they are any more. And as they must look rather sulky, she suggests they go for a drink at a place she knows near Montreuil. Once near Montreuil she can't remember the place, but if they go as far as Porte de Bagnolet they're sure to find something. And while they're at it, it would be so much simpler to push on a bit further, to Bastille, to her flat even, where she can make them a comforting cup of tea. So at 6 p.m., after driving the ritual three times round the traffic-swamped *quartier*, they finally park near Saint-Paul, right outside François's block of flats. With a bit of luck, François could come face to face with Julia on her way home from the swimming pool.

Our travellers glance at each other sheepishly. Their entire story is falling to pieces: on no account were they to return to Paris during the month, that was the rule of the journey, the rule of the game; and now it would be so easy to say goodbye, see you tomorrow, or another day, and to go home, able to swear in cowardly relief that they had done nothing to cause this derailment.

But maybe Karin did them a favour in bringing them down to earth a little, reminding them that calling this a game is all very well and good, but the simple truth is that nothing separates Paris from its suburbs, and that everything else is of trifling importance, including the blisters on their feet.

But they don't dwell on it for now, they just drink up and get out as fast as they can, back to Aulnay and their wretched bedrooms – yes, *their* bedrooms – at the Chinese hotel. Don't give in to temptation and the blinding fact that they're being absurd in not walking the few steps back to the peace and quiet of their own homes. Go and be swallowed up by Le Chemin Vert metro station, direction Gare du Nord. By the ticket office is the blackboard of bad tidings with, written in chalk: 'SUBURBAN SERVICES FROM GARE DU NORD TOTALLY SUSPENDED'.

Disaster has struck.

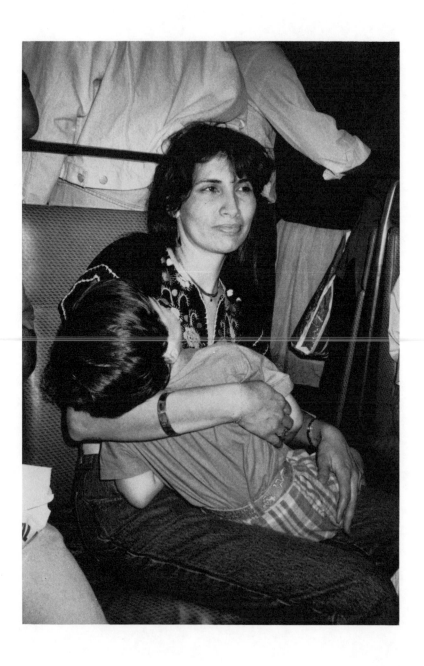

7

Aulnay-Aubervilliers. – The RER inspectors have had enough. – Cité de la Muette at Drancy: a model estate. – From council flats to concentration camp. – The barometer-flower.

THURSDAY 25 MAY. In the end there was no disaster. At Gare du Nord they were swept along by the sullen, silent crowd rushing into the bowels of the underground RER station. The departure boards were dead, the ticket office was empty, and besides, no one was bothering with tickets, they were just tearing towards the unplugged turnstiles in a headlong assault. Our travellers were thrown, flattened and crushed into an unlit carriage, with silence still heavy in the air and no one looking at anyone else. Miraculously the train left. After a nonstop fifteen-minute ride they arrived at Aulnay and hurled themselves, still running, into the flooded underground passage to avoid being jostled and trampled by their fellow travellers, who had launched into a gallop like a herd of bison.

Later they would read in the press that if they had been through the big departure hall at Gare du Nord, they would have been witness to some amazing events. At 6.23 p.m. services were suspended, the boards were jammed and the loudspeakers fell silent. The crowd charged forward chanting 'We want trains!' and 'We have paid!', then, exasperated and bent on demanding an explanation, dashed up the stairs to the interior balcony leading to the management's office. A delegation was received while riot police contained the others. But when the delegation came back out on to the balcony, the increasingly large and rumbling crowd took them for a group of striking railwaymen; it started to shout 'Lazy sods! Bastards!', and to bombard them with beer bottles and cans; upon which the riot police moved in again with their usual tact, bringing the showdown to a finale.

They probably have this delegation to thank for their miracle train.

In the press, the inspectors give vent to their discontent after three of them had been attacked the previous weekend. 'They're ganging up on us more and more. If we check a Black or North African with no ticket, we're immediately racist. . . . We know these gangs of youths on the Bondy line. Inspector-bashing's becoming a game. Management says: If you see some

yobs, change carriages. It's not as if we're going to come down on kids and grannies who've forgotten their passes! . . . For the first time in thirty years in the job, I'm really scared. It's hard, you know, when it comes to that. We want to be a public service, but we're not kamikazes.'

There is to be an increased police presence, and in particular steps are to be taken to lift the restrictions which, for reasons of territorial administration, stop the same police team working along an entire line.

The RER is not safe. At the same time, the latest incidents are brought out into the open. The concrete block thrown from a bridge at a suburban train, killing the driver. And the mad marksman taking pot shots at the Orly airport express. And the rape of a young girl in a carriage between Choisy-le-Roi and Gare d'Austerlitz. And the delinquency: offences on the suburban network are up by 20 per cent so far this year. And of course there are the drug-pushers, who, driven out of the Paris metro, are retreating up the suburban lines to the furthest stations – such as Les Beaudottes? – and, when hunted down in the stations, into the council estates themselves. Monsieur Alain Faujas, writing in *Le Monde*, is not optimistic:

> If the policing solution is not backed up with other measures, it will only push the delinquency a little further away. . . .
>
> The cause of this delinquency is to be found in an urban planning policy that has shut up the most destitute people far from the town centres, though all the while subjecting them to the torment of Tantalus thanks to the RER, which leaves them twenty minutes away from the attractions of the consumer society, like Les Halles. No preventative policy will succeed without a review

of urban planning, of the provision of activities for youngsters from the suburbs, of welfare to people caught in a downward spiral and, needless to say, in the shortage of employment.

*

This morning they depart once and for all, with luggage, for Aubervilliers. The trains are running again, and PAPY whisks them away.

For a long time, François recalls, the wartime child he once was has retained a small but stubborn dread: lurking in a corner of his mind is the clinging fear that everything could once again *stop*. Because he experienced a time when there was no gas, central heating, light or hot water; when food was short. When *things*, like soap and shoes, ran out. And because, years later, he has seen the same thing in so many other countries. He has never sneered at progress, but the suspicion has always remained: don't be surprised by a new and abrupt hiccough in history. So, whenever he is looking for lodgings, he always checks to see if there's a chimney – not because it's picturesque but in case there might be no other way of keeping warm. And likewise, in the country, he sees if there's a well, or if the garden is likely to be good for vegetables. He blames cars for the disappearance of any sort of crankshaft start, and he was alarmed to learn that the last Poitou donkeys might disappear: if there is a car shortage, who will repopulate France with mules? No, he never longs for the old days, he is convinced that the washing machine is a great victory for mankind, and he likes writing on a computer; yet he worries about not holding on to an old washboard, and he has kept his typewriter. And some pencils. Lots of pencils.

So when he suddenly reads 'TOTAL STOPPAGE', as he did yesterday, he immediately imagines disaster scenarios like in those old science-fiction stories where the author writes that, in a flash, the 'electric current' went dead right across the planet. Society today is ten times, a thousand times, more vulnerable than the one he was born into. All the feeble ways of scraping through he saw applied during the war, and which are used today to survive in the Third World suburbs which make up two-thirds of the world, would be useless here to overcome a few days of a general power cut, a total petrol drought, or simply a long-term shortage. Everything would collapse, just like that. It wouldn't just be luxuries and the easy life that would disappear. It might be life itself.

Imagine tropical birds in hothouses suddenly deprived of heat, dropping like flies; rare exotic fish floating belly up when their aquariums break down? They are all precious inhabitants of fragile, oh so fragile Europe.

*

FRIDAY 26 MAY. The temperature suddenly drops ten degrees in the night, and from the tenth floor of the hotel they see that Aubervilliers has donned its suburban clothes: it's a grey early morning, cold and dirty. They put on their woollies.

*

Midday at Drancy. A signpost points to: 'Cité de la Muette – Cité du Square de la Libération – Riot police station'. And further on:

The Public Housing Development Office
is renovating 369 flats here at
Cité de la Muette.
The work is financed by the Regional Council and the State.
The State is investing here for your future.

Grey four-storey buildings, or rather one building composed of three sections stuck together at right-angles in a U-shape, two hundred metres by forty, round a squarish piece of ground; the fourth, south-facing side remaining open. At this hour Cité de la Muette, like the other estates, is empty. The only passers-by are the usual housewives coming back from the shops. A young Tamil waiting for someone becomes impatient and keeps going to the phone-box.

The estate seems bare. Is it poverty? At first glance, this is even more apparent in the cheapness of the constructions than in its age: on the courtyard side, a gallery of spindly grey-painted metal pillars runs round the horseshoe; the iron and concrete structure above is covered by sheets of scabby cemented gravel separating narrow windows and vertical rows of openwork cement blocks, which mark the position of the stairwells. On the garden side, on the outside of the horseshoe, the floors are ringed by a balcony running from door to door like a gangway; there are, of course, no gardens around the estate, at least not any more, but in the far distance are the houses of Drancy. This construction seems to have been shoddily put together, or else over the years the squares of this long vertical chequerboard have warped, the cement has come apart from the iron, and now everything is skewwhiff. The façades are fragile as a house of cards. Never has a 'modern' construction so well deserved comparison with an endless line of rabbit hutches.

Under the galleries, no sign of life. Only outside the estate do you find some local shops, a pizzeria, a dry cleaner's, and other shops that have closed down.

Drancy: Cité de la Muette

The square – the centre of the estate – which boasts a few scrawny trees and a children's playground in poor repair, is shut and locked.

The place isn't poverty-stricken, it isn't a total wreck. It's neither happy nor sinister. The visitor feels only a vague sadness thinned out in the uniform light-grey distemper. And what do the inhabitants feel?

Just where you go in and walk under the right-hand gallery, there are three marble plaques fixed to the wall. The biggest of them reads:

IN THIS PLACE
which was a concentration camp
from 1941 to 1944
100,000 men, women and children
of Jewish religion or ancestry
were interned by Hitler's occupying forces
then
deported to the Nazi death camps
where the vast majority died

Cité de la Muette, 1935, one of the grandest public housing schemes between the wars.

Cité de la Muette, 1941–44, a transit camp on the road to death.

Cité de la Muette, 1989, a decrepit council estate.

Cité de la Muette, a play in three acts. A radiant estate. A deadly estate. An ordinary estate.

Ordinary. It has been made ordinary. And is soon to be renovated.

Because you are told never to give up hope.

*

Je suis juif.

No, not exactly. As they tell you kindly in Israel: 'Nobody's perfect.'

(But, just as the little mouse said to the elephant, the day the Greek colonels decided to arrest all the elephants who didn't leave the country in the next twenty-four hours, and when they were both running, running flat out towards the border: 'But how can I prove to them I'm not an elephant?')

Tu es juif, il est juif, nous sommes juifs, vous êtes juifs.

Ils sont juifs.

In truth, no one can prove he isn't. And neither can anyone who isn't put himself in the place of someone who is.

It's too late.

It should have been thought about before.

Before this:

I, Marshal of France, Head of the French State, Decree:

Art. 1 For the application of the present decree, a Jew is considered as any person descended from 3 Jewish grandparents or 2 grandparents of the same race if the husband is himself Jewish.

Art. 2 Access to and the exercise of the public offices and mandates listed hereafter are forbidden to Jews:

....

Vichy, 3 October 1940.
Philippe Pétain.

You went to register at a police station. The secretary stamped your identity card: JEW. You were a civil servant, you're not any more. You were a shopkeeper, lawyer, doctor, you're not any more. You were an ex-serviceman (and even ready to do service again) – that's a bit more complicated, but basically you're not any more.

Later you went to collect your star, you stood in the queue, you handed over your cloth coupon cut out of your ration book, you sewed it on your clothes and those of your children.

You have done everything: you are in order.

'Before,' wrote Max Jacob, 'no one noticed me in the street. Now the children make fun of my yellow star. Lucky little brat! You haven't got a yellow star.'

Lucky children. French children. Aryan children.

> I, Marshal of France, Head of the French State, Decree:
>
> *Art. 1*   As from 1 November 1940, the Ministry of the Interior will provide supervision of the camps set up in mainland France to guard French nationals and foreigners grouped together as an administrative measure. . . .
>
> . . . .
>
> *Art. 4*   In addition to the funds granted to the Minister of the Interior by the Finance Law of 31 December 1939, a sum of 32 million francs is available for . . .: Cost of supervising camps for undesirables.
>
> Vichy, 17 November 1940.
> Philippe Pétain.

You are a foreign Jew. Or a denaturalized Jew. You are the scum of Europe. On the rubbish heap! Off to the camps for undesirables! French camps. Pithiviers, Beaune-la-Rolande, Compiègne, Gurs, Les Mille, and thirty others. You're going to be sent back where you came from. Or to Madagascar. Or Pomerania. In a word, nowhere. It's not our problem. Somewhere you'll be taught the meaning of hard work. Taught how to live. Immigrants out.

You are a French Jew. You're a French Jew, which means you're Jewish full stop. Maybe you had completely forgotten: the Republic is a lay institution. But we're going to refresh your memory. And if ever you get out alive, you'll never forget it. In the meantime, the UGIF, the general union of Israelites in France, will defend your interests when dealing with the Marshal. He must know you're good Jews. But didn't you know there are no good Jews? To the camps. The UGIF will pay your expenses. Until the UGIF itself is sent to the camps.

Everyone to the camps.

All French people know the camps. All of Paris knows the camps. 'So-and-so's at Drancy': news like that is part of everyday life. People feel sorry for them. Tristan Bernard is at Drancy: Paris exerts itself. Cocteau. Picasso. Drieu. And who else? Everyone. We must go and see Abetz. Tristan Bernard is released. Max Jacob is at Drancy. 'God help him,' writes Cocteau. The Aryan God or the Jewish God? Paris exerts itself. Too late. Max Jacob's already dead. Léon Blum's brother is at Drancy. Who exerts himself this time? He died at Auschwitz.

According to a census by Serge Karsfeld, 73,853 people who passed through Drancy were sent to Auschwitz, Maidanek and Sobidor; 2190 returned.

DRANCY CAMP. MEMORANDUM NO. 77

By order of the German Authorities, it is strictly forbidden for any internee to approach the Aryans working in the camp or to speak to them.... It is forbidden for any internee to enter the Aryan workers' changing-room.

Drancy, 13 August 1943.

DRANCY CAMP. MEMORANDUM NO. 78

The instructions previously given by order of the German Authorities concerning internees' haircuts are to be relaxed in the following way:

cat. b .... shaved head
cat. a-c2-c3-c4 .... close-cropped hair
cat. c1 Normal haircut (hair not falling over the eyes)

Drancy, 14 August 1943.

'We must stay away from the Jews as a whole and not keep their children': Robert Brasillach, in *Je suis partout* ('I am everywhere'), the Pétainist newspaper.

Woken up suddenly during the night, the little ones, drowsy with sleep, started to cry and little by little the others did the same. They didn't want to go down into the courtyard, they struggled and refused to be dressed. Sometimes a whole room of a hundred children, as if gripped by panic and unassailable horror, would no longer listen to soothing words; so they called the gendarmes, who took children screaming in terror downstairs on their arms.

Georges Wellers, L'Étoile jaune à l'heure de Vichy
('The yellow star at the time of Vichy')

*

Cité de la Muette was built between 1933 and 1935. The architects were called Marcel Lods and Eugène Beaudoin. In his excellent history of council housing (*Loger le peuple*, Éditions La Découverte), Monsieur Jean-Paul Flamand gives the following description:

The overall plan combined fifteen-storey towers ('Les Tours') and a 'combing card' of two-, three-, and four-storey blocks, separated by small gardens. This plan reconciled the demand for high-density accommodation with the wish to retain traffic-free public areas for playgrounds, etc. The construction was based on the definition of standardized elements, prefabricated on-site in an open-air factory: the principle behind it was a framework of metal sections filled by concrete sheets.... This was the most 'modern' of designs, both in terms of

142

the architectural picture it offered and in a technical sense, fulfilling the period's desire for productivity. Another sign of 'modernity' could be found in the hyper-rationalized interior layout of the flats: their very small surface area (20 square metres for a two-room flat with kitchen) and the details of their design are not unreminiscent of German projects of the same period, influenced by the research of 'modern' architects promoting the idea of *Existenzminimum*.

Behind the work of Lods and Beaudoin, who have many other pre- and postwar developments to their name, there is of course an ideology which draws both on the tradition of the garden cities (themselves born of experiments like Godin's 'familsteries', and, even further back, Fourier's phalansteries) and of Le Corbusier's plans for 'standard-size living units'. Two grand humanist visions if ever there were. And to embody this ideology came a key man from a working-class background, who was Mayor of Suresnes, President of the Seine Departmental Council, senator, a minister in the Front Populaire, a socialist friend of Léon Blum and even a Communist for a time, and *even* a friend of the Mayor of Aubervilliers, Pierre Laval: Henri Sellier, the man who, between the wars, devised policy concerning the low-rent *HBM* and *HLK* – types of low-cost housing – in Paris, with the brick flats just inside the Paris *périphérique* (it was in one of these that Anaïk managed to be rehoused), and outside Paris, with no fewer than fifteen estates, of which Cité de la Muette was the most successful. The memorial dedicated to him in Cité de Châtenay-Malabry reads:

> May his memory be honoured as that of a friend of the people. He devoted his life to social progress, the glory of the Republic and the happiness of men.

Les Tours and Le Peigne were finished in 1935. They should have been joined by terraced flats, which in fact only reached the planning stage, and by a Cour d'entrée (entrance courtyard), and Fer de Cheval (the Horseshoe), where building continued up to 1939. The courtyard was supposed to be a meeting-place, with shops and public and sporting amenities. All very hygienic and socialist. Only two things were missing (as in most constructions of the period): work nearby and public transport. It's a logical, unchanging fact when you're looking for cheap land.

The first tenants of Les Tours and Le Peigne were railwaymen and workers from the TCRP (today's RATP, the Paris public transport executive). But surprise, surprise: the rents were too high, the insulation wasn't up to scratch, it was boiling in summer and freezing in winter, there were defects galore, and the *Existenzminimum* was really too minimum. And just as the tenants could not get used to their dwellings,

Drancy: Cité de la Muette

the neighbouring population rejected the buildings and their occupants outright. The press, for its part, criticized these 'skyscrapers', visible from Notre-Dame, as a blot on the French landscape. The public amenities were never built. In 1939 Les Tours, by now standing empty, were already deteriorating badly. In 1970 they had to be knocked down for good and replaced. For want of anything better, Le Peigne had been transformed into barracks for riot police and their families. In the space of four years, what had, by its innovations and technical rationalizations, been a big first, an exemplary development, was no more than a pile of buildings rapidly going downhill.

A total failure. But rest assured: after 1945, Lods and Beaudoin were each able to throw themselves into the reconstruction of bomb-damaged France. They and many others, of course, were daddy to all the big developments which, with the 1962 Delouvrier Plan, appeared all over the Paris area. They used the same techniques, but they were perfected now. On a large scale, too. This time they were a success – and how!

So in 1939 the Fer de Cheval was still short of heating or plumbing. Turning it into a concentration camp was a French idea: responsibility lies with the Daladier government, which rounded up German nationals when war was declared. Barbed wire was put up round the open side, then right round the path ringing the three blocks; basic toilet facilities were built with planks across a platform. The scenery was complete. Supervision of the whole place was entrusted to the riot police who lived in barracks just a few yards away. We know that during the 'phoney war', among those arrested and interned under the title of 'German nationals' – enemies, in other words – were the anti-Nazi Jews who had fled Germany. Funny, really.

When the Germans arrived in June 1940, they found the ideal base, two kilometres from the marshalling yard, for locking up English and French prisoners of war on their way to Germany: Cité de la Muette became *Frontstalag III*.

The first Jews arrived at Drancy in August 1941. They were the first victims of a big Paris roundup of over 4000 people carried out by 2400 French inspectors, sergeants and constables from the prefecture of police. Yves Jouffa was one of forty Jewish lawyers among the first arrivals:

> No arrangements had been made for our arrival. They had put wooden bedsteads in the huge bare concrete rooms, but no mattresses or covers. The draughts were such that when winter came, the water froze at night in the bedrooms. There were twenty taps in the big courtyard for 5000 internees, and about as many lavatories. There were no food containers, and we had to clean rusty old cans left by former prisoners with earth from the courtyard.

On that date, then, the 'camp' was surrounded by a double ring of barbed wire with a watchtower in each corner. The ground in the courtyard was covered in cinders, which created thick black dust in summer and flooded in winter. Later they cemented it over and even grew a lawn in the middle. The sanitary block made from planks which blocked off the open side of the Cheval de Fer was nicknamed 'Le Château Rouge' ('The Red Castle'); another block, on the closed-off side, was used for body searches. Round the camp today there are still gardens, open ground and factory sites, but there are just as many in the town centre: as well as the accommodation for gendarmes and their families in Le Peigne, there are lots of *pavillons*, shops, a café, and the town market is only fifty metres away.

Drancy camp was a French camp. Although it was under the high command of SS Dannecker, who dealt with all Jewish matters in France in the name of the Reich, it was placed under the direct administration of the prefecture of police, in accordance with the decree of 1 November 1940 signed by the aforementioned Philippe Pétain. Dannecker's general directives were adopted in French to form more precise regulations, then drawn up and signed by Admiral Bart, Prefect of Police for the Department of Seine, and by General Guibert, Commander of Gendarmes in the Paris area. Up until July 1943 the camp was guarded entirely by French gendarmes, while a police team from the prefecture took care of internal supervision. This responsibility was then taken over by the SS, although until the end the French gendarmes continued to provide an effective guard. In fact, the German presence at Drancy camp never exceeded five men, who represented the 'AA', the German authorities.

As in the German camps and the Warsaw ghetto, internal administration was provided by Jewish officials. The Vichy Government had 'permitted' the UGIF to meet the detainees' needs – a French version of the principle that the extermination of the Jews should be financed by the Jews. The UGIF thus sent to the camp what might help it to run smoothly: sand and concrete mixers which, among other things, enabled the construction of a pigsty for the Germans; and a flow of parcels which didn't all get through, feeding instead the lucrative black market the riot police set up among the prisoners: they sold sugar at up to seven francs a piece, bread at 150 francs for 200 grams. 'Due to a shortage of food, the internees eat peeled raw vegetables or cooking scraps,' notes a prefectural report. In November 1941, 1400 detainees fell victim to a dysentery epidemic. Between 1941 and 1944, forty detainees starved to death without leaving Drancy.

The camp population reached as many as 7000. The buildings had been planned for 700 inhabitants. Today they house 400.

*

In 1942, after the French police's big roundup on 16 and 17 July, a consequence of the Nazi decision to implement the final solution to the Jewish question and launch Operation Spring Wind, Drancy became the one and only departure point for Auschwitz. On Le Bourget station's *quai des moutons* ('sheep platform'), prisoners were loaded into cattle wagons which remained under the guard and responsibility of French gendarmes and railwaymen as far as the border.

When they handed over their money to the camp administrators, prisoners received a receipt written in German which gave the exchange value in Polish zlotys.

*

Max Jacob, a Breton Jew who wrote *Les Poèmes de Morven le Gaëlique*, had been living for twenty years in the shadow of the church at Saint-Benoît-sur-Loire. He said he couldn't see why they would come for a harmless old man who asked only that he might continue to pray and grow carrots. The French police came for him in February 1943. He died at Drancy from a bout of pneumonia caught during the interminable journey there. He used to apologize humbly to his companions for saying his Catholic prayers.

There was, however, one riot policeman who protested against the camp regime. His name was Lieutenant Dhuard.

The last convoy left Drancy on 31 July 1944. On 17 August they still managed to load fifty-one Drancy internees on to the last train taking political prisoners held in Paris to Buchenwald. Paris was already up in arms. The Liberation had begun.

Many riot police took part in the Liberation of Paris.

The Paris police were decorated with the Legion of Honour.

*

Some graffiti noted down after the Liberation:

Arrived at Drancy 19 July 1944. Lucie Fuentes and her mother, 58 rue Sedaine. Deported 31 July 1944. In good spirits.

30-6-44. The last convoy! . . . which will be coming back SOON.

Thank you France, all the same. Greiffenhagen.

The graffiti have been wiped away. Everything has been wiped away.
In 1976 the council unveiled a memorial.

*

Of course the story of Drancy camp didn't stop with the wave of a magic wand in August 1944. The French administration wasn't going to deprive itself so easily of such a fine instrument. Drancy was thus used until 1946, this time to intern collaborators. The same gendarmes guarded it with the same zeal. Such continuity was no exception, and we can beat that: take the camp at Saint-Maurice-d'Ardoise in the Department of Gard, which was used successively to intern Spaniards, German nationals, Jews, collaborators, activists from the Algerian National Liberation Front, and members of the far-right-wing OAS, until the huts were earmarked to house *harkis*, Algerian soldiers who enrolled in the French army during the Algerian War.

*

'Drancy-la-Juive': a French camp shaped like a suburban neighbourhood, cut off from the rest of town. With its French riot police, five Germans to make things run smoothly, its internal administration, its police and its Jewish leaders – its *Judenrat* – 'Drancy-la-Juive' was the Paris ghetto, a little Warsaw ghetto. Both ghetto and *Umschlagplatz*: a boarding-place.

Umschlagplatz: it was a Polish goy called Rymkiewicz who wrote: 'Anyone who thinks that what happened in Niska, Dzika and Stawki Streets will never begin again is a fool. The liquidation has been interrupted. But those of us living near the *Umschlagplatz* know very well that nothing is over yet.'

*

Happy are those who think that time erases everything. There do exist places of horror that have been transformed into havens of peace. The Ile de Gorée in Senegal, which for centuries was used to store slaves from all over Africa leaving for the Americas – another *Umschlagplatz* – is today a tourist paradise. The International Institute is based there. Off the coast of Guyana, the penal colonies on the Iles du Salut and Devil's Island, where Captain Dreyfus went through hell, are picturesque picnic sites for the Ariane rocket technicians. Ideal locations for a Club Med holiday village.

Cité de la Muette was simply restored to serve its original purpose. Little had needed doing to convert it into a camp. They just added the barbed wire and a few plank huts, bricked up a few spaces under the galleries. Even the gendarmes were already there. Little needed doing to change it back from the camp into *HLM*. They just removed the barbed wire and the huts. And finished the piping and the inside partitions. A first 'renovation', in effect. The gendarmes didn't even need moving. They're still there, in the neighbouring high-rises.

There are other places of horror where, on the contrary, everything has been razed, everything has disappeared, at least to the eyes of the unwitting passer-by. Where everything is different, and even the space has changed. On the site of the Warsaw ghetto are rectilinear blocks of flats and avenues of trees; in a part of town that no sign points you towards stands a grand monument which no Pole seems to visit except for official ceremonies, and where from time to time a coach of West German tourists pulls up. The whole world might never be able to forget the Warsaw ghetto, but on the site itself you find nothing but obliviousness and indifference. You need all the inner emotion that grips you and simply tells you you're *there* to imagine, by looking around you, what the ghetto was like.

Here time has covered nothing. Everything is dreary because everything has always been dreary. No imagination is required. In the continually changing scenery of the Paris suburbs, such permanence is actually rare. There are still the same galleries, the same dire façades, the same narrow windows. Still the vague impression of incompleteness due to the poor quality of the materials. The estate might have changed roles, but it has changed neither in shape nor in the indefinable something that must be its true character. Visit it with a former prisoner. He will show you where the children's rooms used to be, the solitary confinement cells, the body-search hut, the Jewish administration centre and office of the successive Jewish commanders – Kohn, Blum. He'll point out the cellar where they dug the tunnel with the help of the Jewish administration, which a 'grass' from Compiègne sold to the SS. No, no effort is needed to see the prisoners queuing ten at a time outside the latrines of the 'Château Rouge'. Here's the exact spot, practically unchanged from the photos that have been preserved, where the riot police unloaded their jostling human cargo off the arriving buses. Today a sad padlocked garden covers the exact area of the former central platform; around it, where there used to be cinders, then cement paving stones, there is now a car park where clapped-out family cars doze, waiting for the weekend. To the west, the barbed-wire fence stretched away from the housing blocks, creating a triangular space: they turned this bare plot of land into a courtyard and made the children play there at certain times of day in sight of the passers-by. Today there is a magnificent covered gymnasium in varnished brick with a huge black slate roof.

As the estate is old and poorly built, its present population is made up of modest people, immigrants mostly. That story is certainly not their story – luckily for them, because who could live there if all the time you had so many repulsive echoes ringing in your mind?

At the entrance, then, there is a monument. It is huge, pink and hideous. This raises the eternal question: how do you stop memorials being the final stone, sealing indifference and obliviousness for ever?

In front of the memorial, a freshly painted goods wagon on its rails: 'Horses 8, Men 40'. It is closed, but when you open it you can see mementoes, photographs and documents inside.

*

A few years back, when the new headmaster of Lycée Eugène Delacroix, Monsieur Jacques Durin, arrived in Drancy, he wanted to see what remained of the camp. His school is two hundred metres away. He thought, 'as everyone does', that there had been groups of huts, the classic dismal set-up, and that nothing remained. He hadn't imagined that. Few people who come to Drancy have. The camp is still standing and intact. Monsieur Durin decided to dedicate to the memory of Drancy camp a monument made not of stone but of paper, with his pupils writing an album which was then printed at Le Bourget. It is the most simple, moving and effective monument there is against forgetting.

But the real monument is all of Cité de la Muette.

*

So before arriving at Cité de la Muette that morning, that grey morning, they had spent the night in Aubervilliers in a hotel whose courtyard was jammed with tourist coaches: *'Wir sind der Mittelpunkt der Welt'* – 'We're the centre of the world' – proclaimed the sides of one of them. But this place was nowhere, a big impersonal hotel a stone's throw from the gates of Paris. At reception you could book seats for guided tours in panoramic buses:

TODAY
VISIT THE MUSÉE D'ORSAY
AND THE JEU DE POMME

Jeu de Paume, even. At breakfast, around large tables in a noisy windowless room, they had found themselves sitting with old age pensioners from Quebec just starting their 'Round Europe in a Fortnight' circuit. Service was by Tamils – or rather wasn't, which had aroused the ire of the Québécois gentlemen: 'We haven't been served over here.' There was no more butter – quite outrageous! Luckily, to brighten things up, there was also a French seminar group, and at their table a delighted sales executive was describing how pleased he had been to spend the night with a pretty young woman (from the same seminar?): 'There's no butter, but you've found a Tampax.' ('Did I hear right?' a prim and incredulous François asked Anaïk. Yes, he did.) After which the delighted executive decided to tell his current conquest about some past conquests: 'She was Dutch. No, she was a butcher's wife. Anyway, she had plenty of meat on her.' Ha! Ha! Or maybe it was the words to a song? The pretty young woman had the distraught look of someone waking up from a bad dream, only to realize it's not a dream. François pretended to look shocked; Anaïk chose that moment to bark to him through the din something about the discreet charms of the bourgeoisie, and – don't ask him why – she had sounded so aggressive that he had taken it personally and started to sulk. Anaïk tried to explain that no, she wasn't getting at him, she just thought she'd seen an ostrich walk through the dining-room, and it had reminded her of Buñuel's film. François wasn't having any of it, and continue to sulk he had.

And of course they had gone to catch the RER at Aubervilliers station, which is a long way from the centre of Aubervilliers, and they'd got off at Drancy station, which is a long way from Drancy. And they had even had to change trains at Le Bourget, because in accordance with the *leapfrog* principle explained above, a train stopping at Aubervilliers doesn't stop at Drancy, and vice versa. After which they had crossed a long concrete bridge, where a lone and melancholic Indian woman in a sari was leaning on her elbows, and walked between *pavillons*, roses and sweet peas. This development is exceptionally large, and remarkable not just for the number of howling hounds but for the number of deterrent signs:

I'm keeping guard.
You enter this property at your risk and peril.

Or for these words on a row of small signs on gates, the first of which shows a highly effective black skull and crossbones on a blood-red background:

DANGER OF DEATH
House protected. Fierce dog. DANGER.

In a yard selling tombstones, nothing but tombstones, two wild beasts were also keeping guard. They had bayed as our travellers went by, making giant leaps alongside the fence. What is there to steal in a marble workshop? Anaïk wondered. A sundial, perhaps, even though it would be heavy to carry on your back. But a tombstone? She had photographed the

monsters, who were howling louder than ever, and the workshop boss had come out on to the pavement opposite and barked: 'Have you finished exciting the poor things?'

They had walked along large brick 'walls', then other more recent flats, and come out on to place de la Mairie, half-administrative buildings and half-shopping centre, with the 1900 town hall, all spruce and well preserved, topped by an attractive pinnacle. They had taken a moment's breather in this forum-shaped square interspersed with white ceramic columns, and admired a large and weird thing composed of a concrete triangle flowing out of which is a solid, brownish-coloured plastic coil which might once have been golden: could it be the river of life? It ends in a well-polished copper tap. 'It's definitely a monument,' was Anaïk's diagnosis, 'because there's no point to it.' And off they had gone again, leaving behind on their right modern white flats with entryphones, and on their left Cité Vaillant Couturier, obviously much older. On the avenue were lots of blackened brick buildings from early in the century, the sort of flats that always remind François of a line by the Québécois poet Gaston Miron:

Le cœur serré comme des maisons d'Europe[3]

A sign had told them: 'La Muette/Le Village parisien/Les Oiseaux', and they had enjoyed their one pleasant encounter of the trip, a gentleman pushing a wheelchair loaded with plaster flowers: 'The Barometer-Rose'. François thought of buying one for Julia, who was expecting him to bring back a souvenir from his travels, but then some lazy spirit had whispered to him that he was bound to find other, better ones. That it wasn't urgent.

After all, what is urgent about this journey?

8

*Aubervilliers: Akim at the Jean Bart. – The La Courneuve
4000: a 'wall' comes down, roots are lost. – Requiem for Le
Corbusier. – Daoud, 'nationality love'. – The Unexpected. –
Aubervilliers fort, workers' allotments. – Forts and 'fortifs'.
– Le Landy. – Pierre Laval, baron of the 'couronne parisienne'.
– 'The little children of Aubervilliers'. – 'I'm not racist,'
she says. – Excursion to Saint-Denis. – Les Vertus lock.
– Living in Auber. – Rachid Khimoune and the artists at
La Maladrerie. – 17 October 1962 and rue de l'Union.*

FRIDAY 26 MAY, CONTINUED. Aubervilliers-La Courneuve station dates
from the time of the Northern Railway Company: you come out on to a
square/car park/waste ground, the site of the future A86 motorway,
which, in one, ten or a hundred years' time, will loop the loop round Paris.
Following the now familiar rule, the station is relatively close to Saint-
Denis, but to reach the centre of Aubervilliers you're better off catching
the bus. And of course they get it wrong, they catch not the 150 but the
150A, which changes everything, for they should know that the 150A is
an *express* which doesn't stop before Porte de Pantin on the edge of Paris.
And so, after travelling a kilometre in twenty minutes and being stuck
in interminable traffic jams, the driver blithely shoots straight past the
town hall bus stop, refuses to open the door during the long waits at the
next lights and, in the end, gives in to the pleas of tearful passengers –
old ladies with shopping baskets and more resigned-looking Africans –
only a kilometre later, on the corner of some unknown crossroads. All our
travellers can do is to get their bearings and walk all the way back.

Aubervilliers is stuck on to Paris, pegged to Porte de la Villette. On
the map, Aubervilliers seems to be just an extension of the most working-
class areas of Paris. Today the metro runs through the town as far as La
Courneuve; the number 65 bus (a two-figure bus number, showing that
it's an authentic Parisian bus, a blue-blooded bus, and not a three-figure
bus, the suburbanite, the proletarian, the bastard) has its terminus outside

the town hall: everything makes Aubervilliers seem like just another area of Paris. And yet.

*

Outside the town hall, a giant slogan celebrating the 1789 bicentenary announces that

THE WORLD HAS CHANGED, AND MUST KEEP ON CHANGING.

The town hall itself is an opulent edifice whose every stone is redolent of the Third Republic, with just that hint of nostalgia for the Second Empire visible in all the *mairies* of Paris's arrondissements.

On the official noticeboards is the latest council by-law: it concerns traffic regulations on days reserved for the First Communions of 1989.

Our travellers have a rendezvous opposite Lycée Le Corbusier, at the Jean Bart. It's difficult to know why this fat Flemish pirate, whose name meant *beard*, should preside over so many *bar-tabacs*, save for the fact that it's a bad pun (Bar = Bart with a silent t) for bistros founded by natives of Auvergne – naturally enough – whose first name was Jean. Their path is paved with enigmas. At the Jean Bart, then, whose owner is Arab, Akim is waiting for them. They are dead-beat and ravenous, and wolf down their hot dogs. Akim's amused: 'I never thought I'd find you so tired.' He had already been amused three months before, when they had told him about their project; but straight away he had been one of those – perhaps the first – to take them very seriously. He was the one who had talked about the variety of landscapes, structures and people they would meet: 'If you really know how to open your eyes. . . .' A few days earlier, they had phoned and asked him to find them a hotel in Aubervilliers – small, pleasant, inexpensive, etc. – and he had reserved them two rooms at Hôtel de l'Imprévu (Hotel of the Unexpected), a name which had had them dreaming ever since. He will take them there in a minute. He doesn't know the hotel, but he frequents the café on the ground floor, because it's on the way to Maison du Peuple Guy Môquet, a community centre in La Courneuve where he is currently rehearsing with the young theatre group with whom he is actor, director and stage manager: Akim is one of the founders of the *ABC* – Aubervilliers Theatre Group – which at the moment is preparing a show as part of the operation 'Coup de cœur à La Courneuve' ('Straight from the Heart of La Courneuve').

When they discussed the journey three months ago, Akim was rehearsing Mrożeck's *The Exiles* with a friend.

Akim was born in Cité des 800, a collection of economical thin grey 'walls' built in the late fifties, not far from Cité des 4000, which went up shortly afterwards. 'When I was a kid,' Akim remembers, 'the real gangs were formed by youths from the 4000. You see, when someone said "I'm from the 4000", and you could only reply "I'm from the 800", already you didn't make the grade.' Aubervilliers is an old working-class town, La Courneuve a young monster which has grown up too fast. Is leaving Aubervilliers for La Courneuve like going where the savages are? In any case, you're from Aubervilliers, not somewhere else. These days, when Akim is working in La Courneuve, he likes to go back to Aubervilliers for lunch: 'As soon as I see the sign for Auber, I feel better – I'm home.'

*

In a small café in place des Fêtes, Akim's mates are playing pool: they are childhood friends. Akim insists that they're not actually schoolmates or friends from childhood: they all grew up on the Auber 800. Our travellers have to wait for the game to finish: the stake is ten francs or a cinema ticket. Introductions: 'We're all Swedish,' says one, to keep things simple.

*

Off they go to the 4000. They cross an avenue: farewell Aubervilliers. The 4000 does not hold the absolute record for the longest 'walls' in France; apparently that goes to one 700 metres long built by B. Zerhfuss in Nancy: quite a feat. But still, the 4000 – four thousand flats for as many families, which makes how many inhabitants: 20,000? – is a fine example of human storage. It is one of the most grandiose results of the Delouvrier Plan. The year was 1960. 'Delouvrier,' said de Gaulle, 'these inhuman suburbs are making the Paris area a shambles – sort them out.' Delouvrier had answered something like: 'Affirmative, General', and he sorted them out. He devised a Plan called the *PADOG*, and Zones, following up the *ZUP* with the *ZAC*, until they were replaced by the *ZAD*; he remodelled the old Department of Seine-et-Oise into several new departments as a prelude to creating the *région parisienne* itself: 'I studied the problem for six months ... in theory, finding the urban planning lever was simple enough: to build housing you need land; to build new towns you need lots of land; to build new railways or motorways you need long pieces of land.' Delouvrier knew all about sort-outs: in 1941 he had passed through the management school at Uriage, which, as we know, was a nursery for top civil servants at the time when France was singing Pétain's theme song *Maréchal nous voilà* ('Marshal, here we are'); the main thing, as de Gaulle used to say, is that they were all good Frenchmen. In short, Delouvrier and his chums sorted out the Paris area. And then later, twenty years later, with Mitterrand as president, they realized that the Plan wasn't working, that it was unbearable, and it was decided to *sort the place out* again. As the new urban planners had finally realized that everything stemmed from a lack of humanism, they looked for a human dimension. And as there was a risk of social discontent boiling over, they decided to dynamite the biggest 'wall', in Cité des 4000 Sud. It was one of the president's first big initiatives. The principle of a big clean-up by a clear-out was certainly not new – the Germans tested it successfully in 1943 in the Old Port of Marseilles – but it's not what you do, it's the way ... : here, there were no unseemly scenes, no cordons of helmeted gendarmes, no exodus or scenes from Armageddon; no, quite the contrary, the event passed off in a mood of delighted consensus. A huge crowd of onlookers came to watch the show, stands were put up for the personalities: the organizers of 'Suburbs 89', who had masterminded the great idea; the mayor and town council; the powers that be from the department and region; the Minister for Housing. Scaffolding was specially erected to give the press and television crews a good view. Naturally there were also large numbers of police and firemen. In this atmosphere of much rejoicing, the French people were able to follow the show on TV in amazement. The big 'wall' needed only ten seconds to fall elegantly down. An on-site reception followed. 'Ten seconds to wipe out high-rise depression', 'The mistakes of the past', headlined the following morning's papers. On the site today there remains a vaguely grassy area and a melancholy little tree planted by the youngsters who were born there: they say that this little tree and this big empty space are all the roots they have left. Because those youngsters are still there – living in other 'walls', which get the sun now. Well, they're not all there, of course. Some of them had to go. The authorities also took the opportunity to 'ventilate' the immigrants. As they said, they're humanizing the place.

That 'wall', the absent, disappeared 'wall', was called Debussy.

*

Today, everyone – at least, everyone who matters; that's to say, the urban planning commentators – seem to have agreed on the guilty party: Le Corbusier, the man who inspired it all. So let's all jump on Le Corbu: 'Everything was built not just cynically but foolishly too, in a kind of stupid adherence to the ultra-rationalist discourse used by Le Corbusier on the machine for living'; this appraisal is thrust in our faces in *L'État de la France-1986* by Roland Castro, who has inspired the President of the Republic's thinking on the suburbs since 1981. Yet Le Corbusier said some wonderful things, which set people dreaming and still do:

A man's house, the mistress of its form, takes root in nature open to the four horizons. It lends its roof to gazing at the clouds, or azure skies, or stars.

He used to say that 'blocks of flats will no longer be pinched lips', and that 'taking possession of space fashions an undeniable harmony, binds human enterprise to its setting'.

Open to welcome
Open too for all
to come and take

the waters flow
the sun sheds light
the complexities have spun their web
fluidity is everywhere

the tools of the hand
the caresses of the hand
the life we have tasted through
its moulding by the hands
the view that is in the palpation

Le Corbusier adored the casbah in Algiers, and used to say that the flats in the *ceinture des Maréchaux* were 'the belt of shame'. In the end he didn't build much in France: just a few experimental residential villas between the wars, a church – Ronchamp – with curved lines 'like conches', and three 'radiant estates' which saw him roundly taunted by the serious people. One must say that almost everyone was against him – well, everyone who mattered (see above), and most particularly the world of promoters and money: wasn't their main complaint about his designs their excessive cost? His radiant estates were built in only three places, and the one at Briey, which you see rise up like a cathedral on the hill in the middle of the forest, came within a hair's breadth of being dynamited a few years ago. It hadn't withstood the black years of the steel crisis and resulting unemployment in Lorraine. It had become so gloomy that Didier Daeninckx used it as the setting for the blackest scene in one of his *romans noirs*.

It is hammered into us today that Le Corbu was the spiritual father of the 'walls' and high-rises; but even so, at the time when they were being built, the same people who found no fault with the creation of all the Sarcelles-style schemes and other big developments shrieked along with the chorus, calling him *'fada'*, barmy, because of a few dozen flats in Marseilles set amongst the trees. (But who remembers that the word *fada* comes from *'fade'*, meaning fairy?) In 1954, the grand master wasn't called Le Corbu but Auzelle, a teacher at the École d'Urbanisme in Paris. Auzelle's principles and creations served as a practical guide for those carrying out Delouvrier's orders. Monsieur Jean-Paul Flamand, whose book is really very useful, defines the practice thus: 'There were two basic operational approaches, though one daren't talk of principles. One was to organize the traffic between a few big public buildings and assign the latter distinct zones; the other, to organize the traffic between the zones. This "zoning" thus distinguished the industrial zones from the office zones and living zones. The gaps left between them were to be "green spaces".'

Zoning + storage = big housing estates. 'Only after these spaces were put into operation and segregation set in did the unbearable truth become clear, namely that it was no longer a town, not even a very poor one, but a simple storage space,' wrote Roland Castro in 1986, readopting the Left's 1970s watchword: 'The bourgeoisie doesn't house its workers, it stores them. The bourgeoisie doesn't transport its workers, it rolls them.' To be fair, he now writes: 'Since 1981 there has been a good way of trying to check this situation.'

*

At this point in his account of the journey, François finds himself faced with a situation he has not yet encountered once since he began to write it. Until now, he has been able to rely on his notes: wordy or succinct, precise or barely indicative, they have always just about done their job. But for La Courneuve, they have suddenly let him down. Not that he didn't take any. The words are there in place, in his crumpled exercise book (exercise book number 3, that is, the one whose prettily coloured cover shows Winnie the Pooh saying to Piglet, 'It's so much more friendly with two'), themselves duly recopied each evening at the hotel from the little notepad he carries constantly in his pocket. But when he rereads these words now, they become inconsistent. They drag behind them only confused images, unconnected snatches of conversations. He knows that they've walked, seen, listened and talked. He knows the places they've been to, the people they've met. He remembers that it was fine and clear that afternoon, but then everything goes misty. Their stay in La Courneuve is a blank.

In the end, maybe that is the hallmark of the 4000: its feeling of emptiness, even if it has the population of a small town. The feeling that no words exist to describe a giant 'development' which brings together and unites nothing, where nothing seems to have a meaning, not even that of a machine for living where nothing is attractive and nothing is ugly: where everything is a big dull zero. One dull 'wall' cancels out the next dull 'wall', and so on, from car park to car park, from paving stones to withered lawns; and nothing – but nothing – has an impact, so that out of so many zeros rises nothing but another zero just like all the rest.

159

La Courneuve: The 4000

In the end, the only remarkable thing about the 4000 is the site of the demolished 'wall', the *cancelled* 'wall'. The 4000's youngsters are right to say, 'It's our monument.'

All that remains is the shapes, lines and life captured by Anaïk's camera. But were these photos really taken at La Courneuve? Or at another estate – Les Courtillières, Les Francs Moisions, Massy-Villaine or Les Ulis? Didn't you mix the rolls up, by any chance? No, it's impossible: you remember those faces, don't you, the retired couple leaning out of their ground-floor window in the sunshine? I asked if I could photograph them, we chatted for a long time, and the woman started to cry?

Yes, that photo has stuck: 'That woman,' says Anaïk, 'seemed to be waiting for something like death.' It was when she talked about the *pavillon* she would so like to live in that the tears came. She had held out through the window three little pieces of nougat. Very hard on the teeth, nougat.

The notes say that they stopped off at Café le Courneuvien, then add soberly: 'gloomy atmosphere of alcoholic dilapidation'. In the past, Le Courneuvien was known not just as a café but also as a major drug-dealing centre. The notes also say that they visited Espace John Lennon, and that 'the cultural amenities are excellent'. There's no way that happened under Giscard, that's for sure. A youth café serves non-alcoholic drinks. Everything is brand new. The recording studio has a magnificent 24-track sound deck: the equipment is far more modern and sophisticated than at the studios of Radio-France, and the technician is a highly qualified buff. Bands can make demo tapes at extremely low prices and, of course, benefit from council subsidies. The disco-videotheque organizer is down in the dumps: he had sixty CDs stolen in the first week; the younger kids distracted the DJs while the others stole and worked out how to slip through the anti-theft system. The idea that the Espace should be open to all without the slightest control has now had to be modified: you have to register to get in, and the CD cases contain only photocopies. The centre has had a concrete slab through the window. It's only natural, says the organizer: the centre is so attractive and new that it's felt to be a window of luxury, a provocation. 'In less than a year it'll all be smashed up,' says Akim. Is it any wonder the organizer is miserable, dismayed? In a place like the 4000, any chance of things changing depends on a few individuals like him.

Madame Merri, the caretaker, walks past dragging a gigantic plywood map of Corsica: tonight a Corsican is being given a party – is he getting a medal? or retiring? – and there'll be a crowd of people. She's lived at La Courneuve for thirteen years. She knows them *all*, she's not scared of *them*: she knows how to handle them, talk to them and tell them what she thinks, and if need be give them a kick up the backside.

Outside, Anaïk photographs an African woman doing embroidery in the sun and looking after children, and they have a chat. Then she walks past some young North African women. They don't want to be photographed. 'You can keep your photos for the mamadous. Yeah, we saw you. Is it for 93 or the town hall newspaper? Why the big interest in the mamadous? They have four wives and twenty children, the mamadous do. There are loads of them just over there if you're *that* interested. Have you been to Africa? Surely not Burkina? Really? But what were you doing in Burkina? It's poor, it's a dump, there's nothing to see in Burkina.'

In late afternoon, the 4000 livens up. Outside Le Courneuvien, the scaffolding is in place for a concert by a band of *beurs*, French-born Arabs. '*Beurs?*' says Akim. 'I'm happy being called an Arab, that doesn't bother me. But the word *beur* just appeared. I didn't – we didn't – invent it. People can pin it on us, but for me it's a meaningless label.'

They have a rendezvous at La Courneuve's Maison du Peuple Guy Môquet, where Akim and Catherine, who created the Aubervilliers Theatre Group in 1987, are moving on to rehearsals for the next improvised show – still as part of 'Coup de Cœur à La Courneuve'. Present are fifteen or so young people who need the energy to emerge from everyday life, work, family and kicking their feet, to plunge into the world of a show which exists only through solidarity and concentration, words, the right accent; and they're in Salle Mentor too, which, when empty, is gloomy and sad, and has awful acoustics: the words get lost up in the rafters.

Still at the Maison du Peuple, there is a TV screening of the film *Mélanges*, shot six months ago by *ABC*. '*Story-Mélanges*: six young people from La Courneuve and a writer combine their biographies, mixing the story of the origins and identity of foreigners born there. These hilarious fragments of comic fiction fuse to create a rare experience.' The writer is Jean-Pierre Renault. What provides the film's *mélange* is a man over forty years old returning to the suburb where he was born; he is searching for roots whose traces have already been worn away. On the doorstep of a council flat, the present tenants, suspicious and hostile, refuse him entry. It's a closed door, closed on 'a society clean out of invention'. All that remains is to listen to the young people who were born there and live there: 'We shot the film where we were born, in an anti-TV style so we could hear some sharp, unofficial talking and silence the people who talk all the time .... This is art, writing and the language of film being used in a salutary way by those who are usually spectators deprived of their own lives; here, they're astonished to find themselves rebuilding an identity.... The suburbs seen through a glass magnifying the surrounding shambles and shameful paradoxes. Roll on the future.'

Those 'mixing' themselves in this film, which they have written and acted in, are J.-P. Renault, Ryade Balaabi, Chérif Boudjeraba, Farid Hamza, Mahmoud Ibrahime, Daoud Krouri, Sayed Soliman, Akim Touchane, Richard Tumeau. Daoud, for example, a leggy lad whose triangular face is too smooth, almost angelic, introduces himself and offers glimpses of his story:

> Nationality: Love. Et cetera, et cetera, et cetera.... I'll always live for the et cetera, et cetera, et cetera.

What about the 'surrounding shambles'? They say: 'Don't confuse the people who live here with those hideous façades. They always have nice names, Debussy, Balzac, but something about those names stinks.... If I could say something to the people who built that, I'd tell them: Next time, think first.'

Akim talks about shooting the film: 'We called it *Mélanges*, but a collection of individual stories doesn't in itself make a story: it wasn't enough to stick them together, we had to create, invent something else from that. Fine, but what can you invent in the 4000? Maybe the film shows that in the 4000, you always come up against the same walls and always bounce back off them?'

*

Night has fallen. A group of them have dinner at L'Orange Bleue in the old part of Aubervilliers, the working-class part, next to the *périphérique*, a few hundred metres from Paris. It is an Algerian restaurant, with paper covers on long tables and menus printed in purple ink. There's human warmth. At the next table, like a home from home, some middle-aged gentlemen are speaking Italian. Or, to be more precise, Piedmontese.

The owner offers them liqueurs.

*

The best thing about Hôtel de l'Imprévu is the official plaque saying 'Tourist Hotel', with one star. 'Ah,' says the proprietor, 'I didn't know there was a lady. To be frank, I advise you to take bedrooms with toilet at 140 francs – not that there's anything wrong with the others, mind, but those are cleaner.' The hotel looks out on to Aubervilliers's avenue Jean Jaurès – in other words, the inevitable Nationale 2 and its motorized cortège, not far from the crossroads where it becomes La Courneuve's avenue Paul Vaillant. The rooms are on the first floor, up a mouldy staircase which opens on to a landing of uncertain levels; and that, of course, is the moment when the automatic light chooses to go off, causing a total blackout. At last, their doors. François's carpet is so rotten that he is scared of sinking into it, as if it were a swamp. Among the stains and cigarette burns, there is one recent, particularly eye-catching streak which splashes its way from the bed to the washbasin with quite extravagant gusto – something like a comet's tail or an ejaculation of a particularly lustful mammoth. The basin is grey with grime, and François can't imagine washing his hands in it – or, indeed, anything else. Anaïk's bedroom is blue: it smells of 'foot cheese', a manly old expression from military service days. Rather dismal. François tiptoes into bed, curls up and remains quite still, as if on an island besieged by jellyfish, giant toads, an oil slick and bubonic plague, waiting to be knocked out by a merciful sleep inhabited by giant squid and the blaring horns of rutting HGVs.

*

SATURDAY 27 MAY. Early in the morning they meet down in the narrow hotel lobby, where, amid (plastic?) greenery, coffee is served on three Formica tables. Alone at her table, there's an attractive young lady wearing a boubou. At another table, an elderly couple exchange a few words in low voices. The lorries are still going past, and the windows vibrate: other than that the place is almost intimate, slightly stifling. The pretty lady gets up and says goodbye to the assistants, who reply politely, 'Have a good day, Madam.'

Barely has the door closed when people begin talking ten to the dozen in loud exuberant voices. 'You see,' the elderly gentleman confides to them, 'the trouble with this hotel is that for a while now they've been taking anybody. It was a good hotel once, but they break everything. You can't spend all your time repairing everything if they go and mess it up again.' The lady of the hotel, who turns out not to be the proprietor, explains that she comes from the Xth arrondissement, that she's had enough, that she wants to leave, that there are just too many clients who get her down. 'That's nice for us,' remarks Anaïk. 'Oh, I don't mean you. Luckily we get pleasant clients too. Luckily there's not just *them*.' She tells them how recently she was queuing for an ice cream in a cake shop: she was offered a 'creole' – no, another name, she can't remember – anyway, you see what I mean, one of *those* names, a name from *over there*; so she replied: No thank you! We get enough round here as it is. 'Well, I can tell you, everyone in the queue laughed; it made us feel better. Well, all except one woman, probably because she's married to a Black, so that'll teach her. And if they're not happy. . . .' 'They only have to hop on the metro,' chips in the elderly gentleman. They roll about laughing. The lady talks about the thieving. All the thieving. 'They wouldn't dare where

164

they come from. Over there, they'd get their heads cut off.' 'Or maybe something else,' adds the client pompously: Ha! Ha! Ha!

It remains only to pay the bill, say thank you and get out into the clean air of avenue Jean Jaurès. 'It's a bit much,' remarks Anaïk. 'They complain about them, but they're quite happy to take their money.'

They walk down the sunny pavement towards Fort d'Aubervilliers metro station. It's Saturday, and the crowds are out. A North African gentleman goes past with a flowerpot: tomorrow is Mother's Day. Phototime for a hairdresser who has painted on his window: *'Chez François le coupeur de têtes* ('Chez François, the cutter [-off] of heads'). The executioner, scissors in hand, squints at them and comes out to ask: 'What's that for?' Anaïk has to explain that her friend's called François, so obviously. . . . They all laugh. They tack towards the sun. To the left, the renovated high-rises of Les Courtillières, dressed in a *flan-au-caramel*-coloured brick-and-ceramic skin. In front of them to the south, behind a long fence with padlocked gates, are the workers' allotments on the glacis of the fort, which is invisible beneath a carpet of vegetation.

The 'Vertus d'Aubervilliers' Association of workers' allotments.

François helps a tall moustachioed man carry a brand-new and very heavy automatic weeding hoe. The man's wide-brimmed hat, which causes a passing colleague to dub him 'The Mexican', shades a hirsute face and eyes circled by small steel-rimmed glasses, making him look half faun-like, half bucolic intellectual; he is wearing grey shorts and a vest. He lives a stone's throw away, at Les Courtillières. He's retired: 'You've got to do something to stop yourself going under.' Ah, if only he had a *pavillon*. He's only just got the allotment: he's tried to clear it with a spade, but it's impossible; he was actually the village blacksmith, but this is the first time in his life he's had blisters. He went and hired the hoe, two hundred francs a day, but it's already broken down, so . . .

They find a gate that's open; above it a sign announces tomato plants for sale. The gate opens on to a path leading straight towards the glacis, between metal grilles surrounding gardens and sheds, and connects with another, perpendicular one which seems to go right round the fort beside a deep ditch where trees have grown. Through gaps in the greenery the ramparts appear on the other side, themselves crowned with lush vegetation. They take this outer covered way, which is also lined by fences. They go through a real little wood with willows, ashes and sprouting plane trees, and walk between hedges of rambling rose, masses of ivy, barely faded lilacs, and more roses, clusters of button roses. 'It's like Château Bagatelle,' says Anaïk. 'Perhaps,' François philosophizes, 'the

Fort d'Aubervilliers

workers' allotment is a certain idea of happiness.' Behind them the big high-rises of Les Courtillières tower over everything. It's 10 a.m. and there's no one about.

Overhanging the ditch is a terrace with a rusty iron trellis and vines – real vines like the ones you once found all round here, whose grapes must make a tart wine like its neighbour from the Butte Montmartre: the abundant clusters are formed from seeds that are still tiny because they have only just finished flowering. And outside the bitumen paper shed, a table and chairs stand ready for a sabbatical breather. At this moment a distant cockerel begins to crow: the first of the journey.

The path goes no further. Retracing their steps, they see a man working down below on his allotment in the sunshine. They talk to him through the fence. There's a drought, he says. It's been like this since last autumn, and in any case the soil here's no good: it's grey and full of stones; try as he might to take them out, they come back every year. Water's a problem too. There used to be pumps, but when Les Courtillières was built they put concrete thirty-five metres down, and that dried out the underground layer. They did get a well-digger in twenty years ago: it cost two million old francs, but he didn't find anything. Yet a river used to flow past here; it's even been marshy in the past. Which just leaves the rainwater. We have to gather and stock it in those blue barrels, and everyone uses them: they come from the washing plant at Pantin, so you've got to mind the soap powder residues or all your vegetables get burned.

'The rats are the real pest. They arrived about ten years ago when they dug the metro under avenue Jean Jaurès. Paris rats. Enormous, they were. In winter you could see them running all over the place. When it got dark, I could see them staring at me from behind that elder; there were twenty, thirty, forty of them. Once I was really scared and did a U-turn. You could hear them whistling, because those creatures whistle, I can tell you. They gobbled up all the animals – chickens, rabbits, pigeons. You don't get them any more. When I saw that I didn't hang about, I was so upset I gave all my animals away. And then, luckily, things calmed down. Maybe it's because they'd eaten everything. There were only vegetables left, and those creatures aren't vegetarians.

'The allotments are shared out by the association, the League for a Piece of Land. It dates from 1922: it was for the proletariat – the workers, basically, as the name suggests. But the land still belongs to the army. The State Property Department. I've had my allotment for seventeen years, and I hear that next year it's all being closed down: there's talk of a riot police barracks. Or a hospital. In the meantime, we're still here.'

He's sixty and was born near Dunkirk. His father skippered one of those deep-sea trawlers they called 'the Icelanders'. His father was also the harbour master at Algiers: before that, during the First World War, he'd commanded an anti-submarine boat, and earlier still – much, much earlier – he started off on a sailing ship. . . . Taking after his father, the son spent ten years as an engineering officer, but he stopped going to sea after his third child was born.

All this leaves our travellers a long way from the workers' allotments, Les Courtillières, Auber and the RER: they're sailing off the banks of Iceland, then they head back southwards towards Gibraltar, beautiful white Algiers, and why not, after that, to the Sargasso Sea. . . . No, let's be serious, let's go about so we're downwind, with a reef in the mainsail, let's haul in the Genoa sheet, then sail as close as we can to the wind without worrying about the breakers, the swell of heavy seas and dripping oilskins; let's tack again, keep tacking, and get back to Aubervilliers fort, which is moored a cable's length from Paris – it's Saturday 27 May and we have clear skies, a force two wind and visibility ten miles: calm weather, very calm weather.

*

The military ring round Paris consisted of about thirty forts, redoubts, depots and entrenched camps which are mostly still there today. Some forts have been assigned other jobs: one example is Châtillon, where the first nuclear reactor was perfected in 1947 – at the time it was called an atomic pile: it was all small and quaint, and its name was Zoé. Others, like Vincennes and the Mont Valérien, are still used by the army. And finally others, like this one, lie abandoned.

It was in 1830 that the idea of giving the capital a fortified wall again became a serious concern. Defending Paris was all very well, but against whom exactly? The plan of the War Minister, Marshal Soult, involved building seventeen forts. Opposition deputies had plenty of opportunities to show that 'a comparison of the distance between the forts in relation to the different *quartiers* behind which they are to be erected, and the range of their cannon, leads one to think that they will become a group of fresh Bastilles, better armed against the people than against foreign invaders'. In opposition to these unpopular forts, the Left proposed a project of a single rampart stretching round Paris. Only after lengthy debate did Monsieur Thiers, who had become Louis Philippe's Prime Minister, manage to get voted through a plan combining advanced forts and a protecting wall. The forts nevertheless remained the object of suspicion and hatred for ordinary Parisians. They knew quite well that by placing his cannon there, Monsieur Thiers was aiming primarily at them, the 'enemy within'. When the project was completed under the Second Empire, it included: an initial line of forts; a second line of fortifications right round the city, which in Parisian lingo became *les fortifs*; and in Paris itself, says an 1867 guide, a third line 'made up of enough barracks and strategic roads that under no circumstances will it be thought necessary to bombard the city'. At least they made no bones about it. And so while Paris, behind its wall, was duly held in check and controlled by the 'second' and 'third' lines, the surrounding area, or suburbs, where most of the new working class was settling, developed under the close watch of the forts' cannon, which were always ready to spray the environs, where factories and buildings were sprouting up.

The forts were effective against the Prussians during the 1870 siege, and therefore completely ineffective at first against the Parisian populace: not only did the latter, up in arms and feeling invulnerable behind its wall, want to lay into the Prussians, but, making the most of the Imperial army's defeat at Sedan, it had declared a republic. No, that wasn't at all what Monsieur Thiers had in mind. And it would have been rather tricky shelling the people of Paris to their senses, watched by the delighted enemy. It was therefore necessary to withstand the siege and, for want of anything better, to see that the Parisian army was, as we know, shelled by the enemy instead. But once the armistice was finally signed, at the first sign of exasperation from the Parisians – on 18 March 1871, when the National Guard went to fetch *their* cannon from the Butte Montmartre to stop them being handed over to the Prussians – Monsieur Thiers was finally able to put his plan into action: all the civil and military authorities, and all legislative and executive powers, were transferred from Paris to Versailles, after which the city was shelled and recaptured. Hence the importance of the forts. The one at Mont Valérien remained in the hands of the pro-Thiers faction, known as the Versaillais. To the south, the Communards held those at Issy, Vanves and Montrouge. To the north, the way out was blocked by the Prussian-held forts. The Commune's fate was sealed for good on 9 May 1871, the day the fort at Issy was abandoned by its Communard defenders. In the days that followed, the Versaillais captured the fort at Vanves, and while Monsieur Thiers was signing his definitive peace treaty with Bismarck, they entered Paris along the Seine by the Point du Jour. It was 'la semaine sanglante', the bloodiest week. Twenty thousand Parisians died.

The forts' military history stops there. In 1914, with the German armies threatening Paris, the fortification commander, Gallieni, took an initiative that changed the course of the war: instead of leaving his garrison protected behind the wall, he sent all his troops out into the open to attack the enemy sixty kilometres away on the banks of the Marne, where the retreating French army had regrouped. General von Kluck, who was commanding the German right flank, wrote that day: 'I cannot believe that a governor of a city under siege could have the audacity to take his troops outside his fortress's field of action.' Gallieni did, though, resulting in 'les Taxis de le Marne': Parisian taxis were requisitioned to transport his reinforcements.

In the 1920s, having become decidedly useless, the *fortifs* were destroyed. The forts were mostly disused. But in eighty years they had made their mark on Paris and its suburbs. To understand why Aubervilliers, no more than the other towns in *la petite couronne*, the inner ring of Parisian suburbs, has not been, is not, and will not be part of Paris for quite some time, you need only read this description, in the 1867 guide quoted above, of the protecting wall's fortifications: these included a 250-metre-wide *constraining zone* in the immediate vicinity which could not be built on; the *military terrain* itself with all its defences (glacis, counterscarp, ditch, exterior talus, upper parapet slopes, interior talus, banquette, and terreplein); and finally, set back from the ramparts, the *military road*, made up of an interrupted line of boulevards named after 'les Maréchaux', which for a long time was reserved exclusively for military traffic. The protecting wall thus stretched thirty-three kilometres round Paris, broken by about sixty gates, which were themselves closed off by the city toll barriers and enclosed an area of eight thousand hectares. The toll barriers marked another division, since taxes were collected there on everything coming into Paris, thus fixing different prices inside and outside the capital. It wasn't the Berlin Wall, but even so, living on different sides of the 'constraining line', the Parisians and *the others* had reason to feel different from each other.

*

Lunch at Akim's father's flat. The travellers are happy to return briefly to a gentle family atmosphere. In truth it's not a big place: an *F2* in a high-rise in the 800. Two rooms linked by a kitchen, with a picture window running all the way along. Akim's father is fifty-nine, got divorced a few years back and has had three children with his new wife; and now he has just been pensioned off after nearly forty years at the factory. He arrived in France in the early 1950s. He knew Aubervilliers when it had fields and gardens, which he used to drive through on his moped to go to work at the Motobécane factory. It's a long time since he returned to Algeria – it's too dear, in any case. His life is here, though it's too much of a squeeze, unfortunately, with five in two rooms; but at the town hall they reply that young couples are given priority. The 800, says Akim, is a poor people's estate. Those who can go and live on more modern estates.

As though it were the most natural thing in the world, Akim's father has decided to welcome his son's unknown friends as if they were cousins

arriving after a long journey: his wife has prepared a princely couscous. Round the table are his two eldest sons – Akim and his brother Sadi, a TV cameraman – and the three little ones. The eldest two talk about how worried they are about the young ones' education: if only they could avoid what they themselves have been through. The problem with the estates, says Akim, is that they don't let go of you easily: they're shut in on themselves, they offer a territory, a form of security. There are kids growing up on their Auber estate who have never really searched for other horizons. Even Paris exists only for the odd excursion. The gang ends up taking the place of a second family, of society, and everything takes second place to the role, status and prestige the youngsters can obtain within it: the most important thing is not to lose face in the eyes of the other members. It's tough living on the estate, but it's tough getting out too. Staying there and going back there is almost easier. So they just have to get by on 4000 francs a month, alternating between odd jobs and unemployment benefit. The gang, Akim goes on, isn't just linked to the economic crisis. It comes from something even deeper. He thinks it goes in cycles: there are periods when you think gangs are going to disappear, that the new generation won't experience them, and then they surface again. 'I'll never come back to Aubervilliers,' says Sadi.

Round the table, a mild afternoon kind of feeling. Family photo-time. Akim's father wishes to explain that he doesn't understand how people can live in a country without adopting its customs, provided they're clean and civilized ones. He knows Tunisians and Moroccans who persist in observing the tradition of eating with their fingers, and he thinks that's stupid.

François's lighter has gone out. The master of the house offers him a new one. 'Come back whenever you like,' he says when they say goodbye, at the foot of the tower block.

*

Anaïk goes to La Courneuve to see Daoud, the angel with the blue-ringed eyes from the *ABC*'s film, the one with the 'nationality: love' and the et ceteras. Photo-time with Daoud in batik bermudas. Daoud tells his story in a way there wasn't room for in the film.

Daoud is twenty-five. He's a child of Debussy, the dynamited 'wall'. He arrived there when he was six. Before that his family lived in lodgings. He has six brothers and sisters. After spending a year in Debussy, his parents went to live in Braque, another 'wall'; he was sent to live with his grandparents in Algeria for four years. At fourteen, he found himself in a children's home in Grenoble. He put in a request to the juvenile magistrate to be sent on an electrician's course: he was put in the bakery section. He ran away plenty of times, always down south. When the police got hold of him, he used to give them the name of his brother, who had done his national service, to make them think he was a major. Until he was eighteen, he spent his life playing hide-and-seek with the 'Wanted' posters, always running away, always being captured, drifting around, obliged to steal and sleep rough. After a final warning from the home's director, he ran away to Paris. At Auber he found a place to live – in a garage under a building near the municipal conservatory. He survived by stealing: 'I thieved and mugged at five in the morning to get money.' In Paris he met young runaways like him, and they helped each other out: 'You start stealing when you're ten, when you've got nothing to do – you want a ball to kick about and you're faced with a stupid turnstile. To start with, I was trying to act grown-up – I needed to prove myself. But after that, when I mugged someone, it wasn't to go nightclubbing, it was to eat, so it was stupid. I tried to be pleasant, I'd say: Be nice and give me a few francs for something to eat. Between sixteen and twenty I only had sandwiches in my belly, hot meals were rare.' He tried to work: 'I'd had enough of that lark. I did two weeks as a detective in a clothes shop. I didn't stick it: it didn't pay any more, I couldn't live any better and it didn't make any more sense. Some mates came to get me and go down south.' He started taking barbiturates with alcohol: five sachets a day, sometimes a whole packet. 'You see, when you've just turned eighteen you think the world belongs to you. People make excuses for you, they say: Oh, he's only a kid.'

In 1984 Daoud spent a month in police custody. When he came out

he met a coke dealer. 'It clears the nostrils. But he told me to be careful. A fortnight with him and I was completely hooked. I needed it to feel good. I started stealing to pay for my habit. I got completely manipulated.'

He lived with an older girl who hawked stuff on the markets. They worked together. 'We bought gear for 1000 francs and sold it for 3000. I liked the Arabs, their buy-anything sell-anything side.' Then came the army, in the Engineers: he asked to sit his driving test, but they put him in the combat section. So no licence. 'After what I'd been through, the army couldn't teach me anything about pulling through.' He deserted. He dreamed of pulling off a big number: he'd go to Amsterdam, buy some 'flake', and with the profits he and his girlfriend would have enough to live on for a while. But in the end he went back to the army: they were through with him, preferring to discharge him quietly after eleven days in solitary and a fortnight at the infirmary.

They lived with various people in the northern districts of Paris – Clichy, Pigalle, Gare du Nord, then Bondy. 'But I always came back to La Courneuve.' Finally they found a three-room flat in the 4000, in Renoir tower block. 'We got by.' He copped six months in prison for stealing a car radio. 'Once you turn twenty, things change. It becomes a weight on your shoulders. I don't regret the experience – if I had to do it again, I would. It's just that there are limits. I always told myself: You're doing drugs but you'll get out of it, you'll find something else. What disgusted me, what I'd had enough of, was ending up scarring people for a few centimes. That had happened to me, and I'd had enough. But then again, what's the point in being honest? The thieves aren't the biggest thieves.'

Daoud was attracted by *ABC*'s activities. He went along to the drama group – and showed lots of talent. Then he took part in the film shoot. He played his role with great spontaneity and passion. People noticed how much care he took with the equipment. And there were plenty of problems with it, like the time an overconfident operator let a youngster look at the camescope and he promptly walked off with it; it took Akim half an hour of tense discussion and negotiations to get it back without a punch-up.

The group recommended Daoud to the director of the council's youth services. Daoud was taken on; for the moment he is a temporary organizer. It's no easy task: similar experiments haven't always worked well, with recruits giving up after getting arrogant and shouting at everyone. But Daoud is hanging in there: 'Organizer is what's marked on my pay slip. Security guard's nearer the mark.' But Daoud, who knows everyone at La Courneuve, is full of plans: 'A real job is making yourself useful in life.' He'd like people to understand that they must get their confidence back. That they should shout less and think beforehand. That the inhabitants of the 4000 must stop dirtying their estate and doing nothing about it, as if it's fate. He's already planning to do drawings in the entrance halls – sixteen tenants per hall ... he's got the go-ahead from the housing office. He does the painting but the tenant chooses the style: palm trees, flowers, landscapes. . . . They're making a huge fuss about the Revolution bicentenary with all the shows and theatre, but we should be having the revolution today. He wants to revolutionize La Courneuve.

If he is taken on permanently, he would like his work to be not supervising but informing people about the activities on offer: people don't know what's going on around them. They have to be brought out of their estates. For example, there are concerts at Saint-Denis, but the kids don't know about them ...

'I want to help La Courneuve change,' repeats Daoud. 'Create a movement, activities, open people's eyes – so no one stays shut up at home.'

'He looks as gentle as a lamb,' says Anaïk.

(FEBRUARY 1990. Daoud has been taken on permanently as an organizer. He lives in the 4000 with his twenty-year-old girlfriend, and they have just had a child.)

*

Quite remarkable! In the centre of Aubervilliers, just a short walk from the town hall and church, Café de l'Hôtel de Ville is also a hotel. It has two vacant rooms on the first floor, overlooking the courtyard: small, a fresh coat of white paint, each with a brand-new blue bedcover and light wood table, spick and span from top to bottom. The perfect traveller's resting-place: rural calm in a grey and drab town centre. After a shower and clothes-wash, François tries to get his notes up to date (in his exercise book, he is still rushing round Aulnay).

They have lots to see and do in Aubervilliers. They have a list of names, places, ideas. Not forgetting the cultural side, which has rather been neglected up to now: it would be unthinkable to stop off here without spending an evening at Théâtre de la Commune. Aubervilliers also boasts a museum, the first on their itinerary to be mentioned in the succinct list of important places on the back of the RER map: the 'Museum of Kitchen Gardens'. Obviously they have to visit it. But where is it? When consulted, Akim looked sceptical. Neither must they forget that Yves Lacoste expressly recommended that François phone a fellow geographer who must show him the site of a quite unique reed-bed, *une roselière* (not to be confused with une roseraie, a rose garden), which is apparently growing wild, with complementary flora and fauna, on the site of the old gasometers.

*

SUNDAY 28 MAY. At 8 a.m. Auber is quite deserted, but in the cafés the horse-racing punters have betting fever. At Notre-Dame-des-Vertus, a large village church renovated in the nineteenth century, the congregation files out of a Portuguese mass in an animated murmur: large families in their Sunday best – black suits and white shirts.

They take the bus to the crossroads at Les Quatre Routes de La Courneuve, still known as place du 8 Mai. It's the big market day and people have come from miles around, because you can find everything here and it's cheaper. Exotic fruits, unspecified roots, lots of second-hand clothes sold by old Mozabites, and miracle remedies like the magnetized copper bracelet that cures rheumatism, arthritis, overweight, stress, tenseness, heavy legs, varicose veins, insomnia, constipation and the *etc.* (which is underlined). But the list doesn't stop at the *etc.*: there are even the *problems of modern life*. On another stall is a tropical proliferation of plastic flowers and barometer-flowers: is François going to buy Julia one this time? No, the slippery customer claims that some of them are steadfastly pink and others steadfastly purple, and so they *don't work*. It's like refusing to buy a watch from a clocksmith with the excuse that each of the clocks in his window shows a different time.

At the crossroads, not far from the mouth of the Paris metro terminus, on a central platform covering a section of the Nationale 2 which runs through a tunnel under the junction, stands a pink monument to those who died in the Resistance: large-headed humanoid protozoa intimately mingle their protuberances and flagella. It's the same sculptor who was responsible for the monument at Drancy, and this one is just as atrocious. To complete the unspeakable object, some doggerel:

> The stone's already thinking where your names are writ
> Already you're but golden words in our town square
> The memory of your names already starts to flit
> Already you are but dead and lost up in the air.

An Aragon composition, needless to say. It's a curious way for the living to show that they leave the stone the task of thinking for them and give pride of place to the men who sacrificed their lives for them.

Sunday afternoon, and a lazy stroll down to the Canal Saint-Denis. On the other side of place de la Mairie, the old part of Landy stretches north past the canal on to the Plaine and west to the A1 motorway and the railway line marking the border with Saint-Denis. The big medieval fair of Le Landit, as it was called then, created by King Dagobert, was, they say, held in those parts until 1522. When Aubervilliers ceased to be solely a market garden town, the first industrial workers came to settle in this maze of flaking brick and cement houses, whose courtyards contained both craft workshops and farm machinery: they were people displaced from Paris, or immigrants from the provinces and later from abroad, men working at the nearby La Villette abattoirs and for companies treating the latter's by-products – glyceride refineries, tanneries, gut-dressing works, charcoal factories: workers from the gas workshops and depots on the Plaine, from the big chemical factories – Ugine, Saint-Gobain, Kuhlman – and hundreds of firms making more or less toxic products, cardboard, bitumen paper, paint and even nitroglycerine. There were so many of them that in 1935 journalists could call Aubervilliers a 'chemical town' and 'land of death'; there were hawkers too, rag-and-bone men and second-hand furniture dealers harvesting their crop and stocking it in the *zone*, at the foot of the *fortifs*. In short, there was a concentration of 'dirty industries' considered undesirable inside the walls of Paris, and a tough race of pieceworkers too, which even today makes people say that Auber's *different*, that there's a *special spirit*, made of a liking for hard work, fierce individual resourcefulness and collective solidarity.

The people of Aubervilliers arrived here in waves, and each new colony took care to keep its cohesion, its traditions and even its language. Beginning with the first arrivals, the Auvergnats, to the latest, the Malians, all identically immigrant and transplanted workers, these people have wanted to save their double roots, their double culture, their double loyalty. Each new wave established its own stronghold and only reluctantly gave way to those who followed: besides the Auvergnats driven out by rural poverty, who in the nineteenth century made Aubervilliers the true economic capital of their region, there were the Alsatians who arrived after Alsace-Lorraine was annexed in 1871, then the Italians – last night it was old Auber folk who were speaking Piedmontese at the Orange Bleue – the Poles, followed by the Spaniards, Algerians and Portuguese. Each generation bred its *nouveaux bourgeois*: people therefore say that the Auvergnats, having become landlords in Le Landy, have let flats and hotels to North Africans who in turn, acting as screens for the former, now sublet to the Africans.

The first worthies were the market gardeners, and for a long time the immigrant Auvergnats played a leading role. When a young socialist lawyer, a Châteldon innkeeper's son, first stood in the legislative elections in 1914, and the voters of Aubervilliers were booing him because of his swarthy appearance and calling him a *sidi* (a North African immigrant) and Algerian Jew, he retorted: 'I am neither *sidi*, Jew, nor Freemason. If I were all those, or just one of them, I would say so, because it's very honourable. But I have a confession to make. I have a defect. I'm an Auvergnat.' As a result he won hands down. In 1921 he became Mayor of Aubervilliers, and remained so until 1944. His name was Pierre Laval.

Laval was therefore Mayor of Aubervilliers for twenty-three years. At the Liberation, when the Communists, led by Charles Tillon, took over the council – the Resistance leader replacing the leader of the collaborators – the new councillors wanted to draw up an 'inventory of fixtures' in the form of an accusation: the town, relates Tillon in his Memoirs, was 'afflicted with run-down neighbourhoods and dingy houses where the deprived people lived. A ministry photographer had brought us back grim pictures, a testimony to Laval's legacy. When he saw them, Jacques Prévert had the idea of a film for which Joseph Kosma would write the music. So at the same time as *La Bataille du rail* ('Battle of the Rails') appeared another moving film, *Aubervilliers*, in which the beautiful voice of Germaine Montero sings the famous song condemning the municipal deeds of the man who wanted the Nazis to win.' This documentary, directed by Eli Lotar, was filmed in the streets of Le Landy; it became the symbol of a world in ruins, 'not the war ruins but the simple ruins of working-class poverty', 'where they burned the rubbish and dead horses from Paris', and where, in the Saint-Gobain factories, 'caustic soda mingled with the sweat of hard graft'.

Laval was well known to Tillon, who, after taking part in the Black Sea mutiny, campaigned in Aubervilliers for the Communist Party under the Front Populaire and became the town's deputy. In his Memoirs he retraces the beginnings of 'Pierrot la cravate', thus dubbed because of his white ties, to which he remained faithful right up until the firing squad:

> He had been seen arriving from his native Auvergne before the war, without a sou in his pocket.... The scrawny advocate scraped a few meals from the shopkeepers of Les Quatre-Chemins, who were weary of their royalist deputy.... Laval the lawyer made his name among the ordinary people by holding a surgery in a Quatre-Chemins bistro where he was lent a small room adjoining the building. He used to sit down at a table with his upturned hat close at hand. Then, chewing on a cigarette end, he would listen to his client and slip him some advice. On getting up, the person would ask sheepishly about the consultation fee. The coarse-featured 'poor man's lawyer' would then reply, revealing his black teeth: 'Oh, put something in the hat if you like.' A few small silver coins thus helped him to scratch a living.... As a deputy, then a minister, his good heart never failed.... Whom do you think the man they were already calling the 'Aubervilliers horse trader' chose to chair the Society for the Protection of Animals? None other than the president of the butchers' union from the La Villette abattoirs.

Not a very flattering portrait, finally, for the electorate of a town which never ceased to re-elect its mayor: were they dim enough to let themselves be taken in for twenty-three years by such a repulsive character? The truth as it appears in the biography of Pierre Laval by Fred Kupferman, who minutely dissected his rise and fall, is less picturesque. Laval got started in politics by giving free consultations in a weekly column in *La Bataille syndicaliste*, the daily newspaper of the CGT, the Communist-backed union confederation. In 1910, the unexpected acquittal of a Paris militant made him not only famous but rich: to thank Laval for his unpaid efforts, the CGT, backed by the Communist daily *L'Humanité*, set up a fund which brought in 50,000 francs. It was as a socialist candidate that he won his deputy's seat in 1914. A pacifist during the war, he publicly voiced his approval of the Zimmerwald and Kienthal congresses, organized by Lenin and Trotsky amongst others, which brought together in Switzerland the internationalists of the enemy countries. At the peace, we find him defending the CGT, which was threatened with being banned. He took part in the Tours Party conference, where, contrary to the Aubervilliers section, he chose to stick with the minority by not rallying round the Bolsheviks, then declared himself an independent socialist. It was under this banner that he won the mayorship, backed by the local bourgeoisie, market gardeners and gut-dressers, but also by the craftsmen, the hawkers, and, of course, as always, by 'Little Auvergne': everyone trusted him to defend their interests, although these were bound to be contradictory. In this he knew how to place all his virtuosity at the service of the horse-trading he had turned into a fine art. Emmanuel Berl (that astonishing character who wrote Pétain's first speeches – 'The soil doesn't

lie . . .', 'I detest those lies which have done you so much harm . . .' –
before they realized at Vichy that having a Jew write the Marshal's
speeches wasn't very kosher), his friend during the thirties, said that 'the
people of Aubervilliers admired themselves in him':

> He used to trip down the street with his white tie and gypsy face, looking like
> a provincial solicitor, stroll through the markets, laundries, cafés and factories
> of this big, gloomy, slum-ridden village, where the nauseating smell from the
> knacker's yards stagnated on the canal banks. He kept many friends there; they
> resented the changes he had made but never ceased to see themselves in him
> because he was like them, hard-working and cheery, fierce and greedy,
> passionately attached to his own people and incapable come what may of
> becoming one of those wits or society dandies from whom they felt separated.

By now he was one of the barons of the *couronne parisienne*, while waiting
to become its leader. At first his peers, friends and accomplices were quite
naturally his political neighbours: socialists and radicals, mayors like
Fischer at Pavillons-sous-Bois, Duchanel at Drancy, Poncet at Montreuil,
Kerautret at Vanves, etc., as well as an even closer and, for a long time,
unshakeable friend – Henri Sellier, Mayor of Suresnes, the apostle of
council housing, the creator of the low-rent *HLM*. From this base he
broadened his circle and won the friendship of right-wing mayors,
weaving a feudal network with the dimensions of the Third Republic. If
Pierre Laval's career had ended in the early thirties – when, as Labour
Minister, he had just had a law passed establishing National Insurance in
France and received a bouquet of roses from the socialist Mayor of Lille,
Roger Salengro, to thank him for the way he had ended the textile strikes
– he would doubtless have been honoured, like Henri Sellier, as a friend
of the people who 'devoted his life to social progress, the glory of the
republic and the happiness of men'. He would doubtless have had his
monument in the square, opposite Théâtre de la Commune, as one of the
first men to set up crèches and develop the *Œuvre de la Goutte de lait*, a
charity which monitored unweaned infants and supplied mothers with
milk. So at what moment did 'Bougnaparte' (*bougna* meaning coalman
and Auvergnat) start to emerge from behind the paternal face of 'Pierrot
la cravate'? At what moment did he start his slide into the dirt? When
and how did the abjectness with which Laval's name remains indissolubly
linked begin? Pass over the fact that he was the man hammered into
submission by Mussolini and Hitler at the League of Nations. He got the
same treatment in the pact with Stalin. But what about the man who
actively collaborated with the Nazis, who governed France for three years
and said time and again that he hoped Germany would win, the man who

sent the Jews to the gas chambers and created the special militia tribunals?

François was biographer Fred Kupferman's friend. Fred was a child of *Le Renouveau*, the Jewish orphanage at Montmorency founded by his mother, a Resistance heroine; his father died in deportation. Fred was an obstinate researcher who refused to be fooled by any legend or cliché, no matter how well accepted; he was affectionate, lucid and often caustic. This man, who loved Alphonse Allais, Queneau and Salinger, had a passion which he had shared with François when, for example, as a student, he discovered in the archives the spicy collection of the underground *L'Humanité* from July 1940 (whose editors used it to try to impress the Nazis to obtain the legalization of the Communist Party): a passion for the irony of History. He found this irony fascinating and atrocious, and unsurpassable; he laughed about it so gently that it made him all the fiercer. The work he was so driven by and published before dying could, through the merciless stripping away of superimposed images, seem like a rehabilitation of Pierre Laval. But the worrying thing (and what feeling is more effective than worry?) is that it ultimately shows us an ordinary politician, *un uomo qualunque*: no, the study doesn't rehabilitate Laval; it is instead an implicit indictment of a whole French political class and behind it a vast body of supporters, both bourgeois and working-class, who for a long time liked to see themselves in Laval.

Laval was not a fascist but basically republican, certainly much more so than Pétain, Franco's good genie. Having come to power in July 1940, and having duly been invested by the Senate and Chamber of Deputies before they dissolved themselves, Laval thought he could settle the problem of peace with Germany as he had always settled everything, be it disputes with the rag-and-bone men of the *fortifs* or the 1935 pact with Stalin: by bargaining and trickery, by putting his morals in his pocket with his handkerchief on top. He was convinced the English were defeated, so the game was all about signing the peace before them, beating them for speed and thus obtaining better conditions from the victor than they did. He saw himself as the official receiver: it wasn't going to be pleasant, so he would just have to hold his nose and swallow. The quicker the French gave in on everything, the quicker they'd get out of it. Afterwards, they'd see: he would know how to play it. 'If you could see my arse,' he confided in August 1944 to his old ally Edouard Herriot, the Mayor of Lyon, who, through greater craftiness or luck, knew how to distance himself in time from the Vichy he had supported, 'if you could see my arse, it's blue from where the Krauts have kicked it.' Maybe he gave himself a stiff neck in the evening, trying – oh so tenderly – to admire his Roquefort-coloured behind in the mirror? Was he a traitor, then, this man who, in 1938, had no words strong enough to condemn Munich? 'The bastards,' he had said, on Daladier's return; 'so they haven't a single ounce of national pride.' He liked to be compared with Aristide Briand, and hadn't *he* finished his life with a Nobel Peace Prize? And he never forgot the people of Aubervilliers: Louis Pagès, his deputy and acting mayor – like himself an Auvergnat who had looked after the municipal band – could never contain his emotion: 'Pierre Laval went on looking after the school canteens and the food at the old people's home. He used to say: "I think too many of the French are scheming with the Germans." He wanted to be the only one.'

Laval, therefore, was not a fascist, and neither was he *particularly* anti-Semitic. He didn't mind admitting that there were too many Jews in France and, for that matter, too many foreigners in general who had come to eat French people's bread, and that getting rid of them was a blessing. We know he wasn't the only Frenchman who thought like that in 1940, and things haven't changed much since. It seems that he even saved Jews personally. Saved them from what? From his own laws. He cheerfully had the first anti-Jewish laws drafted in 1940, making genocide possible, then never stopped taking measures enabling its orchestration. He refused to have the slightest qualms about the Jews' fate. SS General Oberg had given him his officer's word that the Jews would be settled in Poland, and that was enough for Laval: in those conditions, it would have been inhuman to separate children from their parents. The Nazis never needed to complain about his gullibility. He simply didn't care. 'I talked to him about a massacre,' recounted the minister Boegner. 'He talked to me about gardening.'

No: Laval, Prime Minister of the French State, and as such bearing major responsibility for the genocide in France, was not *particularly* anti-Semitic. That is what's so horrific: Nazism, racism, anti-Semitism – for him it was obviously all just a 'detail' of his realpolitik. And through all that he was expressing the feelings, hazy or otherwise, of a host of good Frenchmen. In their eyes Laval was no more dishonest than the next man, no more of a bastard than the next man; or rather, he was as dishonest a bastard as the next man: his dishonesty and bastardly tricks actually reassured a whole host of people, because they showed that he was *human*. He had on his side the huge party of people who refused to be conned, who got more or less shadily by – 'le parti de la Grande Démerde'.

Laval was not alone in adopting a matey tone to help people to accept that piece of everyday baseness which each of us carries more or less shamefully inside, the cockiness, the good-natured cynicism, the most crowd-pleasing argument presented as the height of realism, the cleverly worked pull on the heartstrings – the gut department, in other words.

Aubervilliers: Le Landy

You can understand why, after a botched trial in 1945, the new authorities were in a rush to get rid of him and shut him up with a visit to the firing squad. In the event, that was what really mattered: shutting him up – and fast. This man was dangerous. His former friends – like Herriot – who had, with varying degrees of skill, switched sides at the right moment, were not the only ones whose interests lay in giving the push to this defendant-witness, who demanded quite openly to be provided with the entire collection of the state records, *Le Journal Officiel*, in order to prepare his defence; it was all that thick layer of the French population that had complacently followed him and could not forgive him for showing them their own face, suddenly demasked: the face of complicity in the filthiest, most ordinary trick of all.

*

At the Liberation, then, Aubervilliers council became Communist. And it has remained so up to the present mayor, Jack Ralite. Under the Occupation, the working-class areas took the full brunt of the 'relief' invented by Laval – a scheme to send three French workers to labour in Germany in exchange for one imprisoned soldier – then after that failed, they took the brunt of the STO, the compulsory labour service. These areas produced draft dodgers by the thousand. Le Landy's mazes were a maquis for underground Resistance fighters, including many Spanish Civil War veterans who felt at home there: Fabien, the author of the first attack against the occupying forces, had found safe refuge there after escaping from the fort at nearby Romainville. As we have said, the first Communist mayor was Charles Tillon. He remained in the post until 1952, when the old and overly honest Bolshevik was submitted by the Party, along with the 'cop' André Marty, another Black Sea mutineer, to 'a Moscow trial in Paris'. Between Laval the traitor and Tillon the renegade, that made a lot of skeletons in the town hall cupboards, and you can image how difficult Aubervilliers council must have found it, for a long time, to write the story of its past dispassionately.

*

The houses in Le Landy's mazelike streets are the same as they were when Eli Lotar made his film: buildings are still crumbling, but successive renovations have at least brought the water which in times past, sang Jacques Prévert, trickled along the cobbles, the cobbles of Aubervilliers, stealthy as a little rat, stealthy as poverty, the poverty of Aubervilliers. What became of the little children in rue Heurtault, rue du Tournant, passage de l'Avenir, the little children of Aubervilliers?

184

> Gentils enfants d'Aubervilliers
> Vous plongez la tête la première
> Dans les eaux grasses de la misère
>
> Gentils enfants d'Aubervilliers
> Gentils enfants des prolétaires
> Gentils enfants de la misère . . .[4]

What became of those ragamuffin kids in the film, paddling by the fire hydrant and playing in the stream? It featured two teenage lads who embodied future generations, filmed in the gloomy house of a family whose name the narrator gave: Izzi – is that how you spell it? Sure, it's an Italian name. They were fifteen and sixteen at the time, one an apprentice typesetter, the other a postman. That makes them fifty-seven and fifty-eight now. Anaïk and François didn't find them. But at Auber they did find some people who remember an Izzi family from Le Landy: Madame Marie-Josée, whom Anaïk met and photographed, said one of her husband's cousins married an Izzi. He died a long time ago, murdered at a dance. Was it the typesetter or the postman? She arrived in Auber in 1950, and remembers the things that were said about the Parisian journalists who ran a headline along the lines of 'Aubervilliers: the children of poverty'; people in Auber had been disgusted by the scornful tone.

At the time, she was living in rue Solferino, on the edge of La Villette, with her sister, who left the house at three in the morning to go and work at Les Halles. Marie-Josée worked on Les Quatre Chemins market. It was a cheerful place: the girls selling fruit were never lost for words, and there were acrobats and pavement artists. The markets are dreary nowadays because money's all that counts. The small shops are closing down: her horse butcher, for instance, who's fifty, knows he'll have no successor; people don't eat horsemeat any more because there are no more large families.

She met her husband at a dance hall called The Little Whirlwind, near the Paris cemetery on the edge of Pantin: in those days there used to be dances on every street corner, and beside the canal; there was also the Maison du Peuple with its big orchestra, where the theatre is today; it cost more, but it was fabulous. And as she never goes to the theatre, even though she's the cleaner there, she's got nothing out of the deal. The Party's meetings were held at the Maison du Peuple too.

When she set up house with her husband in rue Jules Guesde, to the west of Auber near the cemetery, there was land there where the ragmen lived and stored their 'tat': some of them in those days did well out of it – very well – and some even built themselves a nice *pavillon*. The handcart era was over, they were already working with lorries. Coming to live with her in-laws wasn't easy: she was twenty-two, pregnant, and as a welcoming present her mother-in-law put a dead rat outside her door. The whole family lived in a three-roomed shack with a small kitchen: the walls were plaster tiles, and it was icy cold in winter. When it rained they had to put billy-cans in the corners: the floor was made of cement, they used to paddle through the mud and the wet attracted the rats. Drinking water had to be fetched from a hydrant in the street. She was always getting sore throats and abscesses. She tried to do the house up, with an orange crate for drawers and a pretty little curtain. When she bathed the children in a tub near the stove, her mother-in-law called her a show-off. She had a rough time of it, looking after four children and her husband, with whom she got up at three in the morning for the early shift. The ragmen then were strong men, able to pull four hundred kilos. But on summer Sundays when they invited friends round, they were happy: they put the table in the courtyard with a white cloth. There were ducks, chickens and fresh eggs. In the afternoon they went to the flea market at La Villette, which isn't there any more: at that time it was '*la zone*', but now there's a home electrics superstore. You could find anything, there was a market with the early fruit and veg, and gypsies in black hats who bought the live chickens.

Then her husband found work with a big paper merchant and they moved to the Danièle Casanova *HLM* block, thanks to Karman the Communist mayor. It was a time when people got on well: 'Everyone was on incredibly good terms. No one ever argued.' Karman was a good mayor, a former turner, a factory lad who'd been deported: he'd been to school in Auber and always lived there. He was one of the people. Ralite's a different breed: what interests him is art, teachers, writers. But tell me who in Aubervilliers can afford the paintings he exhibits.

Everything's changed with the new buildings and people living there. Lots of people from rue Jules Guesde have gone north to the Oise. Where there's now Cité de la Maladrerie, the new estate with the modern wooden houses they call 'The Matchsticks' over on Terrain de la Pierre Noire, that was where the ragmen lived. Behind the swimming baths there were big market gardens. And rue Neuve, which isn't there any more, was so pretty with its old cobblestones and little houses. In rue du Long Sentier, they're going to knock everything down: there used to be a bakery where they roasted our chickens and turkeys when we had a party.

I know life was hard then, she says. I wouldn't like to go back to rue Jules Guesde. At the market we used to give the little tramps a coin for stacking the crates, and we organized races between them, with apples balanced on spoons in their mouths. But what's it like today? You don't see the poverty any more, but that doesn't mean it's not there: it's different, that's all, and believe me, it's not the French who are the worst affected, because the foreigners. . . . What about drugs? You find the white stuff behind the canal, on the edge of Le Landy: you can easily spot the dealers and traffickers, young Algerians and *pieds-noirs* (French settlers in pre-Independence Algeria) with nice cars. It's rotten down there. And the kids on drugs because they've got nothing else in life, they're the real children of poverty today. You should hear them say: 'What does it matter if I die young? Life's stupid, everyone's stupid.' Even in the youth centres I could swear they shoot up. If there are no more dances, it's because everything's been smashed up: nothing's been organized for six or seven years. And doing sport is fine, but it's expensive when you've got four or five kids, so what can you do? If I'd been to school I'd like to have looked after the kids on drugs, because no one cares any more.

I'm not a racist, she says: I come from an Italian family myself. But I'm telling you it's too much: it's a sad thing to say, but you mustn't be amazed if more and more people are voting for Le Pen. Auber's been invaded. By the Parisians for a start, but they don't care because they've got money. And by foreigners too: rue Firmin Gémier used to be so pretty, but now you'd think it was the casbah. In the offices where I clean, West Indians and Africans tell us, the Whites, that we smell like death: they're more racist than we are. Yes, I'm sad to say it, but sometimes Le Pen's right.

*

A mild and lukewarm late afternoon on the Canal Saint-Denis. So peaceful. They have walked through the streets of Le Landy: people on their doorsteps, Portuguese and North Africans washing or repairing cars. Café des Mariniers has become an Arab café. On the opposite bank, the not-so-faraway mass of Sacré-Cœur suddenly appears through a hole in a curtain of tall poplars. Across the canal, the Landy area continues on to Plaine Saint-Denis: a few run-down estates, then industrial sites. Sandboxes on the banks. Looking east from the bridge, on the horizon of the canal running straight ahead to rejoin the Canal de l'Ourcq, you can see on a hill several kilometres away the silhouette of a huge development suffused in a slightly stormy heat haze: it's the constructions surrounding the slopes of the Buttes Chaumont; and a few kilometres away to the west, before the canal swings left and rejoins the Seine near Gennevilliers, is the Saint-Denis basilica's Roman tower, emerging from a cluster of old houses like the belfry of a peaceful village church. A few moored freight barges. In front of a river-boat, the *Arizona*, children are riding bicycles and a man is making a fire for his barbecue. On a wall, some superb

Aubervilliers: The Canal Saint-Denis

blue-and-black graffiti, a half-hieroglyphic, half-medieval *danse macabre*: The Pharaohs' Rap.

Later that night, a stone's throw from their Hôtel de l'Hôtel de Ville, they are drawn to an unusual entertainment inside the door of some flats; the black porter lets them in. They are in Studio 26, and tonight there is a Jewish celebration. In the room where the guests are preparing to banquet, the decibel count is deafening. The waiters are all wearing spotless outfits: our travellers feel that they stick out like sore thumbs, and beat a retreat. The porter advises them to come back on Tuesday – that night there's going to be a West Indian party.

The news from China is worrying: Li Peng seems to be regaining the upper hand. The students are still occupying Tienanmen Square.

Was it in a *France-Culture* radio broadcast, 'Sais-tu si nous sommes encore loin de la mer?' ('Do you know if we're still far from the sea?'), or in *Le Monde* that François found this sentence of Claude Roy's: 'The curious child listens at the doors of the earth'? What was he thinking about when he wrote that down? His notes are definitely getting fuzzier and fuzzier.

*

MONDAY 29 MAY. In the café at Hôtel de l'Hôtel de Ville, each table has its own jukebox: offerings include Sweet Death Cap Queen, *EH Tiphaine*, and the indestructible Julio Iglesias. The morning papers confirm Li Peng's success. In Tienanmen Square the situation is tense. The students cannot decide on their next move: those from the provinces want to stay there come what may. The other important news concerns the situation on the RER B-line: the RATP employees, those who work on the southern part of the line, have refused to change to the summer timetable before knowing the result of talks with management; but on the northern half, the SNCF workers, who have ended their strike, have changed timetables. As a result the *interconnexion* is no longer guaranteed, thus posing some nice little arithmetical problems on a par with the perennial problems of leaky taps and baths.

They set off on foot for Saint-Denis, following the northern bank; on the other side, the Plaine Saint-Denis side, the poplar-lined road, which yesterday was silent, is pounding with roaring lorries, while skips and cranes clang together as they decant sand and gravel from the barges into silos, and concrete-mixers grind, which does not disturb the luckless anglers. Over the road, a brick wall several kilometres long encircles the Plaine.

Lock number five, known as Les Vertus, with its sober little houses, would offer a rural scene were it not virtually in the shadow of the double

metal bridge where the RER and trains to and from the North rumble past. The asphalt path they are taking, by a bare yellow grass divider, is bordered by the canal on the left and on the right, down below, by the first flats of Cité du Clos Saint Quentin, which practically turn their back on the water, as though no one had understood the beauty – and value – of the view; but it's true that in thirty years the view must have changed a lot: when the estate was built it was a forest of factory chimneys whose smoke must have permanently mingled with that from the tugs and steam engines. Now the chimneys have disappeared with the factories, and the air is clear. Further away, the façades of more recent blocks are actually more open to the canal and the sun. The squalor is disappearing and unemployment is rising: each generation has its own forms of poverty, which maybe only the next generation will really know how to comprehend. Exterior poverty, poverty for outside exhibition from the golden age of the picturesque – thank you Robert Doisneau, thank you Marcel Carné – is now only the fate of dropouts, tramps and drifters begging in the metro whom everyone more or less puts up with. But how do you photograph all the poverty behind the smooth walls, the silent walls – the poverty of depression and fear, of all the strains of everyday life, of so much loneliness?

Cité du Clos Saint Quentin backs on to another estate, Les Francs Moisins, with its high rectangular 1960s blocks: its bad reputation is equal to those of La Courneuve's 4000 and the Aulnay 3000.

As you approach the A1 motorway bridge, the estate gives way to extremely run-down brick houses. The renovators have yet to visit these

The Canal Saint-Denis

parts. An old gentleman at his window complains sadly that someone is stealing his plants. A tiny house with a courtyard and a group of huts bears a wooden sign, roughly painted in green and blue, which reads: *Hôtel du Nord*. Photo-time. An old North African coming out just at that moment flares up and insults Anaïk, stubbornly refusing to believe it wasn't him she was snapping.

Several times on this walk, they have met groups of youngsters who have politely asked them: 'Will you photograph us?'

The motorway crosses the canal at an angle. Just below is Lock number 6. You could drive past on the motorway a thousand times without guessing it's there. The sharp angle thus wedged between canal and motorway is filled by a *quartier* of small old houses nearly all in blackened brick, crisscrossed by straight narrow streets which open at one end on to a stretch of water and at the other on to concrete and cars. Down a cul-de-sac there's an old hotel, also in brick. It all creates a strange impression: in this forgotten enclave, in the midst of the incessant roar of the HGVs, a provincial atmosphere reigns. Sticking up on the viaduct is an advertising hoarding with the golden rounded lines of a double giant hamburger splashed across it, calling to mind the sensuality of Ferreri's *Blow-out*.

Kingburger – I've got two!

191

More polluting than the tattiest tag. After all, an ad is never any more than an authorized tag, signed Seguela or Dupneu, with a mountain of money behind it. It makes you want to throw up.

After walking across this timeless island along rue du Canal, they must descend into the hell of a tunnel to go under the motorway and come out on to a huge crossroads teeming with buses: it's the entrance to Saint-Denis, right by the gates of Paris. Behind the old Danièle Casanova Hospital there begins a timeworn *quartier*. They pass an African hostel: the heavy grey metal gate is closed, but through a half-open barrier you can see the courtyard, where there are lots of people and activity for the time of day: refuge, ghetto, oasis or citadel – it all depends on the passport, green card or work permit of the person who walks through the door.

Anaïk discovers that she is in urgent need of some cola nut and doesn't actually know how she has managed to survive since the start of the journey without any. It's a well-known fact that in African hostels you always find cola nut-sellers. A lively discussion ensues: François flatly refuses to follow her – once was enough. He goes and waits for Anaïk a bit further down the road. As it happens, a bit further on the scenery changes into a paradise the colours of sweet France, the grounds of the Institut de la Légion d'Honneur, or at least the part open to the public. François sits down on a bench in the shade and wistfully contemplates the banks of flowers, the large white Institut building, and the green roof and towers of the basilica beyond. Behind the fence, two graceful boarders go past in blue uniforms with pleated skirts, wearing round their necks the fringed sash showing their year. As everyone knows, the Institut de la Légion d'Honneur has been reserved, ever since Napoleon I founded it, for the daughters of those awarded said thingummybob. François knows all about it because Julia has a schoolmate whose big sister boards there; she's the one who has supplied Julia, since she was seven, with most of the stock of rude words without which life wouldn't be worth living, and who revealed to her the naughty chatlines on which you can hear such exciting conversations. Discipline has remained strict, and the learning of good manners is guaranteed. François had foolishly thought that with the times we are living in, the school had become slightly obsolete: wrong, for it seems there have never been so many candidates, and the selection process is tough. That aside, as he looks at the building before his eyes, he remembers that its walls sheltered Louis XVIII when he returned after fleeing The Hundred Days of Napoleon's last stab at reforming the Empire; that the king had to beg to return to Paris, still occupied by the Cossacks; and that they had huge trouble stopping the little girls from shouting 'Vive Napoléon!' under the royal nose. On 7 July 1815, at eleven o'clock in the evening, as he returned from meditating gloomily in the kings' crypt, Chateaubriand saw an infernal vision go slowly past: Talleyrand and Fouché coming to swear allegiance to His Majesty, 'vice leaning on the arm of crime'. Upon which Anaïk reappears, holds out to François a brownish, stringy cola nut, bitter as wormwood, and tells him at length about the tittle-tattle she exchanged with the two vendors after going through the hostel refectories and kitchens.

And so, when the moment comes to queue up with the coachloads of tourists at the window inside the basilica that issues tickets for a visit to the tombs, they are suddenly overcome by an immense, irrepressible and probably scandalous feeling of cultural sloth. Yet since the journey started they have bemoaned the cultural desert they are travelling across: no châteaux, as they were all destroyed after the Revolution; few churches of interest, which have nearly all been jealously closed; no museums, save the aircraft one at Le Bourget and, more and more improbably, the kitchen gardens one. Even so, this would be biting off more than they could chew.

In fact the same goes for all of Saint-Denis. By telling its story since the day its beheaded patron saint carried his head to the Butte Montmartre, talking to it (or soliloquizing?) along the way, we have rather tended to forget two other martyred saints about whose heads history offers no details, up to the reign of Doriot – 'big Jacques', the Communist mayor of the people who, ten years after failing to land the Party's secretary-general job in 1934, also failed to be appointed French Führer by Hitler – and, in particular, to explain the unique role in French history of a town which, from the reign of Dagobert up to the end of the Middle Ages, was for religious power what Paris was for political power; but that's in all the textbooks, and to talk about Saint-Denis today, now as much a university town as a working-class one – no, that would take a book in itself. And they are there only for the afternoon, on a simple excursion slightly out of their way.

They will nevertheless go and visit the town's museum. In place de l'Hôtel de Ville, noon is sounded by a series of chimes: they recognize Big Ben, King Dagobert, Orléans-Beaugency, a particularly discordant *Temps des Cerises* and something that sounds like *L'Artilleur de Metz*. The square surrounding the metro terminus is a vast building site emerging from which are the lines of a new white *quartier*, a monumental urban planning scheme similar to Beaubourg's Horloge *quartier* and the Forum des Halles. A pedestrian precinct takes them on to a large avenue of shops. They are tempted by a café's small sunlit terrace and red parasols. Here everyone is definitely French. Even the hospitality is French. The owner is not amused by Anaïk's coffee-with-a-glass-of-water, managing to bring a half-full glass and bang it down so hard on the table that they are all splashed and the glass is emptied, which does not stop said owner bawling disgustedly: 'Your glass of water!' and asking to be paid immediately. Just in case they do a runner.

Saint-Denis Museum is especially well known for its valuable collections and archives from the Paris Commune. For several years they have been housed with the town's other collections in the old Carmelite convent founded by Louise de France, Louis XV's daughter. It is an unusual and attractive mixture: you walk through cloistered galleries, enter vaulted rooms exhibiting paintings and objects relating to the convent's past and Saint-Denis's history. The walls still bear pious biblical and evangelical inscriptions in sober grey lettering. The rooms of this wonderful place are almost empty. Their regret at not seeing more visitors crowding in is mingled with the pleasure of savouring its charm so completely: surely there are no finer museums than those where one is alone? But still, it's not fair. The part set aside for the Commune is on the first floor: the full story of the Paris people's great rage is there, in posters, prints, photos, uniforms. The place is empty. After all, popular rages are said to be out of fashion. The convent staircase continues into the unknown, and written on the wall is: 'Just a few more steps and we'll be in heaven.' It is 29 May: on 29 May 1871, the Commune lay dying under the last volleys of shots from the Versaillais butchers in Père Lachaise Cemetery.

*

They take the same route back. At Les Vertus lock, the lock-keeper comes down from his hut for a chat. Tall, blond, a few teeth missing, washed-out eyes – '*une tête de Ch'timi*', a real northerner. No, no photo, he says: with his mush he'd mess the film up. He's lived here for four years. He was a bargee before that. He's been around a bit: Germany, Holland, Switzerland. He's been down the Saône as far as Lyon, but he never went to Marseille and didn't do the Canal du Midi – his barge wasn't the Freycinet gauge. He was on a barge called *Rolf*: his boss was getting on and there was no future in it, the freight business had become too uncertain. He took the recruitment exam: he couldn't do it now, the keepers need to speak some English because of the growth in pleasure-boating, especially with the new tourist port at the Bassin de l'Arsenal near Bastille. Canal traffic is dying out, the whole profession's dying out. Without the Belgians the canal would have gone out of service long ago. But as long as the Belgians stick in there. . . . The barges end up in the dead branches of the river by Conflans, or get turned into accommodation, offices, workshops – that way at least they're saved. They're planning to reduce the fleet of independent barges in the whole of France to 700; in the last few years, four barges in all have been built: they cost 5.8 million francs, and even if the State contributes two million, it's too risky. Other countries are building modern fleets.

He's happy here by the water, says the lock-keeper. He was lucky not to go and work in a factory. He knows all the boats and people who sail past: you see that big barge coming from Bondy, they're his friends, he went to their wedding. It's a quiet life. The trains make a noise overhead, of course, but you get used to it. Soon the TGV will be coming past too. And soon there'll be a third bridge, for the A86 motorway. The kids go to school fifteen minutes from here. They could walk it but the parents prefer to take them, what with all that goes on round here . . .

*

(THREE MONTHS LATER: 'With all that goes on round here . . .' They had gone back to Les Vertus lock one Saturday after having a bite to eat at the Spanish hostel on Plaine Saint-Denis. Seeing them arrive, the lock-keeper had come down from his position to say hello. He was upset. A few days before, when he'd just come on duty early in the morning, a man had collapsed at the door of his hut. He'd been knifed, and died there right in front of him. A settling of scores. He'd been seen fighting a bit further down the bank with some men, one of whom had a dog. It was through the dog that they found the knife, the same morning, and the lock-keeper was endlessly questioned by the police.)

*

A little further on, on the edge of a huge car park where apple-green City of Paris dustcarts sit in sensible rows of ten, idle youngsters are larking about and a solitary gentleman is sitting by the water reading *Arcadia*. He is very touched that Anaïk wants to photograph him. He takes off his glasses and gives a faint, sad smile. 'All my friends are gone, and the night of my life is too long.'

The anglers are still there.

> The gallant angler drags his rod
> Back home with untouched fly
> He takes the top off a tin of cod
> And slowly starts to cry.

Coming back into Aubervilliers town centre, they walk past Théâtre de la Commune. François used to go there in Garran's day to see productions of Shakespeare and Brecht. Vilar was king at the time, and in the suburbs and provinces people were putting on plays that spoke of men's life and hopes: Garran, Planchon, Sobel, Mnouchkine, Pinchenat and so many others, they all passed through the suburbs. Some are still there. Alfredo

Aria, director of the TSE, the National Centre of Drama, has now taken over from Garran: at the moment they are performing *Mon balai pour un royaume* ('My broom for a kingdom'). They ask about seats for this evening: there aren't any. This evening there is also a preview of a film starring Sandrine Bonnaire, in the actress's presence. The people waiting look cultural: there's no equivalent in French of the Russian, Polish or Czech word *kulturny*, which means both cultural and well brought up: *bon chic-bon genre* (smart and well-bred), perhaps? They all give the impression that they know each other, and our travellers feel awkward. They will come back tomorrow. Such casualness is not to the liking of the young person in the booking office: you don't just turn up like that at the last moment; they'll have to book now or there'll be no end to it. They book, and the computer shows a half-empty seating plan. They pay their 200 francs, and once outside, sitting by the dried-up fountain among Malian ladies nattering and looking after their children, they compare their respective knowledge of and interests in *Mon balai pour un royaume*. Total confusion reigns: François thought it was a Brazilian dance troupe, the famous Tsé group, which he thought Anaïk was a fan of; while Anaïk was convinced that François was an informed admirer of Marilú Marini, the Argentine actress from Porteña who performs a one-woman show featuring the character of a cleaning lady obsessed with the British royal family.

Evening falls. They are meeting Akim at Les Quatre Chemins in Aubervilliers, not to be confused with the Les Quatre Routes in La Courneuve, a mistake an RATP employee made in place de la Mairie when Anaïk unwisely asked him the way. In the bus they meet the cook from their *café-hôtel*, who's going home from work: forty-five minutes to an hour each way with two bus changes to get back to Dugny, which is past Le Bourget airport. It's hard, especially in winter. Is Dugny really as far away as that? Is it a dormitory town? 'What, you don't know Dugny?' It's very quiet over there, there's some fresh air, you can breathe. They'll have to come to tea when she's moved. At the moment she's got an *F1* but it's unbearable, just one room with her daughter: she put in an application at Dugny and Le Bourget but nothing's turned up, everyone's going in front of her. Why does she always get the worst flats? She's hopeful, all the same. She has damp eyes behind her glasses, a gentle smile, slightly henna-tinted hair. She's Algerian.

It is two kilometres from Les Quatre Routes to Les Quatre Chemins. Fortunately there's the metro. 'What did I tell you,' says François, 'about never asking the way?' 'I trusted him,' Anaïk protests, 'he had three stars on his cap.' Akim, who's waiting faithfully at the meeting-place, voices doubts about the interest of *Mon balai* in general, and about the chances of doing that sort of show in Aubervilliers in particular. They don't expand on this vast cultural debate.

Our travellers finish the evening in Restaurant de l'Espérance near Les Quatre Chemins. The couscous isn't up to Akim's stepmother's, but the welcome is better than at the hydrophobic Saint-Denis café. Despite the fact that it's late, they are shown every consideration. The owner offers them liqueurs – very much a key part of Algerian hospitality.

After returning to the hotel, François notes down in his pad a lengthy digression on *the soul of cities*, the sort of topic which crops up during a long *sobremesa*, the sweet connivance that follows a warm and friendly meal. And then a guest happens to ask: 'If you were given the choice, which city would you like to live in? And in which city would you like to die?' There then follows the evocation of fabulous cities: Rome, Prague with its raindrops, nostalgic Trieste, Leningrad and its frozen canals under the pale sky – which are what they have always been; and Barcelona, whose *barrio chino* is not, under the harsh sky, what it used to be; and let's not talk about Paris, but yes, let's. . . . François's dream is Havana, a city of columns and purple sea, a cave of Tritons and water sprites which the sea has deserted but where parched algae still hide away from the burning sun, coiled up in the sticky tropical heat waiting for the nighttime breeze. But who would choose to dream of Aubervilliers's soul? Yet who doesn't feel that Aubervilliers has a soul – slightly blackened maybe, but alive, so alive, and that the people who live there and talk about themselves not as Albervilliariens (or Albertivillariens?), but as *des gens d'Auber*, 'Auber folk', think of it as one always thinks of one's true homeland, the one which, for those who pulled up roots, has taken the place of their one true homeland, homeland purely and simply, even if they feel excluded, rejected, and maybe for that very reason . . .

In Aubervilliers everyone says Auber. But try boasting about living in Auber. Who knows Auber? 'In Paris, when I say I work in Auber,' a friend told them, 'they always think I mean the area around Opéra – they only know Auber metro station.'

François's notes really are becoming more and more unpredictable. Difficult to follow. Disjointed. And, more than anything, further and further behind. And then there are the increasingly frequent gaps. He has to fall back on his memory, and in this great jumble of images and sounds the memory quickly fails. In his Winnie the Pooh exercise book he is still trying to retrace their steps through Blanc-Mesnil. Fatigue is setting in: he'll see later.

On a small stencilled poster stuck up at Les Quatre Chemins:

On 27 May
Claudine Manuela and Barbara
invite you to their: YOUTH PARTY
Age: 15–20
Entry: 20 francs. Buffet extra
The time: 2 p.m. to 10 p.m.
Respectable dress compulsory Varied music
A warm welcome awaits you
The place: in the basement just next to the Church
Bring your friends. See you there

– a text illustrated by a drawing showing a heart pierced by arrows and flashes of lightning, and a couple dancing in silhouette: written on their sweatshirts are the brand names Naf-Naf, BB, Cacharel. A bubble says: 'We're hear to have a good time and not to bore ourselves stupid.'

*

Still, they mustn't forget to look for the Kitchen Gardens Museum.

*

WEDNESDAY 31 MAY. Anaïk goes off looking for cola nut. The small grocer in rue Heurtault who sells exotic fruit tells her to go to the African hostel a short walk away. In the carriage entrance of the old building, some youngsters are having a chinwag. Yes, you can get cola, but what sort does she want exactly? Small cola? But small cola's only for men, it gives them strength. She needs pink cola. A Malian in a blue cleaning company uniform asks her if she knows Africa. 'I hope you're not like those Whites who travel and see nothing, who go all round Africa and know nothing about us, our customs and culture.' Does he go back? When he can, but it's so expensive. And when he is over there, it's hard being thought of as a foreigner. They imagine that people living in France are rich. It's understandable because Mali's so poor: they can't see that it's very difficult living in France. They think we live like French people. How about a photo? 'Sure, if you send us them.' Yes, Anaïk will send the photos. 'But be careful with the address, because the hostel's closing in two days. This place is finished, they're going to demolish it.' They're being transferred to new premises in rue Félix Faure, but they're worried about what it'll be like there.

Their chat, she said, was very friendly and very respectful.

*

They are meeting Rachid Khimoune at La Maladrerie; he's waiting for

Aubervilliers: The hostel in rue Heurtault

them at Bar L'Expo. La Maladrerie is a very large bare concrete estate with real streets, unexpected recesses, blocks of differing heights giving unexpected salients, high passages under the buildings which come out on to open spaces where paved footpaths meander between yellowed couch grass; staircases, curves running from one roof level to another, balconies decorated with windowboxes in the same concrete in which tenants are growing, depending on their tastes, flowers, shrubs or wild grasses; and crenellated terraces in the style of a medieval citadel. Rachid, who is a sculptor, lives with his wife and daughter in a studio on the ground and first floors. In this high, harmoniously-proportioned space, they feel perfectly happy. The studio looks directly on to the concrete passage where people pass by and children play. The architect planned this kind of studio so that the artist can work in direct contact with the life of the estate, and all the passers-by can follow his labours. Opinions are mixed on this idea of the 'artist-in-residence'), of abolishing the ivory tower. Some people feel that artists still need a minimum of isolation. For Rachid the question doesn't arise because sculpture, and particularly his sculpture, cannot be done in a flat, even if the latter is set out like a traditional artist's studio: the technique of sculpting produces clutter, noise and dirt, which requires storage space, lots of room, the use of bulky materials, trowels and soldering irons. He therefore works in premises inside the walls of Aubervilliers fort, next to the scrap metal dealers. Forty or so artists live and work at La Maladrerie. There, just a stone's throw from the

Aubervilliers: La Maladrerie

Aubervilliers: La Maladrerie

capital, they find studios it is now almost impossible to rent in Paris, where the craftsmen's courtyards are disappearing and very few artists can afford the luxury of an 'artist's studio', which has become the almost exclusive privilege of very wealthy bourgeois.

Rachid is tall and superbly welcoming: he is embarrassed by their unexpected visit but convinced that the duty of hospitality comes before everything. They forewarned him at the last moment, and he has to catch a train to go and prepare an exhibition in Grenoble. This doesn't stop him dragging them off to visit his studio in the fort. They have to go through the scrap yard, piles of rusty carcasses and a pack of baying wolf-dogs. Rachid occupies a long thin blockhouse, well lit from above and sealed by heavy reinforced doors. The army experimented here with toxic products on animals. The technical term for it is gas chamber.

All around grows wild and exuberant vegetation. Here Rachid assembles, solders, models, mixes, interweaves and sticks together everything that makes up the fabric of our urban life: paving stones, sand, asphalt, drainpipe sections; he inscribes their imprint on plastic resin, 'a faithful mould of urban memory'. Rachid sculpts nature, the only nature his generation really knows, the only one it really lives in, the only one that truly speaks to it: the wild nature of the streets, estates, towns, the nature in which he grew up and to which he has known how to remain faithful. Cast-iron drainpipe sections become heads or shields, warriors stand erect, fantastic, bristling, grotesque, gentle or fierce; Don Quixote

Blanc-Mesnil: Rachid Khimoune's children of the world

and Sancho Panza head off on crusade on twentieth-century asphalt roads. It's a superb and tender barbarism, completely devoid of mockery: the barbarism of our civilization. Rachid's dream, which he is slowly making reality, is to erect in every town in every continent a ring of 'children of the world', and to do it in the street, in front of the children, with the children. He has done it in China, and he has also done it near here, at Blanc-Mesnil – Anaïk went there and photographed the kids on the estate who had made these strange and familiar chaps their playmates.

Back at the Expo, over sausage and chips, Rachid and a painter friend talk about life at La Maladrerie. The estate, they say, lends itself to community life: there are lots of associations, the Camille Claudel Cultural Centre plays an important role. For the kids, the streets and surrounding land are a tough, sometimes worrying apprenticeship, but one which will help them develop differently from if they stayed cooped up in a Paris apartment, knowing nothing of the realities of human life; or if they roamed like lost souls round the 'walls' of their estate. Their freedom, it must be said, is threatened by the speculators' ever-growing lust for construction: where will the children play when all the land has been built on?

But even so, all things considered, Rachid and his friend sometimes dream of moving far away, nearer the country. To a *pavillon*.

Rachid was born in Decazeville. When his father first came to settle in Auber, he lived at 15 rue de l'Union. Like Akim's father. Like thousands of others. 'Ask them and you'll see,' Akim had said. 'They all passed through rue de l'Union.' In the fifties and sixties it was the 'address' of the biggest shantytown in the Paris area, along with Nanterre. François remembers it; during the Algerian War he had friends who lived there. It was from rue de l'Union that one of the columns of the big demonstration set off on 17 October 1961.

That day, more than thirty thousand Algerians converged on the wide Paris boulevards for a peaceful demonstration in support of the FLN, the National Liberation Front. Many were wearing their Sunday best. They had no weapons. The immediate motive for the demonstration was to protest against the 8 p.m. to 5.30 a.m. curfew imposed on all 'Algerian Muslim French people' in the Paris area following several attacks on policemen. It was a night of beatings and slaughter. Few demonstrators were able to form a procession. Rachid remembers going with his father as far as Porte de la Chapelle. They couldn't go any further. No one has ever known exactly how many people died under the blows of the Paris police; but by counting the corpses fished out of the Seine in the days that followed and those recorded in hospital morgues, the estimated figure, as given by *Le Monde* in 1982, is 200, to which we must add 400 disappeared. Pierre Vidal-Naquet, a scrupulous historian if ever there was

Aubervilliers: La Maladrerie

one, relates that 'before the eyes of the Prefect of Police, M. Papon, several tens of Algerians were massacred in the prefecture courtyard.' Twelve thousand men hauled in that night were shut up for several days, many of them at the Palais des Sports, then mostly dispatched to Algeria or to concentration camps such as Saint-Maurice-d'Ardoise or Le Larzac.

At the time, the overwhelming majority of the press and the politicians celebrated a victory over chaos: armed gangs had tried to spread terror in Paris, and the butchers' plot had failed. Protests were scarce: mostly the same old little groups of irresponsible left-wing intellectuals and delinquent *porteurs de valises* ('suitcase carriers', volunteer FLN couriers in France). At Charonne a few months later, on 8 February 1962, when the same police corps weighed into a peace demonstration – all good Frenchmen this time – and killed nine people, horrified protests were widespread.

Maurice Papon, the Prefect of Police responsible for this city-wide anti-immigrant attack (this pogrom, wrote Pierre Vidal-Naquet), now stands charged with crimes against humanity. The charge concerns his activities supplying Jews to the death camps at the Prefecture of Bordeaux under the Vichy regime. Crimes against humanity have been declared imprescriptible under a retroactive law. All events relating to the Algerian War are covered by an amnesty.

Rachid thinks the FLN knew perfectly well that it was sending unarmed demonstrators to their deaths; maybe, in the light of the ensuing

story of independent Algeria, many children of Algerians today probably think as he does: that their parents were criminally manœuvred for the needs of the FLN's international propaganda and to demonstrate the movement's power on the eve of the negotiations. François remembers only that no one – French or Algerian – in rue de l'Union or elsewhere could have imagined that the demonstration, which was felt first and foremost as an assertion of dignity, was heading for butchery; and that no one, especially among the activists he knew at the time, had envisaged for a single moment anything other than the peaceful presence of a mass of Algerians in the streets of Paris, for an hour or two, showing by their numbers and determination that they rejected discrimination and wanted freedom for their country. But it remains clear that through this demonstration, the French branch of the FLN wanted to stage a show of strength for the GPRA, the provisional Algerian government.

On 18 October 1961, the curfew was brought forward to 7.30 p.m. for all 'Algerian Muslim French people' in the Paris area.

*

In the evening, our travellers go to see *Mon balai pour un royaume* at Théâtre de la Commune. Nothing to report.

9

*The Plaine Saint-Denis and the Roman
campaign. – Waiting for the barbarians
– Interconnexion – Incident at Gare du Nord.
– Off on new adventures.*

WEDNESDAY 31 MAY. Perched on its embankment, La Plaine-Voyageurs station is a sad place: the narrow, fence-ringed platforms shake with every passing express train from Gare du Nord and every freight convoy leaving La Chapelle marshalling yard, which all rattle through without stopping. From the grey platforms you can see a row of roofs of dull machine-made tiles and rusty zinc, and a forest of crumbling chimneys. The station building down below is a small old brick fort which they have never managed to scrub clean of the soot built up by generations of steam engines. You come out on to the A1 motorway, which at this point runs through a cutting between two rows of decrepit blocks of flats and warehouses weighed down by advertising hoardings. Stretching out behind the station are crisscross streets of peeling houses, cheap *pavillons* and former factories which have been salvaged, to varying degrees, as stockspace by the big Paris stores, or returned to their natural state, namely wasteland. This is a zone where nobody stops, a storage zone, even a '*zone*' (a poverty-stricken area), full stop. This 'crater-tragedy', to use Roland Castro's expression, once used to be rather marshy countryside which began on the northern slopes of the Butte Montmartre. In the 1840s, Gérard de Nerval used to go for quiet strolls down the hill behind Château des Brouillards, where gambolling goats grazed acanthus on the rocks, guarded by 'haughty young girls with mountain eyes'.

> The Plaine Saint-Denis is admirably contoured, the reflections of the sun and clouds varying with each hour of the day.... How many artists snubbed by the Prix de Rome jury must have come here to study the Roman countryside and the aspect of the Marais Pontins. There even remains a marsh enlivened by ducks, goslings and hens.
>
> Nor is it unusual to find picturesque rags on the workers' backs.... Most of the land and scattered houses belong to old landowners who anticipated that

Parisians would have trouble building themselves new homes, and that houses in the Montmartre area would tend, in time, to invade Plaine Saint-Denis.

Gérard had dreamed of building 'a small villa in the style of Pompeii' at the foot of the Butte amidst the vines. Our travellers walk past a high wall topped with barbed wire and surrounded by brambles, then go under the railway embankment. They turn down a cobbled alley where abandoned railway tracks wind through heaps of rubbish. In one courtyard, car carcasses lie rotting in front of low buildings – abandoned workers' accommodation: two floors of thin plaster-and-brick tiles with a caved-in gallery leading to the cramped rooms running along each. Rusty tracks leading nowhere, a courtyard in ruins: two photos to illustrate what the world might be like at death's door, just after the end of humanity.

The alley comes out on to straight streets running up against the embankment where the RER goes past; on either side, tiny brick *pavillons*. On one of them is a tarnished marble plaque on which François makes out:

> Here lived MARIA RUBIANO
> who died at Ravensbrück
> 1944

He asks Anaïk to photograph it. A couple comes out and asks what they are doing. 'Are you from the town hall?' A strong Portuguese accent. They are visibly worried. For them, it seems, any stranger who shows a remotely close interest in their street can only come from the town hall, and everything from the town hall means inventories of fixtures, property deals and rehousing, therefore departure, if not eviction. The travellers explain. It's not easy: diffuse embarrassment and fear hang in the air. François talks about his interest in the plaque. Did they know Maria Rubiano? No, they arrived later. A sad story, says the man:

'It was a woman who lived in the house. There was an air raid – she got out but died instantly.'

Anaïk says how she likes this quiet street at the world's end. She is sincere, and they believe her. Photo-time in front of the plaque, their grandson in their arms.

They have lived here for thirty years, are happy here, and would like to end their days here. They both worked on the Plaine: the man spent twenty years on the production line at the factory that used to be just opposite, which made chemicals and explosives; then the factory was bought and closed. Is he retired or unemployed? It's hard to tell what he's saying: his French is swamped in Portuguese.

Plaine Saint-Denis

Further along, opposite a Portuguese café, Anaïk photographs Madame Pauline's caravan. Again the fear is tangible: Madame Pauline comes out and has to be reassured that they're not from the town hall, that they're not after her dogs, that they're not there to get her out. They end up having a beer together in a café whose customers, gathered at the bar, listen and watch in silence. Anaïk will come back with the photo. It is the start of a friendship.

The only shops here are abandoned, except a chemist's. There's a Spanish church in reinforced cement, its locked-up hostel oozing rust. The hostel opens at weekends. They will be coming again: some people there speak Castilian, though Galician and Portuguese are more common and Cape Verde creole even more so, besides various African dialects. There is a warm atmosphere, you can eat tapas and greasy fried cod, drink San Miguel beer and play extremely lively games of dominoes.

In the late afternoon, Plaine Saint-Denis emerges from its torpor. The children play freely in the quiet streets. Where in Paris can the children still play in the street? The children of the Plaine Saint-Denis are beautiful, like those from Blanc-Mesnil and Les Beaudottes. The Plaine offers an image of a world coming apart, but its inhabitants, who live so badly, are hanging on to life with a vengeance. Many recent arrivals come from the Cape Verde Islands: the Cape Verdian people have some of the most harmonious features in the world: on those volcano splinters scattered a thousand kilometres off the coast of Africa, over several hundred years, all the African races have blended together with those the Portuguese snatched from beyond the Indies. The Cape Verdians have the most delicate features, the most golden skin, eyes ranging from charcoal grey to aquamarine, and bodies straight out of Atlantis. They are as beautiful as a dream of the great final crossbreeding of the human race.

Rue du Landy runs directly north between deserted warehouses and overcrowded houses as far as the Canal Saint-Denis. You leave 'Little Spain' and 'Little Portugal' behind. The closer you get to the canal, the more it seems most people are becoming North African. Narrow housing shared by several families gives way to furnished hotels above cafés which still have names from yesteryear: 'L'Embuscade' ('The Ambush'); or others which have received new ones, such as 'L'Oasis'. Here suspicion is heavy in the air. Slum landlords. Recent illegal immigrants. Drug trafficking. Let us move on.

On the Plaine Saint-Denis, a huge building development is in the pipeline. The calm before the storm. The Plaine is waiting for modernity – or postmodernity? I can never remember, you get lost – as others waited for the barbarians. When it is all complete, you will search as vainly for those beautiful Cape children as for the goatherdesses of yesteryear so dear to Nerval.

Yes, let us move on. Here is Les Vertus lock, and the lock-keeper comes to say hello again. He talks again of his regret at never having sailed on the Canal du Midi.

Was that the day when, late in the evening, in the pizzeria in place de la Mairie, someone told them about alligators collecting in the sewers of La Villette, round an outlet of the urban heating system? François's notes are increasingly hazy.

*

THURSDAY 1 JUNE. Farewell, Auber. Farewell, Hôtel de l'Hôtel de Ville. Can't stop. Must be going. Yet they still had so many things to do. They have seen nothing of Aubervilliers. They didn't ring the reed-bed man, didn't explore with him the wild flora and fauna thriving on the ruins of the prehistoric gasometers, where maybe the bittern heron nests, and the Balearic crane stops off on its way to Norway during the equinoxes. They didn't visit the Kitchen Gardens Museum. Later Anaïk found in her address book the phone number of a Moroccan friend who lives at Les Courtillières: some other time. In Aubervilliers François wanted to meet Didier Daeninckx, author of *Meurtres pour Mémoire* ('Murder in Memoriam'), the only book that describes the 17 October demonstration; he is the man who writes such fine novels – of the sort one is quite wrong to call 'detective stories' – but François never dared telephone him. They must leave Auber with heavy hearts, as you leave a town so far away that you aren't sure that you'll ever come back.

Today they make their longest journey by rail: from Aubervilliers-La Courneuve station they will travel directly to Arceuil-Cachan, jumping ten stations in one go: the one at La Plaine-Voyageurs, where they have already made the compulsory stop; then those they pass through under Paris: Gare du Nord, Châtelet, Saint-Michel, Luxembourg, Port-Royal, Denfert-Rochereau, Cité Universitaire; and finally the first two in the southern suburbs, Gentilly and Laplace, because after lingering in Aubervilliers, this very day they have a rendezvous they can't put off at Arceuil-Cachan. They are expected for lunch. It comes at a good time, for, as François's uncle used to sing in a falsetto voice from the top of his six feet seven, standing on the platform at Gare de Lyon when setting off for the summer hols, amidst a Homeric jumble of rucksacks, hatboxes, butterfly nets and tangled fishing rods:

> A railway ride in the Great Outdoors
> Will make you so hungry you could eat a horse

210

So they choose their train carefully, either SLOW or SUTO, which in a few shakes of the bogies should drop them on the platform at Arceuil-Cachan. In the end it's KOHL which presents itself for duty. Unfortunately their delight is extremely short-lived: KOHL plunges into the Gare du Nord tunnel, coasts along the poorly lit platforms, stops, and lets out a long sigh of relief mingled with anxiety. The lights go out. Then, in the ensuing silence, KOHL's voice can be heard: it turns out to have a Perpignan accent and announces that due to disruptions on the network, the *interconnexion* is not guaranteed and all passengers must get off the train.

Its real name was not in fact KOHL, but KHOL, a Muslim or Asian cosmetic.

As there are masses of people on the platforms (although it's supposed to be the *off-peak* hours), proving that the disruption is genuine; as the crowd is bad-tempered, apart from a small group of multicoloured youths smoking, letting out shouts and sketching dance steps to the sound of a fuzzy lambada on a cassette player; as the electronic departure board has gone dead and no trains are leaving; as a laborious consultation of the timetable shows that the next likely departure is a through train which races directly to Massy-Palaiseau and Saint-Rémy without stopping at Arceuil-Cachan, they decide to go up to ground level, just to buy the day's newspapers and sniff the open air round the main line terminal. They take the opportunity to see if the two Russian carriages of the 16.14 Paris–Moscow train are already in. This brings back nostalgic memories: each of them has caught that train at one time in their lives – Anaïk to go to Berlin, François to Warsaw; his trip was already ten years ago, two nights and a day of slow bumps, and he remembers that at the Belgian border, some railwaymen had asked a young woman leaning out of the window where she was going; one of them held out a slightly faded rose: 'Here, will you take this to Moscow?' The young woman pulled her head back into the compartment, threw the flower on to the greenish-yellow velvet seat and said to François in a sullen German voice a sentence in which he recognized the words *dumm* and *scheisse.*

Yes, the green carriages are there, muddy and rusty as you like, with their yellowed lace curtains and, on the way in, just above the wooden steps, a grille in the floor where you scrape the snow off your boots. Hopelessly naff and falling to bits, these carriages are a small piece of authentic people's democracy which runs aground almost secretly each day in the centre of Paris. But there's no chance of climbing aboard to breathe the smell of dusty old tea and maybe even, with a bit of imagination, a whiff of cold sour cabbage, which for decades has been the odour of true socialism: a driver wearing a schapska is sternly standing guard and doesn't speak a word of French. It's a pity: sometimes you find brochures lying in the corridors and, with a bit of luck, they could have laid hands on a precious Trans-Siberian Railway timetable, a thick booklet where you get lost in the succession of days and time zones: after the white plain, another white plain, leave Krasnoyarsk at 0.18, arrive Irkutsk at 09.03, but is that the next morning or the morning after that, and how many hours must you add on or take off, and is your carriage going straight through to Ulan Bator, and if not, must you change trains to avoid ending up in Vladivostok, although you bought your ticket for Peking five days before?

They dive back into the depths of the RER. The atmosphere has changed. On the platform a mood of strange agitation reigns. An RER train has stopped halfway down the track, doors closed. A dense crowd is pressing round the front of the train. People are screaming. There are men on the line: firemen's helmets appear and disappear below platform level. Policemen shove their way through. 'Did you see it?' asks someone. 'It's not our lucky day,' says a man. 'Couldn't he have done it from the Eiffel Tower?' 'More delays,' says another. 'It's the head, it's horrible.'

It is horrible. As the crowd is brushed aside, the group of youths with the cassette player start talking loudly, screaming, shouting: 'I saw it.' 'It's disgusting.' A boy laughs hysterically. So another boy searches in his pockets, pulls out some hundred-franc notes, lights them, and they frantically watch them all burn, the most absurd challenge to absurdity they could find.

The loudspeakers announce: 'Owing to a serious passenger accident on the Saint-Rémy-lès-Chevreuse line, you are requested to go to platform D.' The crowd pours back out.

An hour later, our travellers are at Arceuil-Cachan.

PART III

Hurepoix

And Monsieur Fenouillard confessed that *he under-stood nothing any more.*

GEORGES COLOMB, known as 'Christophe',
La Famille Fenouillard

10

*Arcueil versus Cachan. – An Arcueil kid's success story. – Tales
and legends of the Ligne de Sceaux. – Welcome to Hurepoix. –
From Camulogenus to Erik Satie: 'Arcueil born and bred'. –
The great climb up the aqueduct. – The grand republican
banquet and what happened next. – Meeting Mar-la-main the
cat and Fifi the canary.*

THURSDAY 1 JUNE, CONTINUED. Here they are, then, in the south, and it's
as though the sun were brighter, the air lighter and nature more gay.
Gone is the Plaine, with its nonexistent viewpoints and minimal
landscapes. Are they in another country? Here the suburbs are green and
undulating. Arcueil-Cachan station sits on the west-facing slope of a
valley straddled by the narrow arches of a high, slim aqueduct with
slender millstone pillars. Facing it on the other slope, *pavillons*, estates and
blocks of brick 'walls'; on the edge of the plateau, you can make out tiny-
looking cars on the southbound motorway and, still further away on the
plateau itself, Gustave-Roussy Hospital, whose massive bulk overpowers
the entire valley like a steel-and-glass fortress, crowned by a medieval
keep.

But this isn't the moment to be interested in the landscape. They have
a 12.30 p.m. rendezvous at Restaurant de la Mère Dubois; they're late,
and would still like to drop off their bags at Hôtel le Relais Bleu in rue
Camille-Desmoulins, the only one where, after many a fruitless telephone
call, they were able to book rooms. The map next to the station giving
the route of the 187 bus shows a bus stop called Camille-Desmoulins.
Fifteen minutes later, the 187 drops them at the bottom of the valley
opposite a very modern brick development grouping together a town hall,
shops and high-quality housing: they set off down avenue Camille-
Desmoulins, which takes them southwards, first through the houses in the
old village, then between the wider-open spaces of the school complexes,
until the moment when, after an interminable trek, they realize that the
treacherous Camille has long since turned into avenue de la Division

Leclerc, and that they are coming into L'Haÿ-les-Roses. About turn. Trickling with perspiration and with their straps digging into their shoulders, they have to face facts: there are no hotels in avenue Camille-Desmoulins. Closer study of their map reveals that they have been duped as if it were still the first day of their journey: the Relais Bleu is in fact in rue, not avenue, Camille-Desmoulins, which is in *Arcueil*, not *Cachan*. And of course this street is situated in quite the opposite direction, on the other slope of the valley behind the motorway. Too late to drop off now, it's 1.30 p.m.; all they can do is rush right across Cachan and part of Arcueil, climb some steep steps past the aqueduct on their way to the finishing post, and land, tongues hanging out, amid the comforting smells of Mère Dubois's dining room, where waiting for them is Monsieur Marin, who is at the coffee stage and cannot hide a certain astonishment at their slightly frantic appearance.

Thank goodness for the Veal Marengo, Rabbit Chasseur and bottle of Brouilly beaujolais served up by Mère Dubois. And it's really not anyone's fault if, in the end, they can't quite eat a horse. Or a rabbit.

Monsieur Marin is Arcueil born and bred. To be more precise, he arrived as an orphan from Asturias at the age of eight, in 1937, and has been here ever since. It was the time when right-thinking French newspapers were proclaiming that curbs should be placed on the number of pinko scum pouring over the Pyrenees – *frente popular, frente crapular* – whilst support groups and working-class councils organized aid for victims of the Spanish Civil War. Arcueil's Communist council accommodated children of Spanish republicans, and over fifty years later, Communist solidarity obviously remains one of the finest human values for Monsieur Marin. He spent his wartime childhood in an alley in lower Arcueil, which is still there today but was packed at the time with wooden and breezeblock shacks. Who could imagine today what poverty there was in Arcueil? How can one explain that in these same little streets, which today are so spruce, only a few dozen years ago there was hunger, mud, damp and cold? The woman who took care of him did so mostly for the town hall subsidies. But the primary-school headteacher took an interest in him: he was top of his class. He found his first job at fourteen with a firm that supplied all of Montparnasse with paints, brushes, canvases and easels. The warehouse and workshop were at Arcueil, in the alley where he lived; the war was on, and he straightened out used nails.

The rest of his story is about the struggle of a kid who clings on to life and wants to win: 'When you escape from poverty, you can fight better than the others, you know the value of things and money.' And the value of life too. Monsieur Marin always comes back to Arcueil's poverty, the poverty he faced so much of, but he also repeats insistently that his story is nothing compared to all the poverty in the world. He now runs a modern business supplying all kinds of artist's materials. Anaïk's painter friends told her it would be unthinkable to pass through Arcueil without visiting him. He knows, loves, and collects modern artists, and is well placed to appreciate their work, which he follows in the greatest detail. And Arcueil can be proud of Monsieur Marin. He has moved the old warehouse into new premises on the other side of the valley, just on the tip of land between the junction of the two motorway branches.

Arcueil has changed, of course. He remembers the time when he used to fetch milk from the farm. The farms and market gardens have gone, as have the quarries, and the slums have been replaced by *HLM*: rehousing people in council flats remains for him a fine victory. 'Say what you like about the Communists, they did that.' Whether they're beautiful or ugly is another matter: if you had seen how people used to live, no hesitation was possible.

*

To reach the Relais Bleu on foot you have to go under the motorway, at the very point where its two branches merge – one coming from Porte d'Italie, the other from Porte d'Orléans. The subway consists of ramps, staircases, deserted tunnels dotted with pools of stagnant urine, abstract sculptures made from cement and broken pots set in stone gardens. The experience of such shabby and absolute horror – a total negation of all humanity – is the most distressingly lonely thing they have come across since the start of their journey: grey, naked death, death unadorned lurking in the subway's bends, whilst up above in another world, the four-road and eighteen-lane traffic thunders on.

The Relais Bleu is a perfectly kept modern hotel where people mostly arrive by the coachload, using some access road imperceptible to the pedestrian. The bedrooms in this blockhouse are arranged so that they all look on to the motorway; the double glazing only soundproofs up to a point, and there is no air-conditioning. A restless night in prospect.

In the late afternoon they go back down to the bottom of the valley, through the redbrick estates, Vaillant-Couturier and Les Irlandais, set out in tiers amid the trees; they follow a street lined with old houses with severe façades, narrow windows – a street that winds as though it were casually following the path of the Bièvre, the river that once flowed past here, where the laundries and tanneries used to be. For a hundred years the Bièvre has been covered over and is now nothing more than a sewer running through the middle of Paris past Pont d'Austerlitz. They walk back under the aqueduct, now aware that it marks the boundary between the rival siblings, Arcueil and Cachan. They dine at La Soupière, the restaurant in the hotel adjoining Cachan shopping centre, one of the Climat chain. They book rooms there for tomorrow. François makes a culinary discovery, a fillet of salmon with sorrel that is hot on the outside but still frozen on the inside: mixed in the mouth this creates a curious effect, with icy crystals crunching under the tooth and a creamy, piping-hot sauce. A modern version of Baked Alaska. Anaïk suggests that he ask for it to be heated through, but François protests: that's what travelling's all about, continually discovering new things. It's the rule of the game. Anaïk points out that they'd rather forgotten it was a game.

We should find room here for some remarks of a gastronomic nature. In this respect, apart from Akim's father's princely couscous, a quasi-regal *andouillette* at the last Auvergnat restaurant in Aubervilliers, just behind the church, and Mère Dubois's good home cooking, this journey has been a disaster.

They walk on into the night, get lost, and find no one to ask the way. After Aubervilliers they are definitely in another country. Will it be like that for the rest of their journey, along the southern branch of the RER B-line, formerly called the Ligne de Sceaux?

*

'In a small way,' says François, 'I'm a child of the Ligne de Sceaux. I was born in the year it was electrified. Of course I only know through photos and people's stories about the days when there was a little steam train linking Denfert-Rochereau and Limours. There are enough *Tales and Legends of the Ligne de Sceaux* to fill a book. For example, the oral tradition concerning the Saint-Rémy-lès-Chevreuse to Limours section is a tangle of contradictory versions: Yves Lacoste – who, as you know, is a great geographer and also a child of the Ligne de Sceaux, since he was born at Bourg-la-Reine – swears blind that this section was never developed: according to him, they built everything – cuttings, bridges and stations, and even, at Limours, a Station and Sports Hotel where we would certainly alight were it still there – but the tracks were never laid, which is why we won't be going to Limours. And yet my farmer neighbour at Milon-la-Chapelle used to tell me that the Germans tore up the rails in 1941. The 1921 Guide Bleu, on the other hand, gives a detailed description of the route taken by the 'ligne de Limours', and even gives the time of the coach connections at Boullay-les-Troux station; so whom should one believe?

'A hundred years ago my paternal grandfather, who spent most of the year in Egypt scratching the Sphinx's feet, bought a house in the Chevreuse Valley for his stays in France. Later, when he came back for good, he kept it. I never knew that grandfather, who died nearly twenty years before I was born: in the photos he is a bearded, portly chap, and I can easily picture him running after the last little wooden coach, one hand gripping the copper handrail, the other clasping an umbrella clamped on his black bowler hat to stop it flying away. At the time – I'm talking about before the Great War – he must have met loads of portly, bowler-hatted gentlemen on the journey: the line had been nicknamed "*le petit train de la Sorbonne*" or "*le train des professeurs*", because lots of academics lived along the route and caught it to go and give their classes in Paris, especially when the line was extended as far as Luxembourg. One was the mathematician Henri Poincaré, who got on at Lozère; another the historian Fustel de Coulanges, who boarded at Massy-Palaiseau. But there weren't just academics: Péguy, for example, who had the bookshop for his newspaper/publishing house, *Les Cahiers de la Quinzaine*, opposite the Sorbonne, lived on the Ligne de Sceaux from his late teens onwards. He did his preparatory class for the École Normale Supérieure at Lycée Lakanal at Sceaux, as Alain-Fournier did after him, then settled in Bourg-la-Reine and finally in Lozère. Péguy regularly took the train, and I'm sure that the steady rocking of the wheels, which must have gone on humming in his ear for the rest of the day, is not unconnected with the astonishing rhythmic drone of his quatrains. The poem *Eve* alone is made up of 1903 four-line stanzas, which go repetitively and insistently by like a long train of 1903 four-wheeled carriages, and one need not be excessively Lacanian to be struck by this obvious semantic detail: quatrain = *quatre trains*, four trains. Moreover, Péguy himself betrayed his obsession with the Ligne de Sceaux in *Les Sept contre Paris* ('Seven against Paris'), in which his pen wheeled out an Alexandrine composed entirely of station names:

Palaiseau, Villebon, Berny, Massy, Lozère

'My grandfather must sometimes have seen Erik Satie get on at Arcueil, though the latter preferred his bicycle. It's fair to add that in this area "*le train des professeurs*" competed with the bean train from Arpajon.

'If you travel back through the mists of time, history and legend concur that this line was one of the first to be built, in the 1940s, and I read that its rails had a quite exceptional gauge, 1.75 metres, whereas the standard gauge, as everyone knows, is 1.435 metres. Just another deep mystery. When and how we returned to normal dimensions I know not. What I do know is that its particularly winding route was used by a scholarly engineer to experiment successfully with the first swivel bogie system, etc., etc.

'I only really got to know the Ligne de Sceaux when I returned from the South of France in 1944 and lived at the house in Milon-la-Chapelle. I was twelve years old and already a connoisseur of the railway arts: at Montpellier I was a habitué of the little Palavas train so dear to Dubout. (Apart from it taking three-quarters of an hour to travel eleven kilometres across flat land and being escorted in the summer months by a thick cloud of mosquitos, one of its features was that it was *always* the wrong way round: when it was pulling the train, the engine went backwards; when facing the right way, it shunted the coaches.)

'Like many love stories, my relationship with the Ligne de Sceaux consists of great affection mixed with a little blood and death. On 6 June 1944 I witnessed the machine-gunning of a train pulling out of Saint-Rémy station. People died. Why did the planes – some say they were English, others French – pick on a suburban metro station? Another Ligne de Sceaux mystery that hasn't been cleared up. It's true that as regards 6 June 1944, "the longest day", historians' attention has been distracted by events more decisive than this trivial hunting accident.

'My adolescence was punctuated by my journeys on the Ligne de Sceaux. I think I used to know all its landscapes by heart: I saw them change before my very eyes from year to year, until today, but it has happened so surreptitiously that I couldn't spot them straight off; and, likewise, when I go through Bourg-la-Reine now, I begin scanning the landscape for the market gardeners' glasshouses.

'This train, it must be said, was extremely modern: so although most suburban coaches of the period had wooden benches, this one's seats were made of dark, gleaming imitation leather. There was a high ceiling and something solemn about the decorations that I've found only in the Moscow underground or the Russian planes I've already mentioned: a pattern of elegant thin brown lines ran along surfaces covered in pale enamel; the window rails rose halfway up from the ground like nickel-plated "T"s with elegant inward-curving wings, and, best of all, the carriages were lit by chandeliers in the shape of upturned mushrooms which wouldn't have disgraced the SS *Normandy*'s third-class lounges. I was very proud of using such a luxurious line. It also had the distinction of belonging to the RATP as far as Massy-Palaiseau and to the SNCF after that, which meant it was called the "metro" or the "train" indiscriminately. I watched its coaches grow old; I lamented the painting-over of their enamelled arabesques; I saw them lose their chandeliers, replaced by mundane, square, plastic fluorescent lights; I heard their electric engines lose their puff and develop tones of pitiful hoarseness. Attempts were made to rejuvenate their exterior appearance by replacing the green colour which so became them by a scheme of two-tone grey. Their transformation into the "regional express network", the RER, with the opening of the Luxembourg–Châtelet section, proved fatal: the incline under boulevard Saint-Michel was too steep, and you could feel their noble skeletons creaking under the strain. But the worst thing was in the final years, hearing the scornful comments of passengers who hadn't known their moments of glory, and their sarcastic jibes when, for instance, the gasping train lost a coach between Bourg-la-Reine and Bagneux. It was all the more unfair because over fifty years of modernization hasn't managed to speed up the journey: it still takes more than forty-five minutes to travel from Luxembourg to Saint-Rémy.

'At the time, the trains departed from Luxembourg station, which was strange in the sense that you went in through the porch of an ordinary building giving no hint that it concealed a station, almost secretly, in its cellar. On the archway you could still see the soot left by the locomotives. At Denfert there was always a packed crowd waiting, and some elbow-work was called for. When the track emerged into the fresh air you felt liberated; you could breathe more easily. And then you knew that you were heading nonstop towards Antony, and it was pleasant to know you were going to race through all those stations and platforms past the mass of suburban ants hanging about for their "stopper". Straight away there was a pretty landscape: courtyards and zinc-grey roofs; a warehouse belonging to Éditions Fayard covered in a large black inscription vaunting the Œuvres Libres charity; and a hoarding for Saint-Raphaël aperitif on the blank wall of a five-storey block, whose red and blue colours had an unusual relief from having been colourwashed on to its uneven rubble stones.

'Very quickly Arcueil aqueduct came into view; all my life I've cherished the impossible dream of walking along its narrow ridge; as soon as I caught sight of it, I unconsciously checked to see if you could walk up there: I had located a small walkway but had never seen anyone up there, and I had also seen that access to it was barred by a sharply pointed fence. Just before the aqueduct, you saw an attractive little goods station where mostly coal was stored, for it's worth pointing out that there was still *freight traffic* on the line. From the train you discovered the Bièvre Valley, where we are now; roofs of red machine-made tiles, tiny gardens and sheet-metal chimneys. In fine weather it made a pretty patchwork, smiling and many-hued, especially at the time of year when lilacs give way to forsythia. In winter it was gloomy, because a thick sooty grey fog hung over the valley. Everything wept coal-black tears – the carriages, the trees lining the track, the houses with their smoking chimneys; for quite a time the facing slope, as far as the terraces of the Hautes Bruyères redoubt, stayed bare; then came blocks of flats, trees, the motorway and the hospital, whose hippopotamus-like bulk managed to crush all the landscape's proportions. Even the aqueduct nearly paled into insignificance.

'Approaching Bourg-la-Reine, the train slowed down and you had time to admire a model market garden: little wagons rode round tracks down the paths between the glasshouses. Going through Bourg-la-Reine was an important moment in the journey. The "express" didn't stop there any more than elsewhere. You just had time to notice the branch forking off towards Robinson. At this moment, drama almost always erupted. All it took was a passenger realizing he was on the wrong train; I'm sure we were all secretly disappointed when nothing happened. When something did, we expressed overdone commiserations: we felt like one big happy family confronted with a person ignorant of the elementary things, and it was then that I realized that there *is* something more oafish than a provincial in Paris: a Parisian in the suburbs.

'Another reason why going through Bourg-la-Reine was an important moment was that I had never – and never have to this day – been to Robinson. I have never taken that little appendix of a line which breaks off westwards: it was unknown territory. All I knew was that at the end of it were legendary *guingettes* built in the branches of century-old chestnut trees, that the food was sent up using baskets and ropes, that "Robinson" rhymed with "*chanson*", song, and that everyone had a ball.

'Leaving Bourg-la-Reine, there was barely time to glimpse a concrete minaret on the right which to me seemed sheer lunacy (I didn't know about Gaudi yet) before the train plunged into a tunnel under Sceaux Park – on one journey out of two the driver forgot to turn on the chandeliers, and for a few seconds it went pitch black. We went straight through La Croix-de-Berny too; for several years, the blue signs announcing the station's name were completed by another smaller one, as if slightly ashamed of the fact, which added: Fresnes. Then Fresnes vanished again just as shamefully. I always wondered about the reasons for this appearance–disappearance. Yet another enigma. Is it because the locals followed the principle: "To live happily, live well hidden"? Is it because the name of Fresnes is too closely linked with that of its prison?

'The train sank – and is still sinking – into the concrete cutting at Antony and stopped there for a minute, at last. It emptied out a little, and you could start making yourself comfortable. Then it re-emerged and rushed towards the plaine at Massy-Palaiseau, whose stations follow on like the cases of a grammatical declension: Massy-Verrières, Massy-Palaiseau, Palaiseau, Palaiseau-Villebon. There were a hundred things to look at on the plaine, in the middle of the first real fields, the first real cultivated land, while outlined in the distance were the first real forests. There was the village of Massy, which was shelled during the war and lay in ruins for several years after; there were the bridges and tracks of the Outer Loop railway which ran alongside for a while after Massy-Verrières, the abandoned route of an enigmatic Paris–Chartres line which was never built, and finally the tracks bursting into flower to form the marshalling yard, which housed countless goods trains. Massy-Palaiseau was a bizarre concrete-and-brick metro station, standing in deserted countryside amid wheatfields and fallow land where horrible henbane could be seen growing; a long spindly concrete footbridge spanned the vastness of the marshalling tracks to allow people to catch their connection on the other line, which you could see on the far side of the tracks. And after Massy the train became a "stopper", went into the Yvette Valley, and we were really in the countryside once and for all, the countryside that Péguy used to say heralded Beauce.

'At Palaiseau-Villebon, on the wall of a millstone house opposite the station, you could read a mysterious message painted in big faded letters:

LA SUISSE PRÈS PARIS
("Switzerland near Paris")

'After Orsay, you finally saw the first cows in the meadows. But you had actually been in the countryside since leaving Paris. For long stretches, the smallest slivers of land beside the line, sometimes coming right up to an apex between the junction points, were occupied by railway employees' allotments: from Arcueil onwards, lettuces and pansies were in fierce competition, and in the summer months, staked peas, dahlias and gladioli would explode like fireworks. The route of the Ligne de Sceaux was thus a horticultural manual whose pages turned with the passing months and years. The embankments that were too steep to be cultivated were covered with copses of young acacias; and they still are in a great many places today. It's really the acacia line, those trees which came from the New World and whose leaves were for a long time worn as a symbol of freedom.

'And on Sundays in springtime, passengers climbing aboard between Saint-Rémy and Paris with thick mauve bouquets made it *"le train des lilas"*, the lilac train.'

*

FRIDAY 2 JUNE. The night was predictably one long to-and-fro: opening and closing the window, oscillating between din and suffocation. During this time, the salmon in François's stomach finally defrosted and started to sing.

It is raining small teardrops this morning. Our travellers are due to meet Gérard in front of Arcueil's former town hall. Gérard, like Gilles, is an old geography student of Yves Lacoste, and, as with Gilles, the latter had told François that if there was one person to see on their trip from Paris to Bourg-la-Reine, it was Gérard; that he knew everything about the area and much else besides.

And so, as they're tearing down the street through brick estates, late as usual, a young man rushes past them in the other direction, and when he draws level with François, shouts: 'Are you Monsieur Maspero? No, of course you're not Monsieur Maspero', not stopping for a moment, which means François has to do a volte-face and gallop flat out as well to try and catch up with him, all the while gasping, 'Yes, yes, I *am* Monsieur Maspero!' Finally convinced, the young man stops and greets them ceremonially: 'Welcome to Hurepoix!'

From that moment on it's a frantic race. Gérard is stricken by the patently obvious fact that one day is not enough to show them all that's important in Arcueil, to explain all its historical and archaeological riches. He knows every detail, every stone, every relic, every tiniest place that contributes to the splendour of Arcueil; especially since Gérard's knowledge and passion are not confined to his home town, nor to the Bièvre Valley, but extend to the huge expanse of Hurepoix, a collection of plateaux interspersed with wooded valleys stretching from Paris to Beauce and teeming with rivers, villages and châteaux.

Gérard is an enthusiast of the past who is excited by discovery, driven to despair by so many wonders disappearing, and tortured by the idea that he will never be able to share so many intense feelings. And yet his passion is infectious: still rushing behind him, they see with his eyes the Bièvre flowing where there is only asphalt to see, châteaux appearing where only brick estates now stand, majestic parks unfurling where a two-century-old tree still grows, the outline of Catherine de' Medici's aqueduct appearing beneath the more recent one. The Gothic church tells them of the pilgrims' road to Compostela. Decorating a former portal under an arch of the aqueduct, a sixteenth-century bust of a woman with two faces evokes the twin origins of Gallo-Roman civilization.

They keep on running, and Gérard keeps on talking, and Anne de Guise, the Prince de Lorraine, Erik Satie, the Gallic chief Camulogenus, the scientist Raspail and his large family, the poet Ronsard, the Marquise de Montespan, the Marquis de Sade, King John II Casimir of Poland, and such a host of other illustrious characters float around them that François ends up latching on to one of them, *le Duc de la Vanne*, maybe because he knows even less about him than about the others. Shame on him! He didn't understand. It was in fact *l'aqueduc de la Vanne*! Let's stop for breath and try to sort it all out.

224

Camulogenus: the year was 52 BC. He repelled Caesar's lieutenant Labenius, who was trying to cross the Seine near what today is quai d'Austerlitz. The Battle of Lutetia was fought along the Bièvre. Having been repelled, Labenius had to go back up the river and cross it at Arcueil to carry out a flanking movement through Montrouge. Upon which Caesar himself took matters in hand, killed Camulogenus on the Plaine de Vaurigard and entered Lutetia following more or less the route of the future rue Vercingétorix. The following year Alesia fell. Why is there no rue Camulogène in Paris?

In his *Sonnets à Hélène*, Ronsard wrote:

> Yes, you had time for Herceuil and to visit
> the gardens with your cousin, and the stream,
> where to division I had touched my lute . . .

But Ronsard was not the only poet to stroll in Arcueil's gardens and sing about its meadows and springs: all the members of the Pléiade could be found here at Robert Garnier's house. They transformed Arcueil into Hercueil, it is said, so as to be able to celebrate the name of Hercules.

Catherine de' Medici: she financed the construction of the second aqueduct. The first had been built under the Romans; it is said that it supplied the Thermal of Cluny, and that its arches gave their name to the village: Archelium. The second one carried water to the Palais du Luxembourg and various Paris fountains. Today it supports the millstone arcades of the third, designed in the nineteenth century by Belgrand (whom we have already encountered on the Canal de l'Ourcq), which carries its waters from the large reservoirs of Montsouris.

The Prince de Guise: his château, of which only a few outbuildings remain, was surrounded by marvellous gardens through which the Bièvre ran, 'feeding the rarest of birds'. By the eighteenth century, the garden already lay abandoned. Gérard is right to say that if you want to conjure up the past, you mustn't think of the château and its gardens as isolated sites but try instead to picture the succession of noble residences which stretched out from Versailles and the heights of Marly and Saint-Cloud, and of which Sceaux remains the nearest. Louis XV went hunting in the woods near Arcueil.

The Marquis de Sade: as late as the 1920s, you could still see the house at 11 rue de la Fontaine, known as 'The Chaplaincy', which Sade tried to rent one Sunday during High Mass for his usual purposes. According to the victim, a woman called Keller, it was a sleazy business. That's always the danger when you get involved in mixing up literary creation and reality. It seems the locals voiced their indignation.

A chemist named Berthollet, and Laplace, a mathematician, lived at Arcueil in connecting houses. In 1807 they founded the Arcueil Chemistry Society. All the intellectual elite of the Empire and Restoration periods – Lamarck, Gay-Lussac, Monge, Alexander von Humboldt, Chaptal – beat a path to their door.

As for Raspail and his numerous family, they exercised huge influence on Arcueil from the time when his grandfather, François-Vincent Raspail, 'the paupers' doctor', settled there in 1864. Though he was already nearing the end of his days, he was none the less sentenced to a year's imprisonment in 1874, at the age of eighty, for writing that the Communards were not murderers. His son Émile started the firm La Liqueur de Raspail, and besides providing work for many local people, whom he employed 'with great skill and human sympathy', he was a fine mayor: he took some daring social initiatives for the period, such as creating a school museum, the first Œuvre de la Goutte de Lait, crèches, and a part-time school for young workers. The other son, Benjamin, set up the Raspail Retirement Home and had a leg cut off by a tram in avenue d'Orléans.

And what about Erik Satie? He is Arcueil's greatest claim to fame and its dearest son. He was very poor and lived in furnished rooms in the house known as 'Four Chimneys', where he died in 1925. The worldly goods found in his bedroom were a hundred umbrellas and an unused piano, all covered in a thick mass of spiders' webs. Satie wanted his music to be edible, but he didn't eat his fill. He used to go to Montmartre and The Black Cat Cabaret Club by velocipede, a contraption whose praises he sang tirelessly, particularly to the Arcueil children whom he took walking on Thursdays. Satie looked after children a lot: legend has it that he never called them by the familiar 'tu' form but always used the formal 'vous'. He ran the municipal youth club, which he occasionally bailed out with his meagre grant, and gave free music theory lessons there. A member of the 'Born in Arcueil' Association – though born in Honfleur – he was a socialist and, in 1920, opted to join the Third International. According to Marcel Trigon, the current mayor, it was Erik Satie who founded the Arcueil branch of the Communist Party. A controversial story. All this takes us some way from *Three pieces in the shape of a pear*.

*

It's still raining. Gérard takes them up to the roof space of the old town hall, a cramped but grandiose pigsty of an attic where he stores all he can salvage: old decorated stone steps and balustrades saved from demolition sites, archives waiting to be read and sorted. Like some archaeological Saint Bernard, he's constantly on red alert so as to be there when the first pneumatic drill starts hammering, since it's often impossible to get hold of things beforehand. In the entrance hall they meet Robert Cluzan, who remembers standing guard at the bookshop La Joie de Lire during the Algerian War, when it was a bombing target. This and other memories immediately establish fraternal bonds between him and François, which calls for a lunch and a toast to old times.

At the time of the Front Populaire government, Robert Cluzan was a socialist on what was then the left of the Left, the Marceau–Pivert tendency. He has known Arcueil since he was knee-high to a grasshopper. He was a militant there, and fought there in the Resistance. After the war he took part in every attempt to forge a united, independent and honest left-wing movement: the PSA, the PSU, the anti-colonialist leagues. . . . Today, at the end of a long itinerary fighting against the tide, he has finally joined the Communist Party, because, he says, 'I want to be able to look at myself in the mirror every morning.' François hasn't followed quite the same path, but after all, maybe Arcueil's mirrors are magic ones . . .

For both Robert and Gérard, 'Arcueil is rather special', especially because even today, 25 per cent of the town's population is from originally local families. (As indeed is the case in several nearby towns: Claude and Jacques Seignolle, who carried out a survey in 1936, thus noted: 'Our main witnesses have a genealogy proving that both lines of their family had been in the area for 321 years.') Yes, in this town of 25,000 inhabitants – a figure unchanged in twenty years, and with an immigration rate the council endeavours to keep under 10 per cent, where from the age of sixteen children are registered on a waiting list for council flats – there certainly is an 'Arcueil spirit'.

This spirit is sometimes a shade subracist, to borrow Robert's expression. We shall see.

In the beginning, Arcueil was the Bièvre: at first a charming river ('a gay little stream which warbled along like a nightingale', sang Benserade in the seventeenth century); then one that was dear to the heart of Victor Hugo, the Bièvre, with its mills, dyeworks and tanneries, became with the passing years a 'filthy cesspool', which in the end had to be covered over. On its banks could be found the highest concentration of laundries around Paris: there were 150 of them in Arcueil and Cachan in 1900. In *L'Assommoir*, Émile Zola described what a wash-house was like at the time. In the laundry Robert Cluzan had known in 1946, the work, even though modernized, remained very hard. He described it as follows:

> The shed was quite high so that the steam wouldn't gather near the ground, from which rose the concrete pedestals of giant boilers, or rather coke-heated steam machines. . . . In front of the bay windows were thick wooden tables on solid trestles used for ironing, for the laundresses in fact mostly do ironing. We still had huge charcoal-heated irons and small cast-iron ones with leather-and-fabric handles which made it possible to grab them from the constantly hot ovens . . .

Until the end of the last century, Arcueil, like all the neighbouring villages, was a land of vineyards. The area south of Paris between Chaillot and Villejuif produced a clear white wine which supplied much of the capital, but didn't travel well further afield. It was a working-class wine – called *tutu* – but a good one too, for since the twelfth century there had been a 'king's wine' at Arcueil. For centuries, up to the Revolution, local peasants went by the title *laboureur de vignes*. Just before 1900, phylloxera killed the vines in Arcueil and the whole area, but large-scale wine production in the South of France had already weakened the vineyards, which were gradually replaced by market garden concerns. The Bagneux *'messiers'* disappeared in 1887; at Arcueil they had gone twenty-five years before. The *'messiers'* were guards armed with sabres who were specially assigned to guard the vines before grape-picking. Robert remembers drinking a Cachan wine. A few vines are still tended at L'Häy-les-Roses. They also replanted some at Bagneux four years ago, accompanied by a great many folklore demonstrations.

Arcueil also meant quarries. It is scarcely possible to imagine what the landscape must have been like in the nineteenth century, when great 'squirrel wheels' towered practically all over the fields around Arcueil, Bagneux and Gentilly. Chateaubriand mentions them in passing, on the road to his estate 'La Vallée aux Loups' ('Valley of the Wolves'); and in his history of Bagneux, Eugène Toulouze describes them as follows:

> In the middle of this grassland crossed by paths through the fields, one could see slight elevations surmounted by gigantic wheels the height of a four- or five-storey building: around the edge of the immense circle were small wooden crosspieces on which several men leaned with feet and hands in turn so as to wind a rope round a central spindle, which brought up from the quarry floor big chunks of stone weighing several thousand kilos; working thus with their feet and hands gave the labourers the appearance of so many squirrels turning in their cage.

The abandoned quarries were converted into mushroom beds. According to legend, you could go from Bagneux to the catacombs at Denfert and even as far as the Panthéon by way of the quarries without once coming up for fresh air. Robert tells how Cité Vaillant-Couturier, which was built on top of these excavations, is still unstable: to strengthen the substratum, they used the concrete-injection method; it was later realized that this was a dangerous process since it compresses the air, thus exploding the cave walls. Today they prefer using piles driven over fifty metres deep.

The extraction of freestone was then accompanied by that of clay, which since time immemorial had supplied a thriving pottery craft industry. The beginning of this century saw the setting up, especially in Bagneux, of industrial brick factories – which explains the use of this material for Arcueil's council flats.

The quarrymen were not easy-going people. Rebels, in a word. And as the presence of vineyards at the gates of Paris favoured the creation of many drinking establishments (at the turn of the century there were 150 in Arcueil alone), the Arcueillais enjoyed a solid reputation as awkward customers who liked a fight. They were called the *Red Guts* and joined forces with the inhabitants of Bagneux, the *Yellow Paws*, to lay into the people of Fontenay, who weren't short of nicknames either; the people of Bagneux were the *Bagneux Asses* or the *Madmen*, for it was said that the stink of the broad beans they grew sent them mad. Over and above this folklore, the fact remains that the quarrymen of the southern suburbs took part in all Paris's big popular uprisings, that Arcueil's population largely sided with the Paris Commune (the Arcueil Communards' red flag has been kept at the town hall), and that they have always felt that the administrative authorities hold them in suspicion. After part of the town was amputated and annexed to Paris and Gentilly in 1922, Arcueil had to suffer the secession of the hamlet of Cachan. For both Gérard and Robert, things are clear: just as the Department of Seine 'punished' the Arcueillais by making them pay for the upkeep of the land round Montrouge fort when in fact it lay outside their boundaries, so the people of Cachan, who were well-to-do bourgeois, despised 'those Arcueil layabouts' for their poverty.

Arcueil was working-class and poor. The valley, with its marshy bed, was an unhealthy place. 'On some days,' says Gérard, 'you can still see the Gentilly fog rising.' A legend from the Middle Ages says that when this happened you could see the outline of the giant Malassis appear. 'In my family,' continues Gérard, 'ten people have died of tuberculosis.' The worst of it was Villa Mélanie at Gentilly: it was a cesspit. The most destitute labourers came to settle there – the Bretons, the Piedmontese, the Armenians. It's true, says Robert, that the first estates they started to build after the First World War were 'rabbit hutches'; but at least people were housed decently. The Arcueil council flats which later took their place were designed not to be gigantic or inhuman. Social conditions came first. They didn't wait for the Delouvrier Plan and the promoters: yes, Arcueil's Communists truly can look themselves in the face. He had known Arcueil without electricity or gas: just putting in the rising main in the 1930s transformed people's lives.

When he was ten, Robert went with his father, who had walked from the XVth arrondissement, where he was living at the time, to his allotment at L'Haÿ-les-Roses. The big thing was cheating on the city tax. All the kids knew dodges: 'It paid for our sweets.' The grown-ups weren't short of a few either. Everything entering Paris had to be taxed, but everything going out was reimbursed with the same tax. They used to measure the petrol level in car tanks. (François muses: 'I wonder how they'd manage today . . .') So the trick was to smuggle products in and bring them out legally. You even saw people organizing fake weddings to get into Paris . . .

*

'Would you like to go up on the aqueduct?' asks Gérard. François can't believe his ears. But yes, he heard right. Gérard is taking care of the bicentenary celebrations for the council's cultural committee. They open tomorrow with a grand republican banquet. For the occasion, Arcueil's strategic points have to be decorated with tricolour banners, and the aqueduct is, of course, one of them.

It's pelting down, but this isn't the moment to be turning up noses. It's now or never. Occasions like this only come along once in a lifetime. Back they go to the old town hall, where Gérard has a 2p.m. rendezvous with the decorating team. They wait. At 3p.m., still no one. What are they to do? Go along anyway, since they've already got the precious banners? Yes, let's go anyway, François agrees, alarmed that the mirage might vanish. We'll easily be able to set them up ourselves. They cart off the three big gauze rolls, which fortunately weigh less than their size suggests. In this rain, let's hope that the dye is fast. They stop off to pick up the caretaker: he's better kitted out than they are, with big boots and a Breton sailor's oilskin to brave the bad weather; he opens the access gate for them.

They head down the narrow path to reach the middle of the bridge, some fifty metres above the valley. Waiting for them, perched shivering on the guardrail, is a small kestrel, a regular visitor to the icy solitude of historic monuments, which flies off only at the last moment. 'To the left,'

230

Arcueil Aqueduct

says Gérard, 'you can see as far as Sacré-Cœur.' 'Take some photos,' says François to Anaïk. 'What do you want me to photograph? There's nothing to photograph,' protests the latter sensibly. She's right: you can see nothing to the left, nothing to the right, just the roofs of Arcueil on one side and those of Cachan on the other; everything else is drowned in the deluge, while the icy spray whips their faces. So they take photos of each other, and François strikes a pose, as happy as if he'd set foot on the summit of Annapurna. They're shivering. Still no cheerful decorators in sight. 'Too bad,' says Gérard. 'Let's get started.' Every roll is several dozen metres long. What exactly is the idea? To hang the three colours down elegantly under the aqueduct? (On the Arcueil side, of course. Those Cachan dogs have no right.) After all, François did spend part of his life arranging bookshop window displays and doing poster layouts, and an aqueduct isn't much different from a display or a poster, it's just a bit bigger. Gérard and François start unrolling the blue one, walking backwards along the bridge away from each other and struggling against the wind, which has the annoying habit of turning the gauze floorcloth into a mizzen sail. François is already preparing a nice granny knot to attach it to the iron railing when the two cheerful decorators come charging up. They take things in hand with such skill that François wonders how he could have imagined for one moment doing it all by his crazy self. Less than an hour later, our travellers are well and truly frozen, drenched, dripping and squelchy, but there it is: the three colours are hanging down.

Less than gloriously, one must say.

Into all great victories there slips a note of bitterness. But François thinks of the face Lacoste will pull tomorrow at Bourg-la-Reine when he tells him, with false modesty: 'I've been up on Arcueil aqueduct.' There's also a fourteen-year-old boy whom he knows would gasp in admiration if he could tell him now: unfortunately it's too late, for he would need to go back over forty years to find that other François, dreaming out of the carriage window as the train trundled through Arcueil-Cachan.

Gérard, taking his role as host more and more seriously, invites them with a magnificent flourish to attend the grand republican banquet taking place tomorrow, Saturday.

*

SATURDAY 3 JUNE. They depart for Sceaux.

The previous evening, after rubbing themselves down but not really warming up, they caught the train to Bourg-la-Reine, hoping to locate a hotel where they could reserve rooms for their next stop. There is no hotel in the village itself – they would probably have needed to look out along the main road. But such things are done only by car. Bourg-la-Reine after dark beat all records for emptiness. One or two restaurants tempted them but, never satisfied, they were put off by the prices. Luckily they found a Chinese. Later they made a few more attempts on the phone to find a hotel between Arcueil and Antony. Everything was full; apparently it's the week of the Post Office entrance exam, at Gentilly Examination Centre, and the candidates are filling up the hotels near the stations. In the meantime, they have decided to spend the following night at Sceaux, where there is room. François is going through a decidedly intense period of discovery, because after the aqueduct, for the first time in his life, he is going to take the branch line to Robinson.

Sceaux station is pleasantly quaint; indeed, Sceaux is pleasantly quaint. But smart. Very smart. You can feel it immediately. Rich is the word. Rich people's villas. Rich people's dogs. Rich people's shops. Rich people's hotels, alas. A place for posh holidays.

In the charming little seventeenth-century church on the edge of Parc de Sceaux, among the usual leaflets on display they find a batch of the newspaper *Présent*, probably left there by a devout militant for the enlightenment of his co-religionists. They grab one and enlighten themselves: at Cergy-Pontoise, immigrant louts are ruining our lives. Rights of man or rights of scum? The Joxe immigration law will quite simply mean the invasion of our country. A message from Mitterrand congratulating the gay magazine *Gai-Pied*. Le Pen in Nancy: the Front National is the party of French people in love with France. Claude Autant-Lara, the film-maker, is standing for the Front National in the European elections: 'True internationalism puts national issues first.'

Parc de Sceaux: a very young warden in a Mexican heavy's uniform, a walkie-talkie in one hand and a chain in the other, is kicking his heels in front of the fence. At the end of the chain, an Alsatian. Quaint towns need burly wardens.

All that remains of yesterday's rain is big clouds scudding above the tall trees through a subdued, damp sky which, despite the showers, smiles from time to time.

From the château terrace, beyond the solitary fountain, the view westwards carries a long, long way, from Meudon to Verrières, over a landscape composed almost entirely of forests.

As in Dufilho's monologue, the château – built in 1597, razed by Colbert, who built himself a nicer one; smartened up by the Prince du Maine, son of Louis XIV and Madame de Montespan; lived in by Voltaire; bought as a national possession and destroyed by the Duke of Treviso to construct another, more comfortable one – is an *entirely period* historic monument.

It houses the attractive Musée de l'Ile de France, whose collections they admire, not forgetting to put on the felt slippers provided free of charge for visitors. There's pottery and earthenware from Sceaux and the area, paintings reconstructing sites now disappeared: Arcueil gardens by Jean-Baptiste Oudry, Huet landscapes, which Victor Hugo loved and which show the dark wild moors around Sèvres; Gentilly quarries in the snow by Léon Mellé, and a magnificent composition which alone is worth the trip, a canvas by J. Veber from before 1914, in his series 'les maisons ont un visage' ('houses have faces'), portraying a Sunday in Robinson: when you look at it, the *guingette* has a nose, eyes, and everything it needs. Best of all, the painting features all the famous visitors of the time: Maurice Chevalier with Mistinguett, Pierre Laval courting Cécile Sorel, Prefect Lépine, Clemenceau, Aristide Briand and, banqueting round a table, Jules Guesde and Lenin in the company of Clara Zetkin (and not Krupskaya? So it wasn't with his lawful wife that Vladimir Ilyich went off to the woods on Sundays to indulge in his healthy velocipedal amusements – on a tandem, say some – nor with his no less lawful mistress, Inès Armand?). There are also archive photos, such as the one of the barge on the Paris–Saint Cloud run via Meudon, and documents relating to local celebrities – Éluard at Saint-Denis, Satie at Arcueil, and Sade too, with a photo of the house of his infamy taken around 1920, just before it was demolished ('By a fitting twist of fate,' the legend points out, 'a health centre now occupies the site'), and one of the novelist Céline at Meudon: here the caption deserves to be reproduced *in extenso* for the education of the reader, who can make of it what he will:

> Known for his violent anti-Semitism and lampoons, Céline held opinions about Nazism in 1940 that later earned him a spell in prison and then exile, from which he returned in 1951, settling in Meudon, where he practised medicine, caring for the poor and deprived. His 'fits of hallucinatory delirium' and the novelty of his mutilated writing with its fake slang earned him a *succès de scandale*.

They walk down by the lawns and wet paths towards the ornamental ponds and Puget statues. There are few strollers about. Near the fountain a fashion photographer, with lights and reflectors, is taking shots of two imitation young newlyweds. Anaïk complains that there are no pictures to take in these parts: 'I wasn't made to do postcards.' She finds the people sullen and monochrome: life is becoming monochrome.

They could leave the park bearing right and, following Chatenay-Malabry's avenue Jean Jaurès, walk all the way to 'La Vallée aux Loups', where in 1810 Chateaubriand planted the beautiful trees which didn't give him shade in his old age, since the cost of being French Ambassador to Rome forced him to sell his estate. If they had more time, they could go and have a rest beneath the sequoias and breathe the balsamic fragrance of the liquidambars. But are there any liquidambars left in 'La Vallée aux Loups'?

They catch the RER again at Parc de Sceaux station and get off at Laplace in front of the modern town hall where the republican celebration is being held. The brick-and-concrete station is a fine specimen in the Palais de Chaillot–public urinal idiom. There are not many people about. In front of the bus stop a bearded young Black in a tight-fitting red sweatshirt hurriedly hides something in his basketball shoes when they go past, then roams off in search of improbable deals. They walk up rue Laplace, pass fifteen-storey blocks adorned with big blue exterior piping, Pompidou Centre-style – is it part of the original, or the fruits of renovation? Opposite the closed shops is a bronze of a man and woman awkwardly raising their arms skywards, wrapped in skimpy tricolour gauze, obviously the work of the fine team of cheerful decorators.

These are two-level celebrations. The people of Arcueil are rejoicing in the street with a row of stands: tenants' associations, early retirers, unemployed, pupils' parents, army veterans, Communist Youth, and so on. The atmosphere is good-natured: lots of sans-culottes and Phrygian bonnets covering the jovial heads of CGT shop steward types. A sans-culotte goes past in his black leather jacket with a large dog on a leash. In another street lower down is a fair. The noise from the popgun stand drowns out everything: quite unbearable. The immigrants are all at the celebration down below.

It's raining. Anaïk is on photo-strike, no doubt about it. They await the opening of the big canvas hall set up for the banquet.

It's a pleasant crush. Then, at last, the stampede. Inside, long tables have been laid for nearly a thousand people at the foot of a large platform. They get settled at one of them with all Gérard's family: Monsieur and Madame, the children, the grandmother, and council workers who are moaning that they've been put there automatically and not somewhere else, when they've prepared everything, but who are very nice, and a couple of slightly wary old Arcueillais. The hubbub is deafening.

It's at this moment that Gérard announces to them that the Chinese army has invaded Tienanmen Square, that there's fighting in Peking, the tanks are crushing the crowd and there are hundreds of deaths. Upon which Comrade Trigon, Mayor of Arcueil, begins to speak. The general feeling is that he'll go on for a long time.

Just under a thousand guests, to whom should be added well over a hundred waitresses in Phrygian bonnets, obligingly allow him to speak, but for all that the good-natured racket of some restless guests does not stop. François holds out his little Sony, while Anaïk, who is rediscovering her taste for photography, clicks away at the family kissing each other affectionately, and the children doing somersaults.

Here's a brief extract from the last three minutes of the tape:

'. . . As in 1789, only a new deal of the cards will turn society the right way round and allow it to advance in the right direction, the direction of progress, of justice, of fraternity. (A voice comes over the tumult, right near the microphone: – *Twist or stick*??? Impossible to tell.) . . . Today we are once again living in a world of injustice. . . . Every day billions and billions fly over the heads of those who so desperately need it. . . . One can understand why every effort is made to hide the true story of the French Revolution. (*"Can you take our table with Trigon at the back?" "What are you saying?" "We can't hear each other. Shout louder." "I can't shout any louder."*) The events are taking place amid a joyful procession of idyllic kings and queens followed by hideous sans-culottes. (*"Come and have a cuddle." "He's the smallest." "He's your favourite."*)

'This huge game of pass-the-parcel with historical truth is even more easily explained when one knows the true aims which, using Europe as an excuse, seek to wipe out another dimension of the French Revolution, that of the establishment of the nation, of the sovereignty of national independence. (*"Absolutely." "Look at those glasses they're bringing round."*) But what European community should we be building? (*"It's very nice." "Is there some orange juice for the children?" "No." "What? Nothing for the children?" "What's that?" "Haven't a clue." "It's a 'royal cocktail'." "A royal cocktail? I've no idea what that is." "Looks dangerous, that does. Coming after the rum, as well. I'd watch yourself if I were you!"*) My responsibility as mayor obliges me to shout to the people of Arcueil: Danger! That Europe and that policy is the Europe of all kinds of danger for your everyday life and your children. (*"Nobody's listening." "It's great, I'm telling you."*) . . . You should realize that in order to bring our education system into line with the situation in other countries, they will abolish infant school, they will make people pay for their studies. They will abolish the essential rights won by the women of France. And they are even heading, as in Portugal, towards authorizing children to work in industry from the age of thirteen. (*"Stop running about. You've played enough, now come and sit down."*) . . . That's why, with regard to all that, I believe, and owe it to myself to say it honestly to the people of Arcueil – and no one will be surprised – that in my opinion, on 18 June, only the team led by my friend Maurice Herzog resolutely opposes . . . (*"I'm sure she's a Scorpio. Aren't you a Scorpio?" "You'd be wise to keep your glass. They're made of Plexiglas." "But can't he see everyone's had enough?" "What's that green stuff in the glasses?" "It's curaçao and I don't know what else." "There's bits of pineapple." "I haven't tried it because I had too much rum." "Our row didn't get any."*) . . . France, the sovereignty she won in 1789.

Arcueil's republican banquet: Gérard

'Letting others decide for France means interference. National sovereignty means the right to self-determination, *here in France*, to be citizens and to act with sovereign power in co-operation with others.... Rights for everyone, not the decline of France. You can be European only if you are patriotic and French. Today our homeland is once again in danger. We must defend it ... (*"They're offering a fill-up." "You take it, honestly, I've still got some rum." "But you're not drinking it." "She hasn't had any." "I'm telling you, rum doesn't agree with me."*) .. the right to live in our town as did our ancestors of 1789 ... list of grievances before a new deal of the cards puts France on the road forward.... Just as Saint-Just concluded ... cried out in 1794: "Happiness is a new idea", so let us dare, dear Arcueil friends, let us dare to say *Liberté, Égalité, Fraternité*, let us dare quite simply to try this new idea called happiness! (Ovation. − *"Another one! Pour me another one!" "Encore!"*)'

What followed became more and more muddled. They ate, drank, and ate and drank some more. They sang *La Butte Rouge* ('The Red Hill'). ('La Butte Rouge,' shouts Gérard, who, against all the odds, intends to maintain his role as chaperon right to the very end, 'La Butte Rouge is just down the road at Fontenay.') But François is already singing *Le Temps des Cerises* − or *La Carmagnole*, he can't remember − arm in arm with his Arcueil neighbour, who's now less wary, thanks to the royal cocktail and the Bergerac wine. Anaïk's gone off to dance − what? A tango? Or the salsa? − with the grandmother, over on the dance floor at the foot of the platform, where the orchestra has taken Trigon's place. They draw the grand revolutionary tombola. Everything's shaking, wobbling, shouting; everything's going crazy. Everything's going hazy.

At 1 a.m. in Gérard's car, his grandmother sings *Sous le soleil de Pantin* with words that cannot be reproduced even here. They part company outside the hotel at Sceaux. Emotional farewells. Everlasting gratitude. Gérard makes them promise to go tomorrow morning without fail and gaze upon the stone urn just opposite in which the Princesse de Maine − or maybe Madame de Montespan? Or who then? − placed the ashes of her cat Malangrin (or Malagrin? Or Malandin?) and her canary Fifi (or Rififi?).

But perhaps it wasn't a cat, but rather a lion or a chimpanzee, and not a canary, but what then? And another day, another night, on another journey, in another life?

11

The fine ladies of rue Hodan. – Ode to the French dog. –
Splendour and poverty of the garden estates. – A long walk. –
The mysterious inn. – That sinking feeling. – When the reader
escapes a fresh calamity. – Wanderings. – Fresnes without frogs,
Fresnes without a prison. – The villains from Villaine.
– Massy-Bucharest. – Les Ulis: a long way over there. – The end
of the track.

SUNDAY 4 JUNE. A single evening like that would have made the whole
journey worthwhile. But this morning they must emerge from the green
nightmares caused by the royal cocktail and the blurred events that
ensued.

First they must go and check the inscription on the stone funeral urn
standing in the square opposite the hotel:

Here lies Mar-la-Main
king of the animals

but they find no trace of Fifi the canary.

They take a turn in and around rue Houdan. If ever the expression *bon
chic-bon genre* was justified, it's here. At The Pink Piglet, *Félix Potin, Golf
& Green, Chantal B., Parc Monceau*, we're among people from the same
world: not one sour note. *Le Roi Lire*: a bookshop at last, the first since
the journey began. François is pleased to find *Journey to the End of the Night*:
he'll be able to check if the fascination-repulsion-admiration exercised by
Céline on so many generations can really be summed up today by the
simplistic trilogy that has been running through his head since the
museum: anti-Semitism – poor man's doctor – *succès de scandale*. What
were they trying to skirt around? He also finds Cortàzar's *Un tal Lucas*,
which has just appeared in French: he is in need of tender and magical
words which, as Comrade Trigon was saying, will turn his head 'the right
way round'.

But what on earth is this? A carnival procession is going past – fifes and tambourines followed by a Punch-and-Judy-esque cortège calling irresistibly to mind the fanfare that used to see off Daudet's folk hero *Tartarin de Tarascon* when he departed on new adventures. It is Sceaux's annual tribute to the Provençal troubadours. Who knows why, in Sceaux Church, there are rows of troubadour busts – Aubanel, Arène, Clovis Hughes, and even Florian. They noticed yesterday that Mistral didn't have a head. Today, miraculously, he does.

Going back that way an hour later, they saw some gentleman carefully putting Mistral's head back into a little basket.

The fine ladies of Sceaux are out shopping in rue Houdan in their four-wheel-drives. They're the fashion. After all, Sceaux's in the country, it's almost mountain terrain. The doggies reappear en masse. We had sort of forgotten about them. Anaïk photographs François in front of the window of *Frimousse, Canine Beauty Parlour*. They're selling jogging sweatshirts for pooches: *'Love me as I love you'*.

Back to the hotel. François claims that he's going to get back to sorting out his notes. They're further and further behind, his notes. But later, all he will find in his notebook at that page is the outline of a grand ODE of distinctly canine inspiration: is it the belated influence of the royal cocktail, Mar-la-main the cat, or the canine beauty parlour? Or the result of reading this *Important Notice* from the French electricity board pinned on a door?

Dog-owners!
Our agents are increasingly being attacked by your faithful companions. Thank you in advance for taking precautions to spare them such problems.

Here, nevertheless, unchanged from the original, is the

ODE TO THE FRENCH DOG

I. PRELUDE

The caring council of Kowloon
Lays on a crèche for young baboons
While polar bears in Anchorage
Can keep their cubs warm in the fridge.

For Sunday lunch in Abu Dhabi
The camels fly in fresh kolhrabi.
Grateful gardeners in Nantucket
Scrape up mule dung by the bucket.

Caged canaries like to sing
To peaceful strollers in Peking.
The liberal folk of Haparanda
Chose as mayor a giant panda.

Kind park-keepers in Havana
Chew the fat with old iguanas.
When spring arrives around Pamplona
The bulls adopt a gay persona.

If zebras shop in Zanzibar
They'll more than likely take the car.
In Widgeegoara Creek the dingos
Love their Tuesday evening bingo.

When punting down the slow Limpopo
Chimps sing gospel songs *con moto*.
Old boars in Mór like playing croquet
While their wives sit doing crochet.

A crocodile caught short in Miami
May do a single backstreet whammy.
For the *Sursum Corda* in Atlantis
The priest invites the praying mantis.

For everyone protects at least
One fish or fowl or bird or beast
With fins, or a beak, or a pouch, or a snout
A koala, marabou, gnu or trout.

REFRAIN: But all you get in this town of ours
Is woof-woof, bow-wow-wows!

(In truth, you also see lots of dogs in Canton: but only skinned ones, dozens of them, hanging by the face in butchers' windows. Dog is much sought after in the province of Guangdong. Who said France really should increase its exports to China?)

There follow twelve cantos and three interludes, one of which is devoted to bullfighting. This takes us away from dogs a bit, but less than you might think, for of course it deals with the relationship between man and bull taken as a model illustration of the relationship between man and animals in general. From bullfighting the author shifts cleverly to rabbit-hunting. He mentions the various forms this takes, and in particular the most noble, which is practised with setters to the sound of Eustachian tubas and appropriate cynegetic songs:

Oh tell me, gentle shepherdess
Hast thou seen the rabbit bouncing by, by, by . . . etc.

It then evokes the final tragic moment, the tragic confrontation between man and beast, the final challenge and the final stare, eye to eye: the nobility of the rabbit's solitude faced with death, and the nobility of man's solitude faced with the rabbit. A few neatly turned Alexandrines must show that rabbit-hunting, like bullfighting, is but a metaphor for life and death restored to their original purity, to the devastating and naked authenticity of that unique moment of the *alternative*, when destiny topples into ineluctable bloodshed but all is still to play for.

There follows a recipe for rabbit in mustard sauce.

This passage must be intensely beautiful.

After which the poet returns to the French dog – or, to be more precise, the dog of the Paris suburbs, by subtle means too long to explain here: suffice it to say that they involve blood, sensual pleasure and death. The ode closes with a lyrical flight of fancy in the form of an apotheosis, and with this final hemistich:

> ... but where's love in all that?

It would also be proper to note that the author, prompted by a sentiment whose delicacy does him proud, does not give the recipe for dog in shallots.

*

'Even so,' says Anaïk, 'you won't persuade me that a country where people love dogs and hate foreigners so much is all there.'

It remains to be seen what *is* a country that's all there.

*

In the afternoon they catch the train to Robinson, a few minutes down a winding rural line. A restful break is in prospect: Raymonde, who was expecting them, gives them tea with the family on the veranda of her *pavillon* at Fontenay. She has always lived there. Her father was a bus driver. She loves the peacefulness of *pavillons*. They talk to Donald, her American companion, about the regrettable lack of contact between the neighbours: things are so different back in the States. She can remember the time when she used to fetch milk from the farm. This milk-from-the-farm story is one of those that people remember most. But when did the fields, farms and cows disappear? It's difficult pinpointing moments in time. She thinks that as recently as ten years ago they used to fetch milk from Plessis-Robinson, a few metres from where she lived. Maybe you still can today? Her son Laurent, who lives in Montreuil, knows a great deal about the suburbs; with François's approval, he launches into a poetic evocation of their climatic mimicry. To the north, he says, you're already in the flatlands; here it's almost Touraine, the garden of France, with a hint of the South; while at Montreuil you can feel the snow and wolves of the eastern steppes, as if the pollution of Paris shields them from the Atlantic gales. Pascale, Laurent's wife, is desperate to know if they've got *an idea in mind*. They had forgotten about that question, it catches them increasingly on the hop, and François feels that replying 'No' elicits merely sarcastic scepticism. Laurent gives them so many friends' addresses for the rest of their journey, they feel that if they wanted to be just a little bit serious, it's by no means over.

They go back down to Bourg-la-Reine, where Camille and Yves Lacoste are waiting for them. They live a hundred metres from the station, just before the ornate minaret which is in truth a *belfry* and was built in 1904 by the engineer François Hennebique with the sole aim of demonstrating the potential of reinforced concrete. The Lacostes' building is a typically Parisian freestone construction from the late 1920s, like those you might find in rue de la Pompe or boulevard Raspail. What makes it slightly strange is that it stands there all by itself: protruding from each of its flanks is rubblework ready to couple with that of neighbours who never came. Yves was born there, and the apartment belonged to his father; his father was a geographer, he is a geographer, his sons are geographers. This solidity of things and permanence of human beings is reassuring.

François likes the way Yves can talk geopolitics and read a landscape at the same time, just as you find in the works of Julien Gracq all the mingled secrets of human anxieties and the folds in the earth's crust.

Before it goes dark, Yves takes them for a car ride: they drive back up towards Sceaux and Robinson. Camille tells them the strange effect Sceaux has on her today: it's like being in a dream similar to a famous American television serial, *The Invaders*, where you see a normal village with normal inhabitants, going about their normal business; and then the spectator realizes that everything is phoney, that it is the village but not the *real* village, and that they are the inhabitants but not the *real* inhabitants. Everything's artificial, slightly off-key: anxiety begins to worm its way in.

At Robinson, all that remains is the skeleton of a tree which housed a *guinguette*, and a big restaurant with a terrace overlooking the valley.

In the 1920s, the plateau at Plessis-Robinson was the site for the first garden estates, which, say suburban commentators today, are the utopia we should return to and make a reality. Was Laurent right when he said earlier that no one wanted to live there – gendarmes had to fill the housing: a familiar story – and that the architect, Payret-Dortal, committed suicide? Today, the few houses in the trees backing on to Parc

Henri Sellier are proud-looking, magnificent cubes with façades à la Chirico and Greek temple proportions. But further away, over the plateau towards the Butte Rouge, is a series of down-at-heel blocks, some of which have the ground floor walled up. A short while ago Laurent, who has never visited Drancy, referred to this kind of estate as a 'death camp'. Stretching out down below, a few hundred metres away as the crow flies, the sumptuous villas in Parc de Sceaux.

When this estate was built, Yves explains, it was far from everything. The rich settled on the valley's slopes and alongside the parks, and the poor were confined to exile on the edges of the plateau or the fringe of the Bois de Verrières, or unhealthy places like Les Blagis, built on a marsh on the edges of three villages: when he was a child, Les Blagis was already doomed to the disapproval of honest people; people used to say – and still do say – 'Blagis louts'. At that time, you could go down to Les Blagis from Bourg-la-Reine by a dirt track between raspberry bushes and nurseries of trees.

Later, in a mellow after-dinner mood made even more languid by the effects of a noble drink or two, a determined discussion rages: François digs in his heels, but Yves Lacoste persists: the Saint-Rémy–Limours section of the Ligne de Sceaux never existed.

The simplest thing would be to go and see.

*

MONDAY 5 JUNE. The tanks have crushed the last occupants of Tienanmen Square. 'They fired on anything that moved.' In Shanghai, a huge student demonstration with placards takes place on the Bund: 'Peking is drowning in blood.' Li Peng has resurfaced, and barely a glimmer of hope remains. President Mitterrand declares that 'a regime that shoots on its young has no future'. Roland Dumas announces that the European Community's foreign ministers are going to 'examine the situation in China in depth': to be continued.

They haven't seen any television pictures from Peking since they set off. This lack of pictures has proved an obstacle neither to getting information nor to emotion.

On the contrary, perhaps.

Today will be a long day. They will go first to Antony, to size up the one hotel, located in avenue du Bois de Verrières, where they have finally managed to call and reserve rooms. If everything is okay, they will come back in the evening to fetch their bags.

More train-changing at Bourg-la-Reine. In olden times they were already changing horses there: it was the first post house out of Paris. And the first hillside too: it was on the road to Bourg-la-Reine, the story goes, on Côte de le Faïencerie, that the busy bee buzzed around: La Fontaine wrote his fable 'La Mouche du Coche' ('The Busybody') at Sceaux. As with Le Bourget, coaching inn status soon gave the village its well-to-do appearance. At Antony, where place de la Gare is a building site – are they already preparing the installations for VAL, the automated metro that will link the RER and Orly airport? – they head off through the old village around Saint Saturnin's Church. The place is one huge building site: houses and streets are being totally renovated, old tiles have been pulled off and skilfully grouped together; it's going to be picturesque, full of shops, probably pedestrianized, smart, and expensive. Isn't there another way of safeguarding old stone?

A long walk towards the Bois de Verrières, whose dark mass can be made out as a distant silhouette. They cross the site of the famous, never-to-be-constructed Paris–Chartres line: in the 1950s the idea was to turn it into a link motorway which would have finished right at the foot of the future Montparnasse Tower. They have now run the TGV through in a cutting which has been covered over, and which, promise the on-site hoardings, will become a 'green stream'. For the moment it's a concrete stream and, as well as vegetation, they're going to need lots of green paint to honour this generous initiative. The hotel is a *café-tabac* set against a background of 1960s estates with grey high-rises. Shut: it's a Monday morning. No matter how hard they knock, the only reply comes from a monstrous hound baying, frothing and making huge leaps behind the glass door. Not a good sign. And this place is well out of the way, far from everything even. They'll come back later, they say. The hypocrites.

Who on earth must stay at this hotel?

Off they trek down the hungry road. In front of them is the massif of the wood, which owes its preservation to the fact that it was a key position in Paris's system of military defences. Today it has the reputation of being the refuge of all the turpitudes driven out of the Bois de Boulogne: don't go walking there at night, they say.

They turn left and leave this area of 'walls' and *pavillons* designed by poor men's architects only to find themselves, all of a sudden, in a newly built neighbourhood amidst a profusion of trees. A nicer sort of area. The buildings' dominant colour is red ochre, and the trees shade parks and gardens. The old village of Verrières is brand spanking new: very dinky. Everything's authentic. Everything's imitation. The château, an attractive little early-nineteenth-century building, was a shelter for the last years of Malraux, and of Louise de Vilmorin. She was heiress to the Vilmorin company of horticultural fame: all the seeds you need. Of all the glasshouses and nurseries famous on the five continents, no visible trace remains.

They stop off in the village. The restaurant is full of local workers and bourgeois, democratically mixed. They are among friends. Anaïk tries telephoning again. She widens the field of inquiry: a hotel at Villebon has rooms – this one is even further away, but seeing how far they've got, why not go and take a look? On the square, François, nose pointing skywards, watches the passing clouds blown along by the ocean winds and awaits the next shower. Water flows from an old pump into a drinking trough.

A car sticker reads:

> Live a stress-free life
> Fifteen minutes of
> transcendental meditation
> is all you need.

In the window of the (closed) tourist office, some small posters:

> Sunday 11 June
> For the Revolution bicentenary
> Pedal-cars
> A revolution at Verrières
> Entertainment, shows, sensations!
> Drinks, sandwiches, spicy sausages, crisps, chips.

And:

> INFORMATION
> As part of the poverty-borderline programme
> The SPF is organizing the distribution of basket-meals
> starting on 11 January 1989 at the Arts and Youth Club from 2 p.m.
> to 5 p.m.
> Proof of status required.

A poster for the Smiling Estates of Verrières-le-Buisson. Verrières has an 'urban property' park of an extravagance and variety that they haven't so far encountered, including concrete flowertubs.

They admire a plough surrounded by flowers behind a garden fence, its wheels and double ploughshare (called a *'brabant'*) artistically painted in bright colours (pink and dark garnet red? Emerald green and absinthe green?); the owner tells of a time when Verrières was strawberry country. Hard work, strawberries: when the pickers were dead-beat after a day's work, they still had to stay up late putting them in baskets, one by one, stalk-up, and covering each basket with sorrel leaves to keep them cool.

It was the same flat-out slog in winter for the Brussels sprouts. His father was a farmer. When the farm was sold, his brother went to farm land in the Loiret. This *brabant* was one of four belonging to the family business. They were still using it in the fifties, pulled by a German army tractor.

Here they are not taken for journalists from the local magazine, or for council shit-stirrers: people think they're house-hunting.

They head back south across the plateau, towards the Plaine de Massy. Farewell pretty village and peaceful *pavillons*. At the bottom is a filthy little artificial lake where a few anglers are lying in wait for degenerate goldfish (the albino roach, perhaps): this is where the Bièvre dives into its sewer. To their right is the green Bièvre Valley, and up above on the other side is the plateau at Saclay, which, thanks to the presence of the nuclear research centre, remains the only farming land so close to Paris. But not for much longer. Beyond the TGV tracks, which at this point run past on an embankment covered with concrete slabs, bleak recent high-rises. Wedged down below is Cité de Villaine with its recent population – in other words, largely immigrant. We're back in the real twentieth century. They have friends in Villaine: they'll be back.

Back to Massy-Verrières on the train, then change again at Bourg-la-Reine: it's the six o'clock stampede. In a recess in the underground passage at Bourg-la-Reine, a policeman is standing guard; he calls to Anaïk, who jumps, and gives her a hearty telling-off: she's crazy to walk around with her camera so visible. François can't entirely blame him.

And finally, two hours later, in a fine drizzle, they arrive back at Palaiseau-Villebon station. The millstone chalet still bears its big faded grey plank sign on which the passing years – a half-century? A century? – have almost erased the black and white letters that are still trying to convince us that Switzerland is near Paris. Let's hope it has been registered on the inventory of historic monuments, just like the one at Honfleur announcing the Ocean Channel Chemist and its infallible seasickness remedy. Naturally the hotel is a long way off – on the boundary with Lozère, the next stop down the line.

They walk through empty streets as night falls, accompanied by a grand canine chorus; sober *pavillons* and small residential flats in the trees. Through the windows, the flickering bluish light of televisions. The hotel is strange: an old mill on the banks of the Yvette, its empty courtyard adorned with wisteria. They are the only guests. At the end of the long dark corridor under the rafters are their huge connecting bedrooms, and the beds are impressively huge, and countless are the glasses in the bathroom. The owner is taciturn and unshaven. There is nothing to eat – the hotel restaurant is closed on Mondays. The place has the bizarre atmosphere of an inn far from human life, outside of time. Something like the Auberge des Adrets. At school there was a classic dictation (from Mérimée? Or Dumas?) which related the fears of a traveller who, alone in his room at an isolated country inn, heard lugubrious preparations in the middle of the night: the innkeepers were sharpening a knife and talking about cutting throats. But whose throat? His? In the morning it was revealed that they had killed the pig, that they were good people, etc. They will sleep peacefully here in Villebon, for the days of killing pigs are gone.

*

Today they have rounded off their third week. This day of long walks went on for ever: grey estates and renovated estates, endless *pavillon* developments, shopping centres, administrative complexes in the middle of imitation old villages, conversations on street corners and in bars, encounters in gardens, behind fences, building sites, face-lifts, depredation, Palais de Chaillot-style stations, Swiss chalet-style stations, public urinal-style stations, streams of vile tags sprayed on the smallest strip of virgin concrete and even on seats in trains, big pathetic graffiti nearly always using dark blue, grey, black, sending out to the millions of gazes that skim past them each year without really seeing them a cry of loneliness, and sometimes of tenderness too.

Anaïk has barely taken any photos, François is now irretrievably behind with his notes. 'This journey,' says Anaïk, 'is as tiring as a film shoot where there'll be no film.' Palaiseau-Villebon is stagnating. Yes, they've got that sinking feeling.

Isn't this inn a charming resting-place? Charming, or rather absurd, this rural and desolate spot, lost deep in the *pavillons* of the new town? François spreads out his playing cards to try a game of patience called 'pharaoh', the only one he knows. Anaïk reads him an old article from *Le Monde*, which, she says, can only pander to his security urges and which they should remember when they catch the RER:

> The main danger encountered by the tourist is of being relieved of his belongings. One very unpleasant method is linked to the thieves' use of scopolamine. This ancient Colombian narcotic was rediscovered in Europe by the Nazi 'scientists' and since then has been used by certain special services as a truth drug. It has the power to neutralize the subject's will and to make him amnesiac for two or three days. During this time, the victim is entirely dependent on the person manipulating him. It is therefore recommended – and this means curtains for conviviality, alas! – to accept no fruit or sweets of any sort from a travelling companion; and also, at stopping places, to keep an eye on your glass of beer or Coca-Cola.
>
> On the other hand, the guerrillas do not attack the tourist.

I know it's supposed to happen in Colombia, but still . . .

François has yet another crack at his notes. In particular he should spell out in black and white what has probably been the most important event of this sad day: at Massy-Verrières they glimpsed the Atlantic TGV emerging from a tunnel. A brand-new TGV, which will not be put into service until next autumn. Their eyes followed the magical blue-and-steel apparition as it disappeared all too quickly – the world's fastest train, a great French success story; they almost had tears in their eyes. To try and control this wave of loco-emotion, François sought to reduce the wonder to more reasonable proportions:

'It's okay, I suppose, but it'll never be a patch on engineer Bertin's airtrain, whose concrete monorail still stretches out its bony silhouette over the Plaine d'Etampes. (Come to think of it, isn't it on the Plaine de Limours where it runs along the route – but of course! – of the Saint-Rémy–Limours section? He'll have to check up on that!) Now that really *did* break new ground. And what about the invention of engineer Brokenface?'

Let us remind ourselves at this juncture that engineer Brokenface's invention was unveiled at the *Columbian Exhibition* at Chicago in 1894. Its creator had got the idea while watching a performance of *Michael Strogoff*: there were horses galloping on a surface moving in the opposite direction, which had the effect of keeping them centre-stage for the greater satisfaction of the audience. Engineer Brokenface then remembered that if two opposing speeds cancel each other out, two speeds going in the same direction could only add up: it would thus suffice to spread out, right along the distance to be covered, a conveyor belt on which, by an ingenious mechanism, would be placed a second belt, on which would be placed a third belt, and so on. By transmitting to each of these successive moving levels a suitable speed – say 180 kilometres per hour, which is really not at all excessive – you obtain, by simply superimposing ten conveyor belts, a constant speed of 1800 kilometres per hour, to which nothing stops you adding the personal speed of each passenger using the upper bridge, if the mood takes him: some prefer to stay inert, while others cannot resist the pleasure of accelerating up to 1818 kilometres per hour by hiring a bicycle at the station of departure.

One can see that this process, simpler and far quicker than the TGV – Bordeaux would be twenty minutes from Paris, Marseille half an hour away – would also have been much more practical and healthy, since it would have spared passengers from being shut up in a confined space, allowing them instead the joy of an exhilarating taster of the great outdoors.

The silence that enshrouded this invention is one of the century's great scandals. Only Alphonse Allais had the courage, nearly a hundred years ago, to brave vested interests by publicly demonstrating the Brokenface process.

Now he is up and running, François decides to trace the outline of an ambitious

GRAND RAILWAY POEM

the details of which we will this time spare the reader.

They'd better be getting some shuteye, each in a bed as vast as Lake Baikal and as deep as the tomb. Birdsong will wake them in the early morning.

*

TUESDAY 6 JUNE. From now on, the wear and tear of the passing days, the tiring walks, the jumble of memories, the rambling nature of François's notes, which will soon disappear completely, all contribute to the fact that nothing remains of the last stages of their journey save a web of which only Anaïk's photos will help to untangle a few threads. That's if they're lucky, for try telling whether this face in close-up or this group of youths is from Massy or Les Ulis; try telling the difference between concrete at Gentilly and at Fontaine-Michalon.

Nevertheless, we can be confident that on that Tuesday and the days

Croix-de-Berny

that followed, they were seen surveying Fresnes and Antony in the rain without really knowing which side of the boundary they were on. They took refuge for a while in the dark and empty Café-Hôtel de la Gare at Croix-de-Berny, to ponder and try to photograph the curious effect created from the café by the RER going over the bridge just opposite: the café forms a spur facing the traffic on the trunk road going to Rungis market and Orly; this road has actually been left to the bulldozers, and when the repairs are finished it will have turned into the A86 motorway; the room is raised and thus on the same level as the RER tracks, giving the impression that every time a train goes past it will barely miss the people drinking at the bar. It seems that our travellers didn't inquire about bedrooms at that particular hotel.

They were seen going on to Antony's university campus, whose occupants are not particularly hospitable towards intruders. François knew it when it was brand new in the sixties. Many students have spent happy days there: the level of comfort was unheard-of for the period; you had peace and quiet there, looking out over Parc de Sceaux; you could work there, eat in the cafeteria – a rare luxury at the time – and do sport. There were study rooms on the ground floor, a library for each subject and a teaching adviser for each subject too. In short, this campus couldn't help but be a great success. A model for the entire world. Today a large part of the buildings has been destroyed, and what is left is appallingly run down. For students from the provinces and abroad, this campus truly heralded brighter tomorrows. For the last ten years numerous campaigns have condemned the campus's lack of security, its being taken over by squatters, etc. The last occupants are waging the same desperate struggle as everyone living in areas that have been declared unhealthy: so here is a university campus relegated to the status of a poverty zone like Châlon. The usual explanations are exchanged: 'They're not real students. They don't pay their rent. The immigrants have wrecked everything.' And in the other corner: 'We've sat and watched everything go to pot. We even helped things along.'

In any case, on the site of B-block rises a gleaming building close to completion:

Coming soon
The ANTONY BUSINESS CENTRE
SOFRACIM is developing
20,000 m^2 of offices.

Antony's council is run by the Gaullist RPR Party.

They were seen walking past the walls of Fresnes Prison, which runs along avenue de la Liberté, and looking for the café called *Ici mieux qu'en face* ('Better here than over the road'). And they noticed that Fresnes is the only place where people never talk about prisons: they met locals who assured them that they still wondered if their neighbours across the landing, whom they had lived next to for fifteen years and who were state employees and sometimes worked nights, might not 'perhaps' be prison officers.

They were seen going up to the ecology museum housed in an old farm, which mounts such fine exhibitions: one of them was devoted to the frog in all its states. They learned that Fresnes was once famous for its frogs, so much so that the locals were called 'froggies'. People used to go there to eat frogs from Paris and elsewhere. Around 1900, more than 30,000 batrachians were being consumed during the frog season, which, as everyone knows, runs from February to Easter. There was even a Paris butchers' society which gathered every year at Restaurant de la Mère Fifine to drink white wine drawn from a tureen with a frog swimming in it.

They were seen getting lost in the vast Antony housing development, which is symmetrically opposite the big Massy development; together they form one of the biggest schemes of the Delouvrier Plan. Its priority was to accommodate repatriates from North Africa. Then came other French people from the overseas territories, West Indians especially. The buildings have been given a face-lift with yellow paint, taking away none of the monotony which here reaches grandiose proportions.

They were seen at their friend Philippe's, known as Fifi, in his ground-floor flat in a Cité de Villaine high-rise, which he has entirely converted to be able to get into and around in his wheelchair. Fifi is a sports fanatic, with a special passion for athletics: he can lift enormous weights. He used to live in the XIVth arrondissement, and is part of the Paris population that has been relocated in the last few years. Here in Villaine, on this new Massy estate which to him seemed like the world's end, he has made all kinds of friends, particularly youngsters, because he's bursting with a lust for life. For and against everything. That evening they chatted for a long time after dinner over a stream of bottles of West Indian rum – at the local supermarket you can find the biggest selection of West Indian spirits in the world – and his young neighbour Faouzi, and Faouzi's mates, told them about life in Massy, and then wanted to know how the journey was going; because several months earlier, Faouzi had been one of the first, along with Akim, to take them seriously: 'It'll be great going everywhere and seeing how people live. There's so much variety.' For him, Massy was almost provincially calm compared to the slightly mythical North: 'It's Zulu country up there.' Even the Villaine gangs don't make the grade. In the South, the only really mean guys are from Les Ulis. It's hardly surprising; they're miles from everything up there. They're out of their minds, coming on raids down here to smash everything up: you have to stand up to them, and people are going to get killed. That lot are real savages. One of these days we'll have to go and get reinforcements from La Courneuve. After all, with the RER the La Courneuve lot will be here in no time. Faouzi was born in Palaiseau. What about the Tunisia where his parents come from? It seems a long way off. Faouzi's thinking about his exams, his electrician's course, his future profession. Having a solid trade, being able to travel from time to time, educating himself, but, like Ulysses, coming back home. To Massy.

They were seen going up to Palaiseau fort, gazing upon the wheatfields in Saclay, walking among the *pavillons*: there they passed a young lad tottering about so badly, so atrociously lost in some nightmare, banging into walls and trees and almost falling over with every step, that they trailed him at a distance through the empty streets, wondering if, and how, they should help him, until a man coming to meet him insulted them violently, asking them to mind their own business; and they didn't know how to explain that that was just what they thought they were doing. And never had they felt so bitter a loneliness as in the well-to-do neighbourhood of upper Palaiseau.

They were seen more than once on the platforms of Antony station, a narrow concrete passageway where the superimposed tags and graffiti were getting extremely dense: one of the greyest, most deprived places in the world. Perhaps it was there, once while they were waiting gloomily for a KNOC or a PSIT, that they deciphered this article from the RATP regulations:

People disabled in both hands may travel free of charge in any class without a ticket.

They were seen reading and rereading the large poster summoning the masses for the GRAND EQUALITY CONCERT, 'Everyone come along to Vincennes on Sunday 10 June', and maybe they could even be heard saying they were upset to have come across so little music on their journey, except the stuff that sticks to you like glue in shopping centres, while all over the suburbs people are making music, real hard-hitting music.

They were seen finding rooms, at last, at Hôtel de la Poste in Massy town centre. They left the inn at Villebon without having been able to shed light on whether the owner really was unshaven or whether it was the combined effect of his skin's usual texture and the pervading murkiness. But in truth they shed no light on any of the secrets of this

hotel, which remained clientless for the three days they stayed there, except for one lone silent guest who, one evening in the huge shadowy dining-room, was perhaps as helpless as they were – a hotel where they passed no one in the corridors except whispering ghosts. A good setting for a Simenon novel?

In Massy they were seen roaming alone round the big pond where frogs and swans have been put, and where reflected in the water are the new glass-and-steel town hall buildings. It was there, as night was falling, that François was panic-stricken to see rushing towards him a group of individuals in jeans, basketball pumps and blousons, carrying various blunt instruments and shouting gleefully. Once the alarm was past, he realized, seeing them go into one extremity of this modern architectural jewel, that they were local policemen.

Sometimes they would mechanically raise their noses and gape at the jumbos and airbuses flying very low over the Plaine d'Antony to Palaiseau, for the latter is on the Orly flight path, and by this one reflex a passer-by could tell that they were new to the area.

They were seen eating pizzas in the huge, half-empty dining-room of an Italian restaurant in Massy's new town centre, a centre made of concrete, glass, ceramics and steel organized round a large square of Ceauşescu-esque proportions.

They were seen walking down the deserted flowering streets of Gif-sur-Yvette, and you could even have heard François mumbling that living behind the fences of the smart *pavillons* must be a fair number of his old

254

authors, from the time when he published people who have since become leading lights at the Centre National de la Recherche Scientifique; but he never dared knock on their doors, he was too afraid that they wouldn't recognize him. And that he wouldn't recognize them either.

They were seen on the premises of the psychiatric hospital at Orsay, where a psychologist friend of Anaïk's works. No one knew exactly what they were doing there, and neither did they. An inquiry into mental health in the Essonne, perhaps? Such a terrible lack of notes . . .

They were seen. . . . When the fine weather returned, they were seen walking up from La Hacquinière station – a long way away, nearly the end of the line already – towards the handsome villas dominating the small valley with Gometz-le-Châtel perched on the side. They even turned down a lady driving past in the car who charitably offered to 'take you a bit nearer' – but nearer to where, and to what?, their refusal proving that they were no longer really looking for contact with their fellow humans. They spent the most bucolic day of their expedition, lost deep in the French countryside. And standing by the church they discovered something as precious as a rainbow: a landscape. The harmonious lines of the woods, footpaths taking flight across fields and meadows, a few villages nestling in the trees, and far away, the high-rises of Les Ulis. They hadn't seen such a complete landscape since Villepinte; just the odd piece here and there, like at Arcueil, like the château terrace at Sceaux, like at Robinson, suggesting that there had actually once been a landscape there in due form. This one was in perfect working order, amazingly well preserved for its age.

Walking through the wood they surprised a squirrel, and they agreed that what was perhaps missing most from the streets of the Paris suburbs was squirrels in the trees, as you find in so many other cities, such as Montreal or Warsaw. Let's face it: humanizing the housing estates depends on squirrels. At Gometz-le-Châtel they also noted that the tags didn't even spare the tombs in cemeteries. From there they walked across the plateau towards Les Ulis. Travelling through the Yvette Valley, near Gif, you discover Les Ulis from the train by lifting your gaze towards the top of the plateau: a few high-rises appear in a dent in the woods – what's that tall far-off estate doing there? When you get there, you find yourself in a new town of fifteen thousand people living by the Aquitaine-bound motorway and the recently built Courtaboeuf industrial estate. Les Ulis was conceived thirty years ago with a view to mixing the scientists working at Gif, where the CNRS was then settling, and Renault workers transported to work by coach. The motorway hadn't yet been built, and the first occupants remember the mud during these years, the train they had to go and catch a long way off down at Orsay, then the slow birth of their town, with its park, its green avenues, its peace and quiet. Les Ulis was all built on a big concrete base: cars are supposed to drive round on avenues in cuttings which you cross over on footbridges. The inhabitants' imaginations have located a thousand phantasmagorias beneath the concrete. Some are real: the lady who told them about the burglars who'd stolen everything hadn't dreamed that they got in through the basement.

At Les Ulis the building continues: flats and *pavillons* 'for first-time buyers'. Buying a home is not necessarily a sign of prosperity: the opposite might be true, for it is often the only way of getting decent accommodation, of escaping from the hell of furnished rooms and dodgy digs for families who have been turned down by all the housing offices. (For many reasons, the most frequent of which is the foreigners quota. Is it a secret? Not exactly.) Unlike the housing offices, private developers and estate agents don't worry about the colour of people's money. People pay them a deposit, though not necessarily a big one, and get into debt for thirty years. Or longer. Don't you need solvency guarantees? It's always possible to arrange one. Then the legal departments set to work until the owner is evicted, if there are grounds. Where are they evicted to? Still further away, beyond the boundaries of the department and region, to other dumping towns – the same old story.

Outside the Jacques Prévert Centre, where newly released films are shown, where you can see international shows on tour, some youngsters told them they were bored at Les Ulis, that Les Ulis was far away from everything; others said how much they liked living in a town that's in the country, in a town where they're close to everything – sports, culture, and so on – and how sick they were of always hearing people say that Les Ulis was the dregs of the suburbs and a dumping ground, of being marked out on the Paris streets as louts up from the suburbs; they had to change all that, they said, and they would do it together.

At Les Ulis, when our travellers sat down in the hubbub of the one open café and Anaïk ordered a coffee, the owner surprised them with the touching reply: 'And won't you be having a glass of cold water as well?'

They were seen. . . . In short, it's time the journey ended.

*

After all, as Anaïk says, journeys aren't just for giving yourself memories. They're for making you want to go back.

. . . And finally, on *Sunday 11 June*, under a glaring sun, they found themselves in place du Marché d'Orsay, where a big second-hand fair is held. A cheerful crowd squeezed between the sad displays of humble, personal things. Stuck on the objects were sale prices far removed from their true value. Here and there, a few broken *vistemboirs*, unidentifiable things. Anaïk acquired on François's behalf a job lot of postcards whose common thread is that they are all addressed by or to members of the Bernart family from Crosnes in the Department of Seine-et-Oise. François had spotted them scattered in a large box which he started to examine absent-mindedly. But the stallholder cottoned on to his ploy and, convinced that François had very good reason to be interested in the Bernart family, not only refused to do one price for the lot but visibly upped his individual price. So Anaïk sneaked back and bought about thirty cards for 100 francs. 'There were definitely others, but he was starting to get suspicious again.' It would then be up to François to piece together the family tree of the Bernarts and their fate, from the first card dated 1910, when young Jean Bernart was a boarder with the good fathers of Compiègne, to the last in 1948, which is addressed to Madame Bernart, his wife and maybe already a widow, who writes laconically: 'Please bring vegetables.' Along the way is a 1918 letter which sees Jean in the army as a squadron sergeant major, and a 1941 'interzone' card ('delete as appropriate') sent by his widow Isorel, who, in the only line free at the bottom of the form, expresses her sincere condolences. For whose death? Jean's? And was his sister Cécile the last of her generation to die? Was it her attic that was emptied to scatter the family's secrets in the four winds of the fair? And what became of little Denise, who was at a holiday camp in 1936? What slightly complicates the untangling of this web of lives is that the Bernart family have this habit of sending each other messages, be it from Suresnes or the XIVth arrondissement in Paris, on cards showing views of Rome, Munich or Brussels; the ecclesiastical uncle is particularly fond of this practice.

Some day, then, François will devote himself to a more precise reconstruction of this half-century of lives, shamefully washed up on the stall of a grasping seller of old things, who was scornful and harsh – so harsh that they were able to save only a few fragments.

Are there any takers (at 450 francs) for this big framed diploma, awarded in 1931 by the Minister for Industry and Commerce to Madame Di Agostino, Maria-Melba, forewoman at Male, Fosse and Sons of Montrouge, 'by way of reward for her long and devoted service to the same company'? Whose living-room walls will be decorated with all that remains of the working life of Maria-Melba, like the stag's antlers on the walls of country houses?

*

The single track at the end of Saint-Rémy station was closed for a long time by a level crossing which was always down. This has now been replaced by a fence, which looks more permanent. The tracks carry on over

the Limours road and disappear into the trees towards de Coubertin's château. A small shed, immediately on the right by the ballast, has for over a year served as shelter for Monsieur Maurice, who is in fact seated in front of his bottle of red wine and his Camembert, and with whom Anaïk immediately strikes up a friendship. Monsieur Maurice has long since lost his job, and catches the RER every day to go begging in the Luxembourg district of Paris; he comes back here away from human beings, unknown to them as they're unknown to him, on nights which, in winter, are hard. They carry on along the rusty rails, passing a scout patrol in Indian file following their trail and holding their totem high; and here is the buffer, the end of the track. Beyond it is a jungle, into which the scouts dive.

Later, Anaïk and François cut through the woods and walked across the Chevreuse Valley, drowsily digesting its Sunday afternoon, climbed up towards the plateau via Château de la Madeleine, trekked through still more woods, and walked back down to Milon-la-Chapelle.

'To talk about Milon,' says François, 'I'd need another entire book.' In the meantime, today's the day Julia celebrates her birthday, and the troupe of children is there, waiting for the worn-out travellers outside the gate of the family home.

The journey is over.

At this moment François realizes that he never did buy the barometer-flower in the end.

Postface 1993

It is now four years since the journey ended, and three years since I finished writing this book. In the meantime both of us, François and Anaïk, have carried on going our own ways. We have often taken the RER line again, separately and sometimes together; and will certainly continue to do so, like our ordinary fellow citizens, until the day we die. We have even glimpsed a passenger reading *Les passagers du Roissy-Express*. In four years the scenery has changed very quickly, and it just keeps on changing. Some places are already unrecognizable. I frequently ask myself the question: Would I write the same book today? Or rather: Would I, quite simply, still be able to write it? When I'm feeling pessimistic, which is most of the time, I tend to reply that I wouldn't, and not only because of the scenery.

What has surprised the authors is not so much that the book has met with a certain success – what author would honestly admit that his work didn't deserve success? – but the very nature of that success. I had foreseen and feared every possible reaction: that the inhabitants of the suburbs who read these pages would not recognize themselves or their world, and would even find it distorted and falsified by the view of this Parisian tourist; that the serious newspapers would find us lightweight and the less serious ones ridiculously pedantic; that the press in general would find us offhand, scornful popularity-seekers with regard to the basic problems – security, drugs and immigration, the eternal trilogy which people on the Left like to precede by unemployment, the root of all evil; that sociologists would be sickened by our aim of skimming over such a dense network of complex detail in a single month, material which requires from them an entire lifetime's study; and that architects and urban planners would be offended to see their work dealt with in a few general remarks worthy of the local launderette. And I was perfectly sincere in these fears. Though I didn't feel beforehand that everyone was entirely right, they had a stack of reasons to be. My fears proved groundless. I repeat: it wasn't so much being showered with compliments which seemed so unusual, but receiving them from all sides, in a touching climate of kindness and fellow feeling which I would describe as ecumenical. Being the miseries we are, we decided to remain suspicious. A few insults would have reassured us. All these people seemed too polite to be honest. It remains to be seen what they were hiding.

*

We have received many readers' letters, and are still receiving them. Some pointed out mistakes in a friendly way: I was too quick to pass the death sentence on Le Corbusier's radiant estate at Briey in Lorraine; by the time I had written my book, it had miraculously been saved. I have rectified this point in the present edition. One reader supplied me with precious information about the Ligne de Sceaux's original gauge. Another gave me such precise details about the famous Battle of the Bièvre between Camulogenus the Gaul and Caesar's armies that I could have sworn he was there. One reader, finally, caused me much shame and embarrassment: she reproached me for not mentioning the debt we owed to Julio Cortàzar and to *Les Autonautes de la Cosmoroute*, his account of the month-long journey he made with his friend Carol Dunlop from Paris to Marseille, from one rest area to another without ever going outside them. How right this reader was, though it wasn't forgetfulness on my part. I owe a great deal to *le grand Conope* – and if I hadn't read that book, perhaps I would never even have dared to write mine. There are, however, major differences between us, beginning of course with the literary dimension. There was a pathetic quality about Julio's and Carol's adventure, living *l'amour fou* in one final race against death – they both knew they were doomed by illness, and it was Cortàzar's last book. This flight into a world where space is reduced to a line a hundred metres wide, where, as on a graph, time and space come together at zero and cancel each other out, was for them the last way to be together, to feel life beating inside them in all its abundance and absurdity. I know that any journey, even the tiniest, is nothing other than an attempt, conscious or otherwise, to flee death. But we, on the other hand, wanted our little journey to be open to life, on the look-out for each piece of ground we covered, eager for encounters in both past and present, outstretched as much as possible towards the future. Ours is not a book of love but, more modestly, a book of friendship. If, under these conditions, I didn't wish to call upon Cortàzar for inspiration, it is because it would have seemed to me almost like a breach of trust.

That said, virtually all our readers' letters were heart-warming. Every one, whatever its length, is like our journey being continued, a chapter being extended, a fresh episode being added – so much so that I thought for a moment of compiling an anthology.

First there are those readers, our brothers and sisters, who love unusual journeys. Of these, first prize unanimously goes to the couple who live in the suburbs and have decided to spend their holidays once a year in Paris: twenty arrondissements in twenty years. But not any old how: they would explore the streets, avenues, squares and boulevards, etc., one after the other, *in alphabetical order*. There is also the railway journey fanatic who insisted on linking Brest (Brittany) to Brest (Ukraine). And having got that far, he took the Trans-Siberian Express to Vladivostok, even making sure, while changing stations in Moscow, to take the tram so as not to go off the rails – and all with the aim of pouring a phial of water from the Atlantic which he had brought with him into the Pacific, and measuring whether their tide levels changed as a result. There is the singing, velocipedal madman from Aubervilliers who rode down the banks of the Seine to Le Havre, handing out the poems he wrote along the way (it seems he practises the art of pedalling without holding the handlebars). There is the Swiss group whose followers, who never meet otherwise, are given a rendezvous every year at some isolated station in the Massif Central: on the appointed day they get off the same train without saying a word, contemplate the landscape, and depart again on the next train, content until the following year. In the meantime they will have penned their strong impressions for a limited-edition bulletin which they do me the honour of sending, for they have made me an honorary member of their association. There is . . .

There are those, more seriously, who wrote to us explaining that as they lived at some point along the line and used it daily, they had long had the same idea without ever deciding to carry it out: weary of contemplating the same stations morning and evening, they dreamed of getting off one day and going to see what lay behind them. They were thanking us for doing it for them. Some have shown more resolve, and I received the account of the journey a class of schoolchildren made, under its teacher's leadership, from Villepinte to Le Bourget.

Last but not least, we have had letters from, and met, people of all ages who, quite simply, seem happy that someone has talked about where they live in terms other than a lament on the theme of 'the problem of the suburbs', and wanted to make their contribution to our story. Many of them are over sixty. That is the age when memories start to compete with the present, and the theme is always the same: 'You could write a book about my life . . .' The book of generations that have seen humanity change more in half a century than in two thousand years. Nostalgia is weighed against clear-sightedness: people are nostalgic for the wide-open spaces of the Ile de France, for the rhythm of the seasons, for the rituals of a society built over the centuries; but conscious that life was hard for humble folk less than fifty years ago, acknowledging, always to their slight amazement, something which is always moving in its banality – that today's comforts, unheard-of for those who experienced the hard times of work in the fields and man-crushing factories, in no way bring happiness but generate fresh worries about the future.

Yes, it's as though the book were never finished.

*

As I said, we were well received by the press, yet strangely, it felt like such a fiasco! The bigger the media audience, the more we could be sure to see the article or interview start with this devastating remark of great sociological import: 'Anaïk Frantz and François Maspero had the original idea of walking round completely unexplored places a stone's throw from civilized life ...' With these few words, all we had tried to do and say went out of the window. What does it matter if most of France's population now lives in the suburbs, to such an extent that France itself, including its remotest subprefectures, is just one big suburb, and that its town centres are but a pale relic of prehistoric times and an artificial shop window of modern times? We had plunged into the unknown, the unknown where all of us live. It was a simple idea. You just had to think of it. I actually read or heard the expression 'the Christopher Columbus of the suburbs' on several occasions. As a result we were bombarded with tempting offers: it was suggested a good ten times that we do the trip again, in the company of a journalist or a television crew. Quickly, of course. In a day, if possible. Visiting the most picturesque spots, getting people to say those essential, moving little things. Our refusal was not appreciated, even less our suggestion: we've done it by ourselves, now you do it. You don't need us. Anyone can do it. It takes just as much trouble as making a family album. A little goodwill, a little openness, above all a little time. But it seems that those people don't have the time.

The well-to-do liked our book because it was reassuring. One of the standard types of discourse on the suburbs is ultimately no more than a continuation of the nineteenth-century line on the lower depths and the dangerous classes. Eugène Sue's *Mysteries of Paris* have been replaced by the mysteries of the suburbs. We came along saying that they weren't as mysterious as all that, and people were relieved; they could breathe again. Here at last was someone who didn't talk in terms of a catastrophe. It seemed that people had only been waiting for us to remark that the suburbs are populated by decent people, and that with decent people you can always get on. This sort of thing reached a pinnacle when the President of the Republic, opening the 'Estates-General of the suburbs' in Bron, near Lyon, quoted our book as an example – inaccurately, of course, telling a cock-and-bull story about bored Roissy youngsters waiting in a bus shelter: they have nowhere to get together. So, says the President, they bravely decide to take matters in hand and create their own youth centre from scratch. The necessary conclusion: take matters in hand, etc. In this edifying story you will have recognized the passage in chapter 1, where Anaïk tells how she had met some bored youngsters. They were bored, full stop. And as I write these words, they probably still are. The rest is presidential humbug. I should add that we were invited to Bron, to meditate on the suburbs and listen reverently to this speech. With loads of competent people. We didn't go. We didn't go anywhere. Either to the urban planning institutes or the think-tanks, or to the meetings of experts who opened their doors to us. It's crazy how many meetings there have been in recent years to reflect on the problems of the suburbs. Their reflections must have been pretty thin if they needed amateurs like us. But we were no longer amateurs: publishing a book had instantly made specialists of us. That's what dismayed us most. If they take people like us seriously, we kept saying to ourselves, they must be further up the creek than we thought. And it's true, they are. But what more could we add? So Anaïk has returned to her photos, to her friends the tramps and to the everyday poverty that's rising, rising, and just goes on rising, without bothering whether it's in Paris or outside; and of course she isn't selling any more of her photos. And François has been off to explore other horizons, in the East particularly, in that Europe in the heart of Europe, which the real Europe, the one with a flag and an Assembly, sees as its limits, its outermost bounds, its suburbs. But that's another story.

*

As I said, the scenery has changed greatly in four years. The enormous efforts – and there is no question of making fun of them – undertaken to homogenize so many 'species of spaces', to join them together, to give them continuity, a meaning – in a word, to make life livable – have been pursued: the A86 motorway loop is progressing; a tramway now connects the prefectures of Saint-Denis and Bobigny; the TGV station at Massy-Palaiseau to the south is open, and Roissy's to the north soon will be; real town centres, such as those at Saint-Denis and Massy, have taken on an authentic urban profile.

For anyone who takes the RER today, the landscapes of the Plaine de France and Aubervilliers are already unrecognizable. New 'poles' are bursting out of the ground. At the same time, the magical towers of EuroDisney have shot up to the east and now attract their share of tourists, who are protected from the miasma outside by watchtowers and barbed wire. Apparently EuroDisney is in a bad way. To give business a boost, its merry cast members should seriously think about including in the ticket price guided tours of the Louvre, the Musée Picasso and the Paris sewers.

In recent years, the suburbs have been studied more than ever before. The creation in 1991 of a Ministry of the Town initially gave great hope to all those working out in the field – urban planners, local councillors, social organizers: at last so much dispersed effort and goodwill were going to be co-ordinated and encouraged. At the same time, the worsening economic crisis undermined those hopes and reduced the best that the Ministry could offer to makeshift solutions. Sporadic demonstrations by young people revived discourse about '*la sécurité*' at the right moment. It's a dialogue of the deaf: in reply to the stereotypical line – now official and quasi-dominant – on the '*insécurité*' of the suburbs, the suburban 'ghettos', young people speak of their own experience of '*l'insécurité*': they feel insecure about employment, which rules out any projects, any thought of the future; and unsafe faced with the violence of tight police control.

The Gulf War in 1991 marked a decisive watershed, a kind of point of no return. We saw a remarkable self-indoctrination of public opinion. The argument was simple: we were waging war against the Arabs (or the Muslims: standard politician-speak makes no distinction between the two), and the suburbs were populated by Arabs, or children of Arabs vulgarly called '*beurs*': so outbursts of violence were to be expected in the suburbs. Yet – what a surprise! – nothing happened. This was reassuring. Our Arabs had turned out to be good Arabs. They had no deep sympathy for Saddam Hussein and his regime. True, but things weren't quite so simple. The Gulf War left a scar which is no less deep for having remained concealed. During this time, faced with the discourse of distrust being addressed to them, French people with a North African name experienced a sense of rejection which many of them felt to be definitive. Although they were born in France, speaking only French most of the time (and of course a little English, since they've all been to the lycée) and nurtured on the fine principles of integration, what had until then only been whispered was suddenly thrown in their faces, or at least spelled out officially: they were suspect. Suspect in the eyes of 'real' French people, of course, but not just them. On the other side of the Mediterranean, they were equally suspect in the eyes of the peoples their parents were descended from; suspect, and even traitors to the Arab cause. Rejected by the French, who refused to let them be French; rejected by the Arabs, who refused to let them be Arabs. Humiliated. With no way out. That scar won't heal in a hurry.

What's become of the characters in the book? I will take three examples. Akim, who had studied theatre, was one of the Aubervilliers Theatre Group's driving forces, and was rehearsing 'Straight from the Heart of La Courneuve' during our visit, decided in a fit of anger to drop everything: he took a cab-driver's licence. His friend Catherine, with whom he used to live, got in his cab by chance one day: he saw her in his mirror, and all through the journey, flushed with rage, he refused to speak to her. He had told us that Aubervilliers was great as long as you'd got out. He hasn't. A reader from La Courneuve has given us news of Daoud, who wanted the tower block tenants to paint the landscapes of their dreams on their landings. He ended up exasperating the council officials whose orders he was working under; he was made redundant and has gone back on drugs – and probably to his thuggish devices. He had never really got out of Aubervilliers, and has now plunged back into it for good. Finally Rachid, big, magnificent and generous Rachid, continues down the road of monumental sculpture and is enjoying international success. He refuses to talk about his origins. He thinks it harms his career. He has understood that the main thing wasn't getting out of Aubervilliers, even though you mustn't return there.

I will also say a few words about other characters in the book, though not in the flesh. I want to talk about those people who, from the most modest up to the highest level, work in the social fabric. First of all the grass-roots workforce, sometimes enthusiastic but often despairing, whether they are based in the local clubs or the various kinds of sociocultural centre. It cannot be said too often, over and above the fine intentions and fine speeches, to what extent they and they alone maintain, in the face of so many difficulties, a social cohesion which is constantly on the verge of breaking down and shattering; and they do it with bits of string, sticking plaster and four sous' worth of subsidies, forever moaning and depressed. Next the local councillors – at least those who still believe, despite the modish devaluing of everything political, that only politics in the etymological sense of the term can forge the towns and help them survive and make progress. Finally there are the architects, tirelessly searching for formulas to help us escape from the 'storage years' which produced all those factories for sleep and depression; and the urban planners who are trying to reconstruct lines of equilibrium in a divided landscape. Among the latter I have often mentioned Roland Castro: a product of the 1968 Far Left, he was the President's valued adviser for ten years, and dreamed of restoring a human dimension to what men seemed to have lost. I might have been ironic about his exemplary transition from red radical – swearing only by the Cultural Revolution – to pink reformer; and it's true that some of the projects of Roland Castro and his ilk – for example, making the old forts round Paris the vehicle of a new network of social interaction – might provoke a smile, with their nostalgia for the great worker-controlled utopias, and their Front Populaire ideology of a 'festive atmosphere' to the strains of accordions, 'rock-ed' up in line with current tastes. But it took courage to hang in there.

For a few months in 1992, the Ministry of the Town came into the hands of the famous businessman Bernard Tapie: we shall see what we shall see, he said. We didn't see much, except a few lightning visits to hand out subsidies to the deserving and the return of the discourse, louder than ever, about the need to break the suburban 'ghettos'. Faced with this kind of demagogy, you either had to put a brave face on it or resign. Reasonably enough, Roland Castro resigned. With him went what little remained of a project, decreed archaic, for a better world made by the Left, which the latter had allowed to collapse. A few months later, the Left itself collapsed.

The Ministry of the Town has been incorporated into the larger Ministry of Social Affairs. Since then, never has there been so much talk of ghettos and the (still) urgent need to get rid of them. As a result, what was largely a fantasy has succeeded in being made reality. The entire arsenal of police checks and repressive measures – of which the most striking are the new identity control arrangements – is accentuating the tendency. When I was writing this book four years ago, I was sure of one thing: that there were no real ghettos in French society, that the suburbs remained extraordinarily open places to live in, of which there are few in the world. But people have so wanted to conjure up these ghettos, and, in doing so, have so believed in them, that they have now finished by making them exist for real, and by persuading those who live there that, as in any real ghetto, no effective help can be expected from the outside. So? So it's every man for himself, a triumph for the 'I'm all right, Jack' school of thought, for an intolerant view of one's nearest neighbours. Or, occasionally, it means the appearance of new and nonsensical modes of taking charge in the community: in certain *quartiers*, for example, such as the Aulnay 3000, drug-dealers have set up their own welfare network and hand out the necessary aid to the destitute, thus ruling out any intervention by the institutions.

*

I certainly don't regret having been for a pleasant stroll among my own people, in this country of mine, in the spring of the French Revolution bicentenary year. I still think it is there, not elsewhere, that my country's life is being lived, played out. That is where its life force is. Its future. I'm simply more pessimistic about the future than I was four years ago. I hope with all my heart that I'm wrong.

Translator's notes

1. This common French term has been kept throughout. In everyday conversation it can often be translated simply by 'house'; but 'house' is employed here to translate *maison*, used by Maspero to describe modest, often terraced housing, a clear cut below the detached *pavillon*.
2. This version will not attempt to match the versatility of *boîte* in the French:

> Seed box Egg box
> Oxygen Box Naive boxes
> Cartons of milk
> For the children!
> Schools to know what you need to know
> Gearboxes Pictureboxes
> Boxes conditioned
> Against your dreams.
> Idea boxes Question boxes
> The agony of it!
> Adapted boxes No-way-out boxes
> Letterbox A box of desire
> To communicate.
> Nightclubs
> Roulette chambers Killing chambers
> Chambers for nutters!
> It's your oppression.
> Ballot box Wedding-ring case
> Reproductive box
> For a standardized citizen!
> HLM boxes Sardine cans
> Toolboxes Machine boxes
> Metro Hard slog Shut-eye!
> Canned food *Café-tabac* dives
> Dives for forgetting Dives for gambling
> High hopes Moneyboxes Bailiffs
> One sad pile of shit!
> Retirement homes From one box to another
> The last box!
> ... A few voice-boxes say to you:
> DON'T SHUT THE BOX!

3. With a heart pinched tight as houses in Europe.

4.   Nice children of Aubervilliers
                    You dive headfirst
                    Into the greasy water of poverty

                    Nice children of Aubervilliers
                    Nice children of working-class people
                    Nice children of poverty . . .

This version uses quotations from translations by William Weaver and Hubert Wolfe.

*

I wish to thank Liz Heron and particularly David Bellos for their valuable work on the manuscript.